Debunking Preterism

How Over-Realized Eschatology Misses the "Not Yet" of Bible Prophecy

Brock D. Hollett, B.S.Ed., M.Div., D.O

Debunking Preterism
How Over-Realized Eschatology
Misses the "Not Yet" of Bible Prophecy
Copyright © 2018
Brock D. Hollett, B.S.Ed., M.Div., D.O

Cover art by Phil Norcom. Used by permission.

Unless otherwise indicated, most Scripture quotations are
taken from the English Standard Version (ESV) of the Bible.

ISBN: 978-0-9889316-1-9

FOR INFORMATION CONTACT
Brock D. Hollett
brockhollett@yahoo.com

Printed in the United States of America by
Morris Publishing®
3212 E. Hwy 30 • Kearney, NE 68847
1-800-650-7888 • www.morrispublishing.com

Contents

This book is dedicated to my friends at Colleen's garage. May they, and all preterists, discover a thoroughly biblical eschatology.

1

What is Preterism?

Preterism is a view of eschatology, or the study of last things, that sees most of the prophecies of the New Testament as having been fulfilled by the end of the first century AD. The word preterism comes from the Latin word *praeter* which means "past." Most preterists place great significance on the events of the First Jewish-Roman War (AD 66-70) and their supposed fulfillment of the prophecies of the Holy Scriptures. Most preterists interpret the events prophesied in the Olivet Discourse and in the book of Revelation as having been largely fulfilled during that historical period. They see the Roman destruction of Jerusalem and its temple in AD 70 as the climactic event that finalized the replacement of the old covenant with the new covenant.[1]

Preterism posits an alternate view of prophecy that is vastly different than traditional futurist readings of Scripture. For example, many preterists deny that the Olivet Discourse and the Apocalypse even address the topic of the Second Coming of Jesus. Preterist author David Chilton claims, "The Book of Revelation is *not* about the Second Coming. ...In fact, the word *coming* as used in the Book of Revelation *never refers to the Second Coming.*"[2] As we will see in Chapter Seven, preterists reinterpret the biblical phrase "the coming of the Son of Man" to refer to an event that occurred in the first century. Much of this book will explore the differences between preterism and futurism, that is, the view that these prophecies will be fulfilled in our future.

Preterism exists in two primary forms, partial and full. Partial preterism agrees with the traditional Christian teachings

---

1 DeMar 1999, p. vii.; Gentry 2010c, loc. 122-27; Gentry 2010b, p. 21; Leithart 2004, pp. 1-2; Wright 1996, p. 323
2 Chilton 2007, p. 166

that the return of Jesus, the resurrection of the dead, and judgment day will occur in our *future.* By contrast, full preterism, the so-called "consistent" preterism, sees these events as having been fulfilled in AD 70. Full preterists, unlike partial preterists, reinterpret the traditional Judeo-Christian understanding of the *nature* of these events; for example, they deny the doctrine of the individual, bodily resurrection of the dead. Many full preterists also deny that God will finally and completely eradicate human sin in the new heaven and new earth (cf. Rev. 21:1, 4). Such positions contrast sharply with the historic church's understanding of these biblical doctrines as defined in the ecumenical creeds. It is no surprise, then, that Christianity rejects full preterism as heterodox, even heretical. This book primarily critiques partial preterism and does not interact extensively with full preterism, dealing with it only briefly in Chapter 15.

Many prophecy pundits advocate partial preterism. Gary DeMar, a postmillennialist and the former president of the Christian Reconstructionist organization, American Vision, published multiple preterist books and videos. Similarly, the Reformed postmillennialist Dr. Kenneth L. Gentry has advanced preterism among popular and academic audiences. More recently, Hank Hanegraaff, the talk show host of the *Bible Answer Man* radio broadcast and president of the Christian Research Institute, popularized preterism through his books and radio programs. R. C. Sproul was perhaps the most famous proponent of preterism. He founded Ligonier Ministries and hosted the *Renewing Your Mind* broadcast. A minority of other scholars and pastors have embraced preterism.

Preterists frequently attempt to normalize preterism. For instance, DeMar labels all Christians as "preterists" for believing that the prophecies about the first advent of Jesus Christ were fulfilled in the past, and he calls traditional Jews "anti-preterists" for denying that these prophecies have been fulfilled.[3] He indicts modern Christians for not embracing preterism by arguing that

3 DeMar 1999, p. vii

3

they seek the future fulfillment of prophecies that have already been fulfilled, similar to the manner in which first-century Jews rejected Jesus as the Messiah.[4] DeMar also points out that many futurists have failed to correctly predict the timing of "the end" and that many reputable Bible scholars have endorsed preterism during the last several centuries:

> ...today's speculative madness related to repeated failed attempts at predicting the end must be a gross misunderstanding of Bible prophecy. As I soon learned, I was not alone in coming to this conclusion. For centuries great Bible expositors had taught that many New Testament prophecies had already been fulfilled. They taught that many texts that are often futurized actually describe events in the first century. This literature made sense of the passages that millions of Christians struggle to understand.[5]

Many preterist authors adopted their preterist eschatology after becoming disgruntled with dispensational premillennialism. This perspective is the eschatological view that Jesus Christ will rapture his church prior to a seven year tribulation period that is followed by 1,000 years of world peace. It maintains a strict distinction between Israel and the Christian church. DeMar is a former Roman Catholic who, prior to his conversion to Christianity, was introduced to the pretribulational school of dispensationalism while reading Hal Lindsey's *The Late Great Planet Earth* in 1973.[6] He explained, "My dissatisfaction with the Lindsey system forced me to go digging for answers to solve the hermeneutical puzzle."[7] He laments, "I soon learned that today's prophetic scenario, so popular with radio and television evangelists and multi-million-copy best sellers, has a short history. The system of prophetic interpretation that is familiar to most Christians had its beginning in 1830."[8] Similarly, Gentry discusses his

---

4 DeMar 1999, pp. 36-37

5 Ibid., p. 15

6 Ibid., p. 13

7 Ibid., p. 14

8 Ibid., p. 15; cf. p. vii

4

years as a disgruntled dispensationalist who was finally delivered from this eschatological system by a professor who introduced him to preterism.

As well, these authors attempt to establish the veracity of preterism by contrasting it with the excesses and flaws of pretribulational dispensationalism, and they rarely interact with other eschatological positions in any meaningful way. For example, Hanegraaff argues his preterist position by contrasting it with dispensationalism throughout the entirety of his book *The Apocalypse Code.* Consequently, preterist works typically highlight the fallacy of limited alternatives, where the only option besides dispensationalism is preterism. Their arguments frequently imply the straw man argument that futurism itself must be invalid because the claims of pretribulational dispensationalism are erroneous.

DeMar and his colleagues have lost faith in modern prophecy experts who claim that our contemporary generation will witness the fulfillment of end-time Bible prophecy. He correctly points out that some Christians in every generation have believed this of themselves. He is also appropriately critical of preachers who "cry wolf" by espousing false doomsday predictions.

Yet he goes further by asserting that the failed speculations of prophecy pundits have resulted from their failure to embrace preterism. He warns, "The events in Waco [Texas] serve as a tragic lesson for those who maintain that the judgment themes depicted in Matthew 24, Mark 13, and the Book of Revelation are still in our future. How many more such tragedies will it take before Christians realize that these prophetic events have been fulfilled?"[9]

This critique of futurism represents the guilt by association fallacy. Furthermore, the cautious reader will not assume that the careless speculations and predictions of some futurists assumes a wholesale failure of futurist eschatology. At any rate, the failure of many believers to correctly ascertain the timing of the fulfill-

---

9 Ibid., p. 28

5

ment of Bible prophecies has contributed to preterism gaining adherents.

DeMar is essentially pessimistic about the practice of looking to current events as fulfillments of Bible prophecies, and he employs pejorative terms such as "newspaper exegesis" to describe this method.[10] However, he fails to recognize that the continued search for fulfillment of prophetic events undermines preterism and is evidence of their non-fulfillment in history. Prophecy teachers may not have calculated the precise date of the *eschaton* (i.e., the eschatological end), but it is clear that these events have yet to be fulfilled as preterists suppose. We hope to demonstrate this throughout this book.

But in fact, preterists are guilty of the very "newspaper exegesis" that DeMar criticizes. They rely heavily on the works of the first-century Roman historian Josephus to validate their claims of prophetic fulfillment. James Stuart Russell, a nineteenth-century preterist, asserts, "The only indispensable *apparatus criticus* is Josephus and the Greek grammar."[11] Gentry praises this approach, saying, "I highly recommend reading the Book of Revelation, Chapters 6 through 19, then reading Josephus, *War*, books 4-7."[12]

It is certain that historical events found in secondary sources should be used to validate whether prophecies have been fulfilled. However, we will see that it is equally certain that preterists engage in the same overly-realized eschatology as their futurist counterparts who engage in prophetic speculation, using a first-century historiography instead of twenty-first century newspapers. As we will see, preterism cannot adequately account for the prophetic details required by the biblical prophecies, and they are responsible for the same kind of force fitting as the prophecy experts that they criticize.

---

10 Ibid., p.15
11 Russell 2003, p. 535
12 Gentry 2010b, p. 31

DeMar audaciously claims that preterism is a continuation of the Reformation of the church, and to achieve this goal, he asserts that a Christian "should never fear having his [eschatological] 'system' scrutinized by the plain teaching of the Bible.[13] The purpose of this book is to evaluate the exegetical claims of partial preterism in light of solid biblical hermeneutics. My prayer is that the reader will arrive at a more comprehensive understanding of biblical eschatology by recognizing that preterism is not an adequate solution.

Soli Deo gloria

---

13 DeMar 1999, p. x

2

The Time Indicators
as the Key to Preterism

The time texts of the New Testament are the primary weapon in the preterists' arsenal. The time texts, variously called time indicators or time statements, are passages of Scripture that preterists utilize to demonstrate that eschatological events must have been fulfilled in the first century. None of the vast majority of the hundred or so passages specify a time or date of fulfillment, but most of these texts convey the meaning of nearness or imminence.

Many preterists describe the time statements as the "key" to understanding preterism. J. Stuart Russell wrote, "It may truly be said that the key has all the while hung by the door, plainly visible to every one who had eyes to see; yet men have tried to pick the lock, or force the door, or climb up some other way, rather than avail themselves of so simple and ready a way of admission as to use the key made and provided for them."[1] Gary DeMar argues that these time texts play a "defining role" in a proper understanding of Bible prophecy. He explains, "The additional study that went into this edition of *Last Days Madness* has continued to solidify my conviction that the time texts are key indicators of when certain prophetic events will take place. Most books of prophecy do not interpret time texts literally. In fact, some books ignore the time texts altogether….To the contrary, 'the time element' plays a major role in prophecy. In fact, it plays the defining role. Without precision of meaning for the time texts prophetic pronouncements are meaningless." [2]

---

1 Russell 2003, p. 367
2 DeMar 1999, pp. viii, 379

DeMar charges non-preterists of mishandling the time texts. He states that "failing to recognize the proximity of a prophetic event will distort its intended meaning" but then accuses futurists of abusing the biblical text, stating, "There is no getting around this language, that most of the verses that many believe are yet to be fulfilled already have been fulfilled. Forcing the following verses to describe a time nearly two thousand years in the future is the epitome of 'Scripture twisting'".[3] He contends that "an honest analysis" of these texts "jeopardizes" all futurist eschatological positions and that some of these systems arbitrarily deal with Scripture since "the entire thesis of futurism rests on a non-literal reading of the time texts."[4] He goes further by accusing the early church fathers and their contemporaries of erroneously believing that they lived in the last days "because they misapplied the time texts."[5]

The entire system of preterism is built around the primacy of the time indicators; therefore, our evaluation of preterism must include a thorough appraisal of these biblical texts. We will begin by evaluating many of the time statements concerned with the nearness of the Lord's return and the day of the Lord. The evidence presented in this chapter will demonstrate that preterism fails to consider the time statements in their proper biblical framework and historical understanding.

Near, Soon, and At Hand

The apostle John provided the reader with several primary time statements in the book of Revelation. These verses demonstrate the *nearness* of the return of Jesus:

> The revelation of Jesus Christ, which God gave him to show to his servants *the things that must soon take place.* (Revelation 1:1, emphasis added)

---

3 Ibid., p. 37, 38
4 Ibid., p. ix
5 Ibid., p. 427

Blessed is the one who reads aloud the words of this prophecy, and blessed are those who hear, and who keep what is written in it, *for the time is near.* (Revelation 1:3, emphasis added)

I am coming soon. Hold fast what you have, so that no one may seize your crown. (Revelation 3:11, emphasis added)

These words are trustworthy and true. And the Lord, the God of the spirits of the prophets, has sent his angel to show his servants *what must soon take place.* (Revelation 22:6, emphasis added)

And behold, *I am coming soon.* Blessed is the one who keeps the words of the prophecy of this book. (Revelation 22:7, emphasis added)

Do not seal up the words of the prophecy of this book, *for the time is near.* (Revelation 22:10, emphasis added)

Behold, *I am coming soon,* bringing my recompense with me, to repay each one for what he has done. (Revelation 22:12, emphasis added)

"Surely *I am coming soon.*" Amen. Come, Lord Jesus! (Revelation 22:20, emphasis added)

Seven of the above time statements appear in the introductory and closing sections of the Apocalypse. This type of literary device is an *ellipsis* or parenthesis. This device functions to inform the readers that the issue of the nearness of the Lord's coming is intrinsic to the book's main theme. Preterists correctly teach that these word groups "soon" (ταχύ) and "near" (ἐγγύς) frequently convey the idea of temporal nearness and likely do in the particular context of the book of Revelation,[6] yet preterists define these words in a particularly restrictive manner that differs from the historical understanding of these texts.

Russell asserted that these time statements are "the key" that unlocks the prophetic events described in the book of Revelation so that John's original audience could recognize the book's

---

6 Ibid., p. 384; Gentry 2010b, p. 19; Danker, Bauer, and Arndt 2000, pp. 992-93

"connection with the events of their own day." He stated that this true key has always been visible, but it has been "allowed to lie rusty and unused, while all kinds of false keys and picklocks have been tried, and tried in vain, until men have come to look upon the Apocalypse as an unintelligible enigma, only meant to puzzle and bewilder."[7] According to Russell, these statements combined with the book's then-contemporary relevance mean that modern readers are "absolutely shut up by the book itself to the contemporary history of the period, and that, too, within very narrow limits."[8] He chides, "How could an event be said to be near, if it was actually further off than the whole period of the Jewish economy from Moses to Christ?"[9] He continued this discussion by accusing futurists of defying the grammatical rules regarding the time statements:

> it seems unaccountable that scholarly and reverent students of divine revelation should either overlook or set aside the explicit declarations of the book itself with regard to its speedily approaching fulfillment... and that they should then, in defiance of all grammatical laws, proceed to invent a non-natural method of interpretation, according to which *'near'* becomes *'distant,'* and *'quickly'* means *'ages hence,'* and *'at hand'* signifies *'afar off.'* All this seems incredible, yet it is true. Language serves only to mislead, words have no meaning, and interpretation has no laws, if the express and repeated declarations of the Apocalypse does not plainly teach the speedy and all but immediate fulfillment of its predictions.[10]

Preterists unanimously agree that futurist interpretations violate the plain meaning of the time indicators by maintaining that John's prophecies would be fulfilled in *our* future. Gentry argues that any view that sees a fulfillment in "the distant future, thousands of years away, is expressly contradicting John's opening

---

7 Russell 2003, pp. 532-33

8 Ibid., p. 374

9 Ibid., p. 41

10 Ibid., p. 534

and closing statements."[11] Hanegraaff retorts, "Are we really to suppose that the angel was referencing a time more than two thousand years hence? Of course not!"[12] Chilton conveys their mutual concern, writing, "John's first-century readers had every reason to expect his book to have immediate significance. The words *shortly* and *near* simply cannot be made to mean anything but what they say. If I tell you, 'I'll be there *shortly*,' and I don't show up for 2000 years, wouldn't you say I was a little tardy?"[13]

Gentry contends that a preterist interpretation of the Apocalypse is "demanded" by John's time statements.[14] His reasoning is that a first-century fulfillment logically follows from the concept of near fulfillment.[15] He notes that John's "stated expectation regarding *when* his prophecies will transpire" is "absolutely essential" to a proper understanding of the book of Revelation.[16] He warns that the "most destructive" mistake a reader can make is "overlooking the apostle's clearly-stated temporal expectation."[17] Gentry means by this that readers should avoid the mistake of avoiding a preterist interpretation of the Revelation.

Hanegraaff states that the meaning of the word "soon" in the Apocalypse is "self-evident" and that any attempt to place the fulfillment of these prophecies into the distant future should trigger our "baloney detectors." He believes that the futurist understanding of the time statement violates the grammatical principle of hermeneutics, and he is amazed that prophecy experts "could possibly be mistaken about something so basic."[18] DeMar agrees with Hanegraaff and argues that non-preterists deny the *literal* and *plain* interpretation of the words "near," "shortly," and

---

11 Gentry 2010b, p. 139
12 Hanegraaff 2007, p. 92; cf. p. 94; Similarly Sproul 1998, p. 109
13 Chilton 2007, p. 166
14 Gentry 2010b, p. 137
15 Ibid., p. 57
16 Ibid., p. 15
17 Ibid., p. 33
18 Hanegraaff 2007, p. 73; cf. p. 91

"quickly."[19] He accuses futurists of inconsistently interpreting these statements, claiming that they interpret these words figuratively when they appear in the Apocalypse and rendering them literally when they appear elsewhere in Scripture:

> Supposedly, while "near," "quickly," and "shortly" are used in a literal sense in every other New Testament passage where they occur, in the Book of Revelation we are told that they should be interpreted figuratively, except, of course, when they need to be interpreted literally. This line of argumentation is surprising when it is put forth by those who insist on a literal interpretation of Scripture. Why don't the literalists want to interpret "near," "quickly," and "shortly" literally in the Book of Revelation when they interpret these same words literally elsewhere in the Bible?[20]

DeMar and his colleagues teach that the book of Revelation was fulfilled no later than Jerusalem's destruction in AD 70. This conclusion is based upon statements in the book that its prophetic fulfillment was *near* for John's original audience and on the fact that the apostle wrote the book, as preterists suppose, during Emperor Nero's reign (circa AD 64-68).[21] DeMar believes that futurists simply "ignore the time texts that speak of a *near* coming of Jesus in judgment upon an apostate Judaism that rejected its Messiah in the first century."[22] Gentry essentially agrees with this assessment. He argues that preterism alone adequately accounts for the *Sitz im Leben* ("setting in life"), that is, the cultural and historical context that allows John's message to serve a function for his original audience, the seven churches of Asia Minor. He thinks that a futurist interpretation of the Apocalypse is "a mockery of their historical circumstances", even a "'be thou warm and filled' comfort of little help to these churches."[23] He writes, "Surely, he is not telling these persecuted saints that the time is near, that they

19 DeMar 1999, pp. 206, 382; cf. Hanegraaff 2007, pp. 17, 90; Sproul 1998, p. 148
20 DeMar 1999, p. 390
21 Ibid., p.21
22 Ibid., p.37
23 Gentry 1998, pp. 139, 140

must heed that which he is writing, that God is concerned with their persecution—but He will avenge you thousands of years in the future!"[24]

The Prophetic Perspective

Despite the claims of preterists, the historic Christian church has affirmed for over 2,000 years that Jesus will return *soon*. Robert Mounce, a preeminent Greek and New Testament scholar, explains, "The most satisfying solution is to take the expression 'must soon take place' in a straightforward sense, remembering that in the prophetic outlook the end is always imminent. Time as chronological sequence is of secondary concern in prophecy. This perspective is common to the entire NT."[25] The idea is that the *eschaton* is always being pressed into the present and portrayed as a "foreshortened time of the end."

Several other commentators have embraced this prophetic perspective.[26] George Eldon Ladd, a distinguished New Testament professor at Fuller Theological Seminary, described the *tension* between the immediate future and distant future in Bible prophecy:

> The problem is raised by the fact that the prophets were little interested in chronology, and the future was always viewed as imminent. Biblical prophecy is not primarily three-dimensional but two; it has height and breadth but is little concerned about depth, i.e., the chronology of future events. There is in biblical prophecy a tension between the immediate and distant future; the distant is viewed through the transparency of the immediate. It is true that the early church lived in expectancy of the return of the Lord, and it is the nature of biblical prophecy to make it possible for every generation to live in expectancy of the end. To relax and say "where is the promise of his coming?" is to become a scoffer of divine

---

24 Gentry 2010b, p. 35; cf. Russell 2003, pp. 384-85, 396
25 Mounce 1998 p. 41
26 Hughes 1990, pp. 16, 241; Ladd 1972, p. 22; Osborne 2002, pp. 55, 59, 781

truth. The "biblical" attitude is "take heed, for you do not know when the time will come (Mark 13:33).[27]

The New Testament reflects the eschatological view that "the end of the age" had arrived during the apostolic period. The apostles taught that they were already living in "the last days" and at "the end of the ages" because the Son of God and his eschatological Spirit (i.e., the Holy Spirit) had arrived (Acts 2:16-17; 1 Peter 1:20; Heb. 1:2; 9:26; 1 Cor. 10:11). Prior to the Christian era, the Jewish nation did not understand the new covenant mystery of a *twofold* advent of the Messiah, namely, that Jesus of Nazareth would arrive to die for sins and ascend to heaven only to return thousands of years later. This meant nothing less than an unexpected and mysterious "breaking in" of eschatological realities *before* the return of Jesus on the day of the Lord. For example, the apostle John saw that the then contemporary presence of antichrists signaled that "the last hour" had in some sense arrived (1 John 2:18; cf. Rom. 16:20). This reinforced the concept that the day of the Lord was "at hand" (Rom. 13:12; cf. Heb. 10:25) and also, the apostolic admonition for believers to patiently wait because Christ's return was "at hand" (Phil. 4:5; Heb. 10:37; James 5:7, 8, 9). The apostle Peter taught that Christians should live in holiness because "the end of all things is at hand" (1 Peter 4:7; cf. 1 Cor. 7:29, 31; cf. 2 Peter 3).

This prophetic perspective portrays "the end" as pressing into the present age and is divinely intended to compel believers in Jesus Christ to live in continual readiness for his return. The passages conveying *nearness* function to remind believers of the Lord's admonition to "stay awake, for you do not know on what day your Lord is coming" (Matt. 24:42; cf. vv. 36, 44; 25:13). DeMar even admits that "the near and soon coming of Jesus in judgment [is used] as a way of spurring the church on to greater works."[28] Such exhortations have enabled Christians *in every era* to constantly live in patient, eager expectation of his glorious

27 Ladd 1972, p. 22
28 DeMar 1999, p. 30

return. The historic church has always maintained this eschatological understanding of these biblical texts.

Figure 1:

The Prophetic Perspective

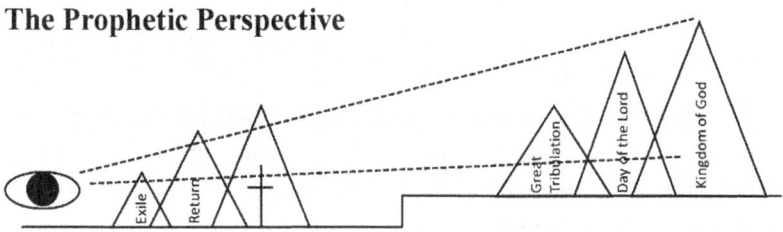

The historic church has maintained that the prophetic events
in the book of Revelation were "near" and "soon" even in the
first century, although the fulfillment of these events would not
take place for more than 2,000 years. This historic understanding
of the time statements was crucial for John's contemporary audience and has remained relevant for every subsequent generation
of Christians. The statements provide the theological *reason* why
God's people can faithfully endure persecution, namely, the persecution will soon end and find its divinely-intended purpose when
Jesus returns. The immediate context of these statements consistently reveals the theme of patiently enduring tribulation that has
resulted from a faithful adherence to the gospel (e.g., Rev. 1:2-3,
5, 9; 22:12).

The book's theme is further developed in the letters to the
churches in Revelation 2-3; the persecuted saints can "overcome"
by "holding fast" to the gospel and remaining faithful in spite of
false teachers and tribulation *because* the Judge is quickly coming
to reward them and punish their persecutors.[29] The idea advanced
by preterists that this coming refers merely to a first-century
"judgment coming" of Jesus robs the *post*-AD 70 church of this
theological basis for their faithful endurance.

Consistent with this theme of the encroaching return of Jesus
Christ, the apostles contrasted the transient, temporary suffering

---

29 Rev. 2:3, 5, 7, 9-11, 13, 16-17, 19, 23, 25-28; 3:3, 5, 8-12, 20-21

("light momentary affliction") of the saints with "an eternal weight of glory beyond all comparison" that will be ushered in at his return to vindicate and glorify them (e.g., 2 Cor. 4:16-18). Consequently, a few thousand years is only "a little longer" for those who partner together in "the patient endurance" of the persecuted saints (cf. Rev. 1:9; 3:10; 6:11; 14:12). The glorious return of Jesus is always *near* when seen against the backdrop of the eternity that God has placed in our hearts (Eccles. 3:11). People living at every period of history sustain an impinging, existential proximity to this day of the Lord, being either preserved for salvation or reserved for judgment. Believers should avoid deliberate sin, but pursue love and obedience to Jesus while encouraging our fellow Christians as we see the day of judgment drawing near (Heb. 10:24-27).

As Some Count Slowness

The modern reader of the Apocalypse faces the challenge of reconciling the time statements with an *apparent* delay in the Lord's coming. Theologians often call this dilemma "the problem of a delayed *parousia.*" Sproul claimed, "The crisis of 'parousia-delay' eschatology has been fostered in large measure by this problem. Perhaps no other problem has spurred the revival of different strands of preterism and realized eschatology more than has this one."[30] The apostle Peter addressed this issue when it first arose during the lifetime of his disciples:

> This is now the second letter that I am writing to you, beloved. In both of them I am stirring up your sincere mind by way of reminder, that you should remember the predictions of the holy prophets and the commandment of the Lord and Savior through your apostles, knowing this first of all, that scoffers will come in the last days with scoffing, following their own sinful desires. They will say, "Where is the promise of his coming? For ever since the fathers fell asleep, all things are continuing as they were from the beginning of creation." For they deliberately overlook this fact, that the heavens existed long ago, and the earth was formed out of water and through

30 Sproul 1998, p. 57

water by the word of God, and that by means of these the world that then existed was deluged with water and perished. But by the same word the heavens and earth that now exist are stored up for fire, being kept until the day of judgment and destruction of the ungodly. But do not overlook this one fact, beloved, that *with the Lord one day is as a thousand years, and a thousand years as one day. The Lord is not slow to fulfill his promise as some count slowness, but is patient toward you, not wishing that any should perish, but that all should reach repentance.* But the day of the Lord will come like a thief, and then the heavens will pass away with a roar, and the heavenly bodies will be burned up and dissolved, and the earth and the works that are done on it will be exposed. Since all these things are thus to be dissolved, what sort of people ought you to be in lives of holiness and godliness, waiting for and hastening the coming of the day of God, because of which the heavens will be set on fire and dissolved, and the heavenly bodies will melt as they burn! But according to his promise we are waiting for new heavens and a new earth in which righteousness dwells. (2 Peter 3:1-13, emphasis added)

Peter reminded his readers that scoffers would cast aspersion on the prophetic certainty of the Lord's promise to return quickly. They will mock, "Where is the promise of his coming?" (2 Peter 3:4). The apostle responded to this charge by explaining that the *apparent* failure of Jesus to return quickly is not an *actual* failure to faithfully keep his promises. Furthermore, the fact that he did not return *immediately* does not indicate a failure to return *soon*. The apostle affirmed that the Lord "is not slow *as some count slowness*" (v. 9, emphasis added).

The actual problem is a *faulty perception* of slowness, based on an erroneous reckoning of time by those who fail to appreciate the depth of God's patience towards his elect who have not yet repented (v. 9). Some (not all!) of Peter's contemporaries accused Jesus of failing to return quickly, but this is based entirely on their faulty human reasoning. The apostle alluded to Psalm 90:4 ("a thousand years in your [God's] sight are but as yesterday when it is past") to demonstrate that a divine reckoning of time is different than mere human reckoning; the idea is that the readers should recognize God's timetable and divine perspective instead of relying on their own understanding.

The apostle Peter explained that the Lord's return will take the scoffers by surprise because he will "come like a thief" (2 Peter 3:10; cf. Matt. 24:43-44; Rev. 3:3; 16:15). They follow "their own sinful desires" and "deliberately overlook" the fact that the same word of God that created the world that was later destroyed by the flood has also reserved the world for fiery destruction at the day of the Lord (2 Peter 3:3, 5-8, 10-12). The motif of Jesus returning "like a thief" during the night means that he will appear suddenly to those who are not expectantly waiting (1 Thess. 5:1-8). The Judge will appear sooner (read "soon" and "near") than many have estimated, and the wicked will be taken unaware and unprepared into eternal judgment (Matt. 24:39, 48-51; 25:11-13, 19, 30).

The apostle Peter's criticism of the scoffers in 2 Peter 3 echoes the sentiments of Jesus himself in the Olivet Discourse. Jesus warned, "But if that wicked servant says to himself, '*My master is delayed*,' and begins to beat his fellow servants and eats and drinks with drunkards, the master of that servant will come *on a day when he does not expect him and at an hour he does not know*" (Matt. 24:48-50; cf. Luke 12:45-46, emphasis added). He emphasized the idea echoed by Peter that Christians should patiently obey and prepare for the Lord's return because it will occur at an unexpected hour (i.e., soon, near, at hand). Although Jesus predicted a delay of sorts (Matt. 25:5, 19), he rejected the idea of a *long* delay (Luke 8:7). He warned, "But watch yourselves lest your hearts be weighed down with dissipation and drunkenness and cares of this life, and that day come upon you suddenly like a trap. For it will come upon all who dwell on the face of the whole earth. But stay awake at all times, praying that you may have strength to escape all these things that are going to take place, and to stand before the Son of Man" (Luke 21:34-36).

The preterist objections to our 2 Peter 3 argument lack substance. Russell contends, "To have intimated that time was a variable quantity in the promise of God would have been to stultify his argument and neutralize his own teaching, which was, that 'the Lord is not slack concerning his promise.'"[31] However, the apostle did not suggest that the timing of the promise was variable but only that it was soon and certain. Gentry acknowledges that Peter was concerned with God's perception of time but he rejects the 2 Peter 3 argument on the grounds that the apostle was facing the "*slowness* of God's judgment" whereas the Apocalypse provided directives to people in history.[32] Gentry fails to notice that Peter also gave directives for his readers, namely, to reject the false teachings of the scoffers and to prepare for the Lord's arrival. In addition, the apostle was certainly *not* "facing the slowness of God's judgment" despite Gentry's claim! The apostle specifically taught that "the Lord is not slow to fulfill his promise" (2 Peter 3:9).

DeMar completely evades the evidence from 2 Peter 3. He claims, "There is no indication in the Book of Revelation or the entire Bible that 'at hand' and 'near' are relative terms. There is no passage that points us to viewing time 'from the perspective of God' as if when God says 'near' He actually means an indefinite period of time. To make such a claim is practicing the fine art of *eis*egesis—reading an interpretation *into* a text so that it will say what you want it to say."[33] Yet as we have seen, the apostle Peter contrasted God's reckoning of time ("with the Lord one day..." in v. 8) with the scoffer's reckoning of time ("as some count slowness" in v. 9) as the primary reason to reject the scoffer's claims that the Lord failed in his promise to return soon. Furthermore, the apostle John used the time indicators in the book of Revelation ("near," "soon," and "at hand") in the precise manner that the prophets employed these time indicators in the Old Testament. We will now examine this evidence from the Prophets.

---

31 Russell 2003, p. 323
32 Gentry 2010b, pp. 43, 44
33 DeMar 1999, p. 383

Time Indicators in the Prophets

Despite DeMar's charge of eisegesis, the historical manner of interpreting the time statements finds its origins in the Old Testament Prophets. The prophets warned of an *impending* judgment upon the wicked at the day of the Lord:

> "Wail, for the day of the LORD is near; as destruction from the Almighty it will come!" (Isaiah 13:6)

> "…its time is close at hand and its days will not be prolonged" (Isaiah 13:22)

> "For the day is near, the day of the LORD is near" (Ezekiel 30:3)

> "Alas for the day! For the day of the LORD is near" (Joel 1:15)

> "the day of the LORD is coming; it is near" (Joel 2:1; cf. Isaiah 9:9; Malachi 4:1)

> "For the day of the LORD is near in the decision" (Joel 3:14)

> "For the day of the LORD is near upon all the nations. As you have done, it shall be done to you" (Obadiah 1:15)

> "For the day of the LORD is near" (Zephaniah 1:7)

> "The great day of the LORD is near, near and hastening fast" (Zephaniah 1:14)

> "…in a little while" (Haggai 2:6)

Many of the prophecies concerning the day of the Lord refer to a localized judgment that was fulfilled *in part* during the centuries following its announcement, but as we will see in Chapter Six, these prophetic expectations will be *entirely* fulfilled at the day of the Lord when Christ returns. These prophecies convey the theme of a certain expectation of judgment for the original hearers and strongly suggests that the day of the Lord is nearer than their stubborn, unrepentant hearts realized. The idea is that the wicked live as if they will live forever and will not be required to give an account for their deeds on judgment day (cf. Job 27:8, 17-22; Luke 12:19-20).

Preterist Keith Mathison admits that the Old Testament prophets "regularly used terms implying 'nearness' to describe events that did not occur for centuries."[34] This concept of a distant "nearness" illustrates our point and undermines preterism. Mathison provides an overview of how the prophets utilized the time statements when referring to relatively *distant* historical events:

> Isaiah 13:22 and Habakkuk 2:3-4, for example, speak of the imminence of the judgment to come upon Babylon. It is interesting to note that Isaiah was writing between 740 and 701 B.C., while Habakkuk wrote sometime between 609 and 598. Yet both spoke of Babylon's judgment using short-term time texts. Isaiah says it is "near." Habakkuk tells the people that "it will not tarry." Babylon fell to the Persians in 539. . . . Isaiah 56:1 says that God's salvation is "about to come." Writing in the early sixth century B.C., Ezekiel says that "the fulfillment of every vision" is "at hand" (12:23). Writing after the Exile, in approximately 520, Haggai proclaims the following word from God: "Once more (it is a little while) I will shake heaven and earth, the sea and dry land . . . (2:6-7). If this prophecy was fulfilled at the coming of Christ, as Hebrews 12:26-28 seems to indicate, then "a little while" was more than 520 years.[35]

Preterists are faced with a critical dilemma. They insist that the time indicators "near," "soon," and "at hand" in the Book of Revelation must refer to first-century events and not to events that will immediately precede the Lord's return. Nevertheless, as Mathison explains, the apostle John borrowed these time statements from the day of the Lord passages found in the Old Testament Prophets, passages that prophesied events that did not take place for *at least several centuries after the prophecies were written.* These same preterists condemn futurist interpretations of John's time indicators on the grounds that they require several centuries for fulfillment! In addition, a general consensus exists among biblical scholars that the "little while" of Hebrews 12:26-28 is an allusion

34 Mathison 2004, p. 202
35 Ibid., p. 165

to the "little while" prophecy of Haggai 2:6. Consequently, preterists must either admit that the writer of Hebrews referred to a different "little while" than Haggai intended or that such day of the Lord passages can have both a *near* and a *far* fulfillment. This would mean either a dual fulfillment or an "already and not yet" aspect of fulfillment of Haggai's original prophecy, both of which are devastating to common preterist thinking about how prophecy is fulfilled.

Do Not Seal Up the Words

Preterists often note the contrast between the angelic command for the prophet Daniel to seal the scroll of his prophecy "until the time of the end" (Dan. 12:4, 9; cf. 8:26) and the command for the apostle John *not* to seal up his prophetic scroll because "the time is near" (Rev. 22:10).[36] The essence of their argument is that futurist positions inconsistently consider 2,000+ years from John to be in his *near* future while maintaining that 2,500+ years from Daniel was his distant future. Preterist Don Preston emphasizes the contrast. He argues, "This means it has now been *four times longer* from John to the present, than it was from Daniel to John. Yet, Daniel was told fulfillment was far off, and John was told it was near.... Was 400 years a 'long time' to Daniel, yet John's vision, that was 'at hand,' has not been fulfilled 2000 years later? This contrast in temporal perspective is *prima facie* proof that the time statements of Revelation must not be 'elasticized' into meaninglessness."[37]

This argument fails to consider the different intended audiences and theological purposes between the book of Daniel and the book of Revelation. Daniel's prophecies were initially intended to *conceal* mysteries from the obstinate nation of Israel. The prophet followed the prophet Isaiah's pattern of preaching a message of divine judgment that reinforced the nation's inability

---

36 Adams and Fisher 2000, p. 111; Chilton 2007, p. 167; DeMar 1999, p. 390; Gentry 2010b, p. 19
37 Preston 2011, pp. 45, 192

to understand his prophetic visions. Daniel, like Isaiah, described this message as an incomprehensible, "sealed scroll" that would not be opened and understood by the nation until messianic times (Isa. 6:9-13; 8:16; 29:9-14; Dan. 8:26; 12:1, 4, 9-10; cf. Rom. 11:7-8). Consequently, the nation would not welcome the message of salvation until the time of the end as it was *far* removed and inaccessible to them *due to their spiritually-hardened condition* (Isa. 6:9-10; Dan. 12:10b).

However, Jesus has now given the secrets of his kingdom to the New Testament church (Matt. 13:11; Luke 8:10), and the messianic secret of Jesus of Nazareth has been revealed as an "open scroll" to all whom God has given "eyes to see" and "ears to hear" (Matt. 11:15; 16:16-17; Mark 4:9, 23; 8:8; 14:35; Luke 10:23; 14:35; 1 John 1:1). Unlike the recipients of Daniel's prophecies, John's receptive audience was comprised of Christians who had been given this open scroll of the Gospel (Rev. 2:7, 11, 17, 29; 3:6, 13, 22).

The eschatological realities of the day of the Lord have been brought near into the present. For example, the New Testament presents Christians as an eschatological people, a type of first-fruits of God's new creation (2 Thess. 2:13; James 1:18; Rev. 14:4; cf. Rom. 8:23), who have received the Messiah and have been transferred by the Spirit into his kingdom *prior to* the day of the Lord (Col. 1:13). Those who are "in Christ" are in one sense *already* participating with him in the resurrection from the dead (Rom. 6:4; Eph. 2:6; Col. 3:1). The "the times of ignorance" when God previously overlooked ignorant sin have given way to the new covenant era when "now he commands all people everywhere to repent because he has fixed a day on which he will judge the world in righteousness" (Acts 17:30-31). The eschaton that was *chronologically* distant for Daniel's audience had drawn near *existentially* by the revelation of the mysteries that had been hidden from previous generations.

3

Two Questions at Olivet

A proper understanding of the Olivet Discourse is essential for any evaluation of preterism. The discourse is found in all three Synoptic Gospels, primarily Matthew 24, Mark 13, and Luke 17, 21, and each account parallels and augments the others. A preterist interpretation of this discourse and the Apocalypse formally sets one apart as a preterist. For preterism, as with most other eschatological systems, the Olivet Prophecy typically serves as the *crux interpretum* through which many other eschatological passages can be understood. According to preterism, this discourse was fulfilled through the events surrounding the Roman destruction of Jerusalem's Second Temple in AD 70. Most futurist interpretations see these first-century events as forming a prophetic *backdrop* upon which Jesus spoke about *future events* that will immediately precede his glorious return, including the destruction of a third temple in Jerusalem.

The Lord Jesus delivered his Olivet Discourse to his apostles while sitting on the Mount of Olives that overlooked Jerusalem's temple from the east. This location was well known as the place where King David wept after leaving the city due to losing the widespread support of the Jewish nation and being threatened by the superior military force of his treasonous son, Absalom (2 Sam. 15:30-31). When Jesus delivered his discourse, he had also been rejected by the nation and was about to be crucified. As the ultimate Son of David, he wept prior to giving his final discourse, knowing that the consequence of the nation rejecting him would be the destruction of the temple and the nation itself. He approached the city and wept with the following words on his lips:

> Would that you, even you, had known on this day the things that make for peace! But now they are hidden from your eyes.

For the days will come upon you, when your enemies will set up a barricade around you and surround you and hem you in on every side and tear you down to the ground, you and your children within you. And they will not leave one stone upon another in you, because you did not know the time of your visitation. (Luke 19:41-44)

The structure of the Olivet Discourse proper begins with the Lord's statement that the temple would be destroyed, and it continues with his lengthy response to the apostles' follow-up questions regarding this event. Matthew recorded this encounter: "Jesus left the temple and was going away, when his disciples came to point out to him the buildings of the temple. But he answered them, 'You see all these, do you not? Truly, I say to you, there will not be left here one stone upon another that will not be thrown down.' As he sat on the Mount of Olives, the disciples came to him privately, saying, 'Tell us, when will these things be, and what will be the sign of your coming and of the end of the age?'" (Matt. 24:1-3)

Several important observations should be made about the questions posed by the disciples. First, their questions were in response to their initial observations about the Second Temple complex and Jesus' statement that its stones would be completely dismantled, an event that occurred when the Romans destroyed Jerusalem in AD 70. Second, the content of the questions reveal that the apostles did not know the *timing* of these prophetic events. Third, the disciples *thematically* connected the destruction of the temple with the coming of Jesus and the end of the age. This is seen by the fact that the disciples asked him about these two latter events *although Jesus had not mentioned either in the immediate, preceding context.* Fourth, the grammatical form of the questions in Matthew's Gospel and the parallel accounts in the other Synoptics show that the topics of "the sign of your coming" and "the end of the age" comprise *one* question and not separate questions per se. This is evident because Mark and Luke combined these two questions into the solitary question "What will be the sign

27

when all these things are about to be accomplished" (Mark 13:4; cf. Luke 21:7). Most commentators, whether preterists or futurists, do not consider these observations to be controversial.

Preterists disagree over the meaning of Jesus' phrase "the end of the age." Those who see the *entirety* of the Olivet Discourse as having a first-century fulfillment believe that "the end" (συντελείας) means, as DeMar defines it, "the *end* of the Old Covenant redemptive system and nothing else."[1] DeMar and several of his colleagues teach that "the end" signaled the termination of "the temple, the city of Jerusalem, and the covenant promises that were related to the Mosaic system of animal sacrifices, ceremonial washings, and the priesthood" in AD 70.[2] Other preterists favor the traditional understanding that this phrase refers to the end of the age at the return of Jesus Christ.[3] For example, Gentry argues that the phrase "appears first in Matthew 24:3 and points to the end of history. It appears in the disciples' questions which are packed with their assumption that the world will end when the temple ends."[4]

Gentry contends that the apostles' questions arose from their supposed assumptions and misunderstanding of the teachings of Jesus. He conjectures, "Thus, even though he [Jesus] is now nearing the end of over three years of teaching them, their two questions betray their eschatological confusion. They misconstrue matters by uniting the destruction of the temple with the end of the world."[5] Gentry imagines that the apostles "wrongly associated" the destruction of the temple with "the end of the world."[6] Kik comments, "There is no doubt the disciples believed that the destruction of the temple and the end of the age were one and the same thing."[7] These preterists would have us believe

---

1 DeMar 1999, p. 68
2 Ibid., p. 69; Similarly Sproul 1998, p. 37
3 Kik 1971, p. 89
4 Gentry 2010c, loc. 1037-1043
5 Ibid., loc. 2150
6 Ibid., loc. 993; Similarly Calvin 1984, p. 117; Kik 1971, p. 88
7 Kik 1971, p. 88

that the disciples incorrectly connected these two events *despite having spent three years under the Lord's direct tutelage*! But as we will see, this connection is derived from the prophetic timeline as established in the Prophets.

While Gentry admits that the disciples' prophetic expectations about timing were "largely due to the famous prophecy in Daniel 9,"[8] he fails to appreciate that the prophet Daniel connected the temple's desolation with "the time of the end" (Dan. 11:31, 45; 12:1-4, 6-12). This will be further demonstrated in subsequent chapters of this work. Daniel also located the Son of Man's coming with clouds at the time of several eschatological events, including the destruction of the final beastly kingdom, the consummate arrival of God's kingdom, and judgment day (Dan. 7:13ff; cf. Matt. 24:30). Contrary to Gentry's claims, the apostles (and Jesus!) followed Daniel by connecting the destruction of the temple with the eschatological time of the end.

Which Temple Destroyed?

Preterists correctly note that Jesus prophesied the dismantling of the Second Temple, the holy edifice that was before their eyes ("*these* great buildings ... not be left *here* one stone" in Mark 13:2; "As for *these things* that you *see*" in Luke 21:6).[9] However, they incorrectly argue that this *proves* that Jesus did not speak about a future rebuilt temple (i.e., Third Temple). DeMar contends that Jesus could not have had a future temple in mind because it "would have to be rebuilt with the same stones that made up the temple that was destroyed. Not just any stones will do. Jesus said that 'not one stone *here*'."[10] Gentry laments that futurists "create another suppressed premise" by positing that Jesus referred to a future rebuilt temple in Matthew 24:16.[11] DeMar echoes these sentiments:

8   Gentry 2010c, loc. 1347
9   Kik 1971, p. 83
10 DeMar 1999, p.52; cf. Chilton 2007, p. 87
11 Gentry 2010c, loc. 1177; Similarly Kik 1971, p. 72

To propose that Jesus was describing a *rebuilt* temple must be proven from Scripture. The New Testament mentions *nothing* about a rebuilt temple. There is nothing in Matthew 24 that even hints at the rebuilding of the temple. Why would Jesus confuse His listeners and those of us who read His recorded prophecy by leaving out a crucial detail like a rebuilt temple? It does not make sense.[12]

Admittedly, Jesus did not specifically lay out the details of the Second Temple's destruction to be followed by the Third Temple's construction and desolation. The concept that the temple will be rebuilt again can only be understood *in retrospect* after it became clear that the events of AD 70 did not fulfill the *entirety* of the Olivet Prophecy. As this author will prove in subsequent chapters, Jesus prophesied in the discourse that the destruction of the temple will *immediately* precede his second advent, the resurrection of the dead, and the repentance of national Israel. Consequently, the rebuilding of the temple after its destruction in AD 70 is *an inferred necessity* given that the prophecies connect these events. This leaves the interpreter with three options: (1) the skeptical view, which claims that Jesus and/or the gospel writers were incorrect, (2) the preterist approach, which denies that these prophetic events must occur in tandem, or (3) the futurist view, which argues that Jesus had in mind the mystery of the Third Temple.

It will be argued in this book that the questions at Olivet arose because the disciples did not have the schema needed to conceive of the possibility that *two* temples would be destroyed before the Lord's return. Jesus answered their questions by prophesying the destruction of the Third Temple as preparation for his second advent; however, the disciples could only identify this mystery after their contemporary generation ended without witnessing the Lord's return (cf. Matt. 24:34).

We should consider that the apostles were also ignorant, at this point, of an extended inter-advent period of 2,000 years. This

---

12 DeMar 1999, p. 94

new covenant period is an outgrowth of Paul's doctrine of "the mystery of the gentiles," that non-Jews who trust in Christ now share in Israel's promises (e.g., Rom. 11:25-26; Eph. 3:6; Col 1:27). Therefore, it should be obvious, then, that the apostles did not foresee these mysteries, since they could only be understood *in retrospect* of historical circumstances (cf. Dan. 12:4, 8-10, 13), including the destruction of Jerusalem in AD 70 which occurred apart from any final redemption. This mystery would be further clarified by the creation of the modern state of Israel in 1948, the Jewish reacquisition of Jerusalem and the Temple Mount in 1967, and the current preparations for the Third Temple by such organizations as the Temple Institute.

Jesus was operating within the normal limits of biblical expression by describing "*the* temple" (without any numeric qualifier) in the Olivet Discourse to speak of the Third Temple. We know that the Jews who lived during the Second Temple period conceived of their own temple as a continuation of Solomon's Temple because the Scriptures describe its construction simply as a rebuilding of "the temple" (Ezra 1:3, 5; 5:2, 11, 15, 17; 6:3, 7-8; Hag. 1:2; cf. Matt. 26:61). Similarly, Jesus answered the disciples' questions regarding their own historical circumstances and the looming destruction of *their* temple by providing a prophecy concerning the desolation of the eschatological temple that will precede his glorious appearance. Preterists are historically anachronistic when they require Jesus to have used the numeric qualifier "third" to reference a third temple, especially given the fact that such an understanding while the Second Temple stood would have undermined the unknowability of the timing of the Lord's return.

Preterists vehemently reject the historic church's position that the Olivet Discourse is concerned with events that are future to the modern reader. Russell summarized the traditional interpretation: "The commonly received view of the structure of this discourse, which is almost taken for granted, alike by expositors and by the generality of readers, is, that our Lord, in answering the question of His disciples respecting the destruction of the temple, mixes up with that event the destruction of the world, the universal judgment, and the final consummation of all things. Imperceptibly, it is supposed, the prophecy slides from the city and temple of Jerusalem, and their impending fate in the immediate future, to another and infinitely more tremendous catastrophe in the far distant and indefinite future."[13] Gentry considers this interpretation of the discourse to be a tragic mistake. He laments, "Indeed, the average evangelical approach to the Olivet Discourse is so seriously misconstrued that it places its fulfillment at the wrong place in history, misses Christ's whole point entirely, applies its judgments to the wrong people, and spreads its catastrophes far beyond its intended focus. Thus, the popular conception has the wrong time, purpose, objects, and scope for its judgments."[14]

If preterism is correct, the reader should expect the historical events of the first century to adequately account for the prophetic details of the Olivet Discourse. However, throughout the next several chapters, we will discover that the preterist paradigm fails to account for these details, and that the events surrounding the destruction of the Second Temple did not exhaustively fulfill the Olivet Prophecy. Conversely, the traditional, futurist interpretation of the prophecy satisfactorily accounts for these prophetic details and provides an awe-inspiring rationale of the most explanatory power.

---

13 Russell 2003, p. 55
14 Gentry 2010c, loc. 161

4

The Beginning of Birth Pains

The ancient rabbis, following the tradition of the Old Testament prophets, taught that "the birth pains of the Messiah" would be a period of increasing distress and tribulation that would come upon the Jewish nation and the world prior to the arrival of God's kingdom (*Sanhedrin 98b and Shabbat 118a*).[1] In the Olivet Prophecy, the Lord Jesus began answering the apostles' questions by reminding them that the birth pains must arrive before the end.

> And Jesus answered them, "See that no one leads you astray. For many will come in my name, saying, 'I am the Christ,' and they will lead many astray. And you will hear of wars and rumors of wars. See that you are not alarmed, for this must take place, but the end is not yet. For nation will rise against nation, and kingdom against kingdom, and there will be famines and earthquakes in various places. All these are but the beginning of the birth pains." (Matt. 24:4-8)

> And he said, "See that you are not led astray. For many will come in my name, saying, 'I am he!' and, 'The time is at hand!' Do not go after them. And when you hear of wars and tumults, do not be terrified, for these things must first take place, but the end will not be at once." Then he said to them, "Nation will rise against nation, and kingdom against kingdom. There will be great earthquakes, and in various places famines and pestilences. And there will be terrors and great signs from heaven." (Luke 21:8-11)

Many events that occurred in the mid-first century AD could be said to represent the conditions that Jesus termed "the beginning of the birth pains." For example, the New Testament and

---

1   Isa. 13:1, 6-9, 17-19; 26:17-19; 33:11; 37:3; 66:7-9; Jer. 4:31; 6:22-26; 22:18-23; 48:41; 49:22; 50:41-43; Hos. 13:13; John 16:21; 1 Thess. 5:3; cf. Gen. 35:18

the Jewish historian Josephus related accounts of contemporary false messiahs and false prophets.[2] Josephus and Philo recorded accounts of several battles, civil wars, and "rumors of wars" that raged throughout the Roman Empire during the same period.[3] Tacitus recounted several battles in *The Annals of Imperial Rome* as did Suetonius in *The Twelve Caesars*. The book of Acts (in 11:27-29) mentions a famine that affected the Roman Empire, especially Judea. Tacitus wrote about famines that occurred in Rome and Greece and about several earthquakes that happened during the years leading up to AD 70.[4] Many Jews within the vicinity of the Jerusalem temple felt an earthquake during this period.[5] Tacitus mentioned two comets that streaked across the empire in AD 60.[6] Josephus reported the appearance of a comet, a star "resembling a sword," and lightning flashes over the temple precincts and the presence of chariots and armor-clad soldiers in the clouds over Jerusalem.[7]

Preterists present this historical evidence as proof of preterism;[8] however, it should be noted that such catastrophic events have and do occur in *every* period of history. DeMar admits no less, explaining that "wars, earthquakes, famines, and plagues have been a part of the human condition since the Fall. … This means that their contemporary manifestation does not necessarily carry *any* prophetic importance."[9] At least at some level, the normative nature of these initial portents ("the beginning of the birth pains") proves that they do *not* signal the end of

---

2 Josephus, *Antiquities* 20.8.5; 20.97-98. Acts 8:9-11; 13:6; 20:29-31; 2 Cor. 11:13; 12:11; 2 Tim. 2:16-17; 2 Peter 2:1; 1 John 2:18; 4:1; Rev. 2:2.

3 Josephus, *Antiquities* 18.6.10. Philo of Alexandria, *Flaccus*, Vol. 25. 3.8; 4.21. Philo of Alexandria, *On the Embassy to Gaius* 31.213. Josephus, *The Wars of the Jews* 2.14.5; 4.9.2.

4 Tacitus, 1989, p. 271. Cf. Matt. 27:54; 28:2; Acts 16:26

5 Josephus, *The Wars of the Jews* 6.5.3

6 Tacitus, *Annals* 14.20

7 Josephus, *The Wars of the Jews* 6.5.3

8 DeMar 1999, pp. ix, 73-86; Gentry 2010c, loc. 1337-1534, 1570-1612, 1944-1989; Kik 1971, pp. 91-97

9 DeMar 1999, pp. 340, 342, emphasis added

the age. Chilton concurs: "In themselves, Jesus warned, they were not to be taken as signals of an imminent end".[10] Gentry argues that Jesus used the phrase "the beginning of birth pains" to warn against "false starts" concerning the end and that this phrase has "no specific referent and is not reserved for final-eschatological events."[11] He explains in more detail:

> In my fuller analysis of the text, I will show that early in the Discourse he warns them not to become confused by pre-liminary signs, for "that is not yet the end" [Matt.] (24:6b) and "all these things are merely the beginning of birth pangs" (24:8). So in answering their question regarding "when will these things be" he cautions them against being misled by the initial signs. This means he is in fact answering their question as to "when these things will be" but has not arrived at the answer yet.[12]

Jesus warned against a premature identification of these initial signs, most likely because these type of events occur *to a lesser degree* in every period of time. Nevertheless, the Scriptures predict *a particular intensification* of these labor pains in the years leading up to the end of the age. For instance, the Apocalypse predicts hail, fire, and blood destroying a third of the trees and all grass, a fiery mountain being hurled into the sea that destroys marine life, a falling "star" poisoning the water system, and the sun, moon, and stars being struck with darkness (Rev. 8:7-12). The apostle John also foresaw that a fallen "star" will open a large shaft in the earth, resulting in smoke that darkens the atmosphere (Rev. 9:1-2). John also described various earthquakes (Rev. 8:5; 11:13, 19) and a famine (Rev. 11:6). None of these events happened in the first century, but this has not deterred many preterists from engaging in exegetical gymnastics to argue that they did occur.

Jesus continued his discourse by enumerating other events that continue the birth pains of tribulation. He taught, "Then they will deliver you up to tribulation and put you to death, and you

---

10 Chilton 2007, p. 90; Similarly DeMar 1999, p. 179
11 Ibid., loc. 1337 and 1534-1540
12 Gentry 2010c, loc. 1156; cf. Gentry 2010c, loc. 2081

will be hated by all nations for my name's sake. And then many will fall away and betray one another and hate one another. And many false prophets will arise and lead many astray. And because lawlessness will be increased, the love of many will grow cold. But the one who endures to the end will be saved" (Matt. 24:9-13).[13] Preterists correctly note that the book of Acts relates how the apostles and some of the other early Christians were persecuted, flogged, beaten, brought to trial, imprisoned, and killed for their faithfulness to the gospel.[14] The external evidence from church history confirms similar occurrences.

However, Luke's version of the Olivet Discourse includes the phrase "but before all this" (Luke 21:12), which tells the reader that this persecution would begin *prior* to the birth pains described in the preceding verses (vv. 8-11). In addition, as admitted by preterists, this persecution of Christians has *continued unabated for 2,000 years beyond the first century!* This fact argues against the limited specificity advocated by preterism, that is, a persecution that refers *only* to the apostolic period prior to AD 70.

This portion of the Olivet Discourse (Matt. 24:9-13; Mark 13:9-13; Luke 21:12-19) should be understood as a warning of abiding persecutions and tribulations that Christians will experience during the inter-advent period. This understanding is strengthened by Jesus' temporal indicator "before all this" (Luke 21:12), which prohibits the reader from equating this earlier tribulation with the *unprecedented and unequaled tribulation* that will occur at the end of the age (Matt. 24:21ff; Luke 21:22-23; cf. Dan. 12:1-2).

The apostle John also differentiated between general tribulation experienced by believers (Rev. 1:9; cf. 2:9-10) and the future period of "great tribulation" (Rev. 2:22; 7:14; 12:7-17; 13:5-8). He related that early Christian martyrs were instructed to "rest a little

---

13 Cf. Matt. 10:17-22, 34-39.
14 DeMar 1999, p. 120; Gentry 2010c, loc. 1570; See Acts 5:17-20, 25-26, 30-33, 40-42; 7:58-60; 8:3; 12:1-5; 14:19; 16:22-24; 17:5-6; 18:17; 20:23-25; 21:32-36; 22:24; 24:23; cf. John 21:18-19.

longer" until their fellow saints experience martyrdom (Rev. 6:9, 11) during "the great tribulation" (Rev. 7:14; cf. Rev. 20:4). The biblical evidence indicates that the initial labor pains, including the persecution of the saints, will intensify and reach a crescendo as the end approaches, consistent with the Lord's statement that "the end will not be at once" (Luke 21:9).

The Gospel to the Entire World

Jesus continued his Olivet Discourse by prophesying about a worldwide preaching of the gospel prior to the end. He explained that "this gospel of the kingdom will be proclaimed throughout the whole world as a testimony to all nations, and then the end will come" (Matt. 24:14; cf. Luke 21:26). Preterists argue that the word here that is nearly always translated "world" (οἰκουμένη) is a technical term referring to the civilized world and that it referred to the Roman Empire during the first century.[15] They contend that the gospel *had already* been proclaimed throughout "all nations" belonging to the empire during the apostolic era, and they support these claims by appealing to statements made by the apostle Paul.[16]

> your faith is proclaimed *in all the world*. (Rom. 1:8b, emphasis added)

> Their voice has gone out *to all the earth*, and their words *to the ends of the world*. (Rom. 10:18b, emphasis added)

> For your obedience is known *to all* ...My gospel ... has been made known *to all nations*. (Rom. 16:19, 25, 26, emphasis added)

> the gospel, which has come to you, as indeed *in the whole world* it is bearing fruit and increasing ... which has been proclaimed *in all creation under heaven* (Col. 1:5b-6; 23, emphasis added)

---

15 E.g., Gentry 2010c, loc. 1641; Jordan 2014, loc. 126, 357, 132; Russell 2003, p. 265; cf. Sproul 1998, p. 56

16 E.g., Chilton 2007, p. 91; Gentry 2010c, loc. 1662; Ice and Gentry 1999, p. 45; Kik 1971, pp. 99-100; Sproul 1998, p. 44

Several objections can be made to this preterist interpretation of these passages. First, unlike the verse under consideration (Matt. 24:14), these Pauline passages simply *cannot* be understood literally and should be taken figuratively.[17] The apostle Paul utilized hyperbole or exaggeration in these verses to emphasize the evangelistic success of the gospel. Luke also used such figurative expressions. For example, he explained that devout Jews "from every nation under heaven" were staying in Jerusalem on the day of Pentecost (Acts 2:5). Certainly, the reader should not think that Jews from Germania or Armenia were in town for the festival! Luke also wrote about unbelieving Jews who accused Paul and his traveling companions of turning "the world upside down" with the gospel (Acts 17:6). In each of these cases, it is simply inappropriate to render these Pauline and Lukan expressions literally.

The apostle Paul used hyperbole in the above verses, a point that becomes more apparent when we consider that he employed the term κόσμος (*not* οἰκουμένη as in Matthew 24:14!) in all but one of these references. First, Colossians 1:5-6 substitutes κόσμῳ ("world") for γῆς ("earth"/"land") and is an allusion to Genesis 1:28 (LXX), a verse that speaks of God's command for mankind to multiply and subdue the entire created world (i.e., the earth). In other words, this term is *not* limited to a geographical region such as a territory, empire, or kingdom. The apostle alluded to this text in the Colossians passage to show that the gospel was spreading vastly and successfully *wherever it was being proclaimed.* Second, New Testament scholars dispute the meaning of the phrase that is often translated "to all the nations" in Romans 16:26. Many suggest that the preposition εἰς in this verse, often translated "to", expresses *purpose or intent* and more accurately conveys the meaning "*for* all the nations."[18] The idea is that the gospel is not limited "to" the nation of Israel or to a particular group of nations. This suggests that the intended scope of the gospel is "all

---

17 E.g., Bruce 1984, pp. 42-43, 79
18 Seifrid, Mark A. in Beale and Carson 2007, p. 693.

nations," and it does not suggest that it had already accomplished this purpose in the first century. Third, while the term οἰκουμένη *can* refer to the Roman Empire (e.g., Luke 2:1; Acts 11:28; 17:6; 19:27; 24:5), it does *not* denote such a limited geographical region in Romans 10:18. This verse is an allusion to Psalm 19:4 (LXX) which was written during the reign of King David, hardly during the time of a civilized empire. In addition, this psalm speaks of "the heavens" and its celestial bodies declaring God's glory to "all the earth" and to "the end of the world." This strongly suggests that Paul borrowed the language of this psalm to express the idea that the heavenly message--the gospel--is intended for Jews and gentiles alike without distinction (Rom. 10:18; cf. 10:12). Fourth, the phrase usually translated "which has been proclaimed" in Colossians 1:23 is in the aorist tense, which often carries a continuous aspect (i.e., "which is proclaimed"). John Piper explains the implications for this meaning of the verse:

> The fact that the [substantival] participle "proclaimed" is aorist tense does *not* mean the proclamation has already happened in the past. That is not the way aorists in substantival participles work, as Daniel Wallace makes clear in *Greek Grammar Beyond the Basics* (note 8, 615). The aorist tense in such uses denotes no specific time. ... So the simplest reading of Colossians 1:23 is that Paul is *defining* the gospel as the kind of gospel that is unbounded and global in scope, and therefore is preached, by definition, in all the creation. There is no statement here that it has already happened. So I would translate it ... *the gospel which is proclaimed in all creation under heaven.* I happily note that N.T. Wright suggests the same interpretation.[19]

The figurative language employed by Paul and his travelling companion, Luke, to describe the non-discriminant intent and victory of the gospel contrasts with the literal meaning of Jesus' words in Matthew 24:14. There is no compelling reason to interpret the Master's words in Matthew 24:14 in a figurative manner.

19 Piper, John. "Has the Gospel Been Preached to the Whole Creation Already?" On March 14, 2017. *Desiring God.* http://www.desiringgod.org/articles/has-the-gospel-been-preached-to-the-whole-creation-already.

Instead, the gospel will be proclaimed "to all nations" (i.e., "to all ethnic groups," πᾶσιν τοῖς ἔθνεσιν) throughout the entire world to provide them with a testimony (Matt. 24:14) prior to the judgment at the end of the age, a judgment that will include "all the nations" (πάντα τὰ ἔθνη in Matt. 25:32). The book of Revelation also conveys the concept that the everlasting gospel must be proclaimed to "every nation and tribe and language and people" (Rev. 14:6) prior to the glorious revelation of Jesus.

On the other hand, the preterist approach to Matthew 24:14 imports an unintended meaning into the words of Jesus and thereby distorts the very basis for worldwide evangelism. Additionally, the preterist interpretation of Matthew 24:14 unwittingly undermines the Great Commission (Matt. 28:18-20; cf. Mark 16:15-18). The reason for this is twofold: First, Jesus promised to be with his disciples in their evangelistic endeavors until "the end of the age" (Matt. 28:20), an age that many preterists believe ended with the destruction of Jerusalem in AD 70. Second, Jesus commanded his disciples to make disciples of "all nations" (πάντα τὰ ἔθνη in Matt. 28:19). Based on their interpretation of "all nations" in Matthew 24:14, hermeneutical consistency demands that preterists understand this commandment as having been fulfilled no later than AD 70.

In addition, preterists cannot demand that we import the meaning of Pauline passages onto the "all nations" of Matthew 24:14 *while arguing that this exact language means something very different when it appears a few chapters later in the same Gospel (Matt. 28:19)!* Other preterist arguments, such as Kik's contention that Matthew 24:14 is about "witnessing" and the Great Commission is about making disciples is unconvincing.[20] Even the preterist, R. C. Sproul, famously taught that the *solitary imperative* for Christian evangelism is the commandment of Jesus in the Great Commission. Consequently, a Great Commission that was supposedly fulfilled in AD 70 leaves preterists without an imperative for worldwide evangelism.

20 Kik 1971, p. 101

5

The Abomination of Desolation

T he previous signs that Jesus prophesied were too general to predict the onset of the end of the age. However, the Master provided one specific sign, the abomination of desolation, to signify the arrival of the great tribulation and the end.

> So when you see the abomination of desolation spoken of by the prophet Daniel, standing in the holy place (let the reader understand), then let those who are in Judea flee to the mountains. Let the one who is on the housetop not go down to take what is in his house, and let the one who is in the field not turn back to take his cloak. And alas for women who are pregnant and for those who are nursing infants in those days! Pray that your flight may not be in winter or on a Sabbath. For then there will be great tribulation, such as has not been from the beginning of the world until now, no, and never will be. And if those days had not been cut short, no human being would be saved. But for the sake of the elect those days will be cut short. (Matt. 24:15-22)

DeMar admits that the abomination of desolation mentioned by Jesus was the sign demonstrating the arrival of the end.[1] However, he also asserts that the first disciples had "no doubt" that the setting up of this abomination "was fulfilled in events leading up to the temple's destruction in A.D. 70."[2] The Jewish historian, Josephus, and many ancient and modern rabbis, have adopted the view that Daniel's prophecies of the abomination were fulfilled in the destruction of the Second Temple.[3] Most preterists teach that an abomination (i.e., an idol or idolatrous event) was set up "in the holy place" (i.e., the temple), which ultimately resulted in the

1 DeMar 1999, p. 179
2 Ibid., p. 101; Similarly, Gentry 2010c, loc. 1764
3 Josephus, *Antiquities* 10:11:7

destruction of Jerusalem in AD 70. Gentry explains, "Although the 'abomination of desolation' involves the destruction of Jerusalem (beginning with its encircling), it culminates in this final abominable act within the temple itself. Thus, the 'abomination of desolation' prophecy finds complete fulfillment in AD 70 during the events leading up to and including the August/September destruction of the Temple by the armies of the Roman general Titus."[4] Of course, many futurists disagree with this identification and maintain that the abomination refers to the Antichrist's idol that will someday be erected in the Third Temple in Jerusalem.

Jesus reiterated the phrase "the abomination of desolation", a concept first introduced in several places in the book of Daniel (Dan. 8:11; 9:27; 11:31; 12:11), which is why he directed his audience to properly understand this event by reading Daniel's prophecies ("let the reader understand" in Matt. 24:15). The following four references to the abomination of desolation are from the book of Daniel:

> It became great, even as great as the Prince of the host. And the regular burnt offering was taken away from him, and the place of his sanctuary was overthrown. (Dan. 8:11)

> And he shall make a strong covenant with many for one week, and for half of the week he shall put an end to sacrifice and offering. And on the wing of abominations shall come one who makes desolate, until the decreed end is poured out on the desolator. (Dan. 9:27)

> Forces from him shall appear and profane the temple and fortress, and shall take away the regular burnt offering. And they shall set up the abomination that makes desolate. (Dan. 11:31)

> And from the time that the regular bunt offering is taken away and the abomination that makes desolate is set up, there shall be 1,290 days. (Dan. 12:11)

Preterist scholar N. T. Wright teaches that Daniel 9:27 is "the crucial determining reference [for the abomination of Matt. 24:15],

---

4   Gentry 2010c, loc. 1839

with the others [Dan. 11:31; 12:11] being subordinated to it".[5] Gentry affirms Wright's assessment that the primary reference for the abomination of Matthew 24:15 is Daniel 9:27.[6] This is a weak argument because the wording of Jesus' phrase "the abomination of desolation" is found in Daniel 11:31 and 12:11 (LXX) and *not* Daniel 9:27! In addition, it is preferable to see all four references to the abomination of desolation in the book of Daniel as referring to the same abomination. This view is supported by the chronological and thematic similarities of the accounts and the fact that Jesus referred to Daniel as having spoken about a solitary abomination ("the abomination") without providing any further qualification.

Figure 2: Overview of Daniel 9:24-27

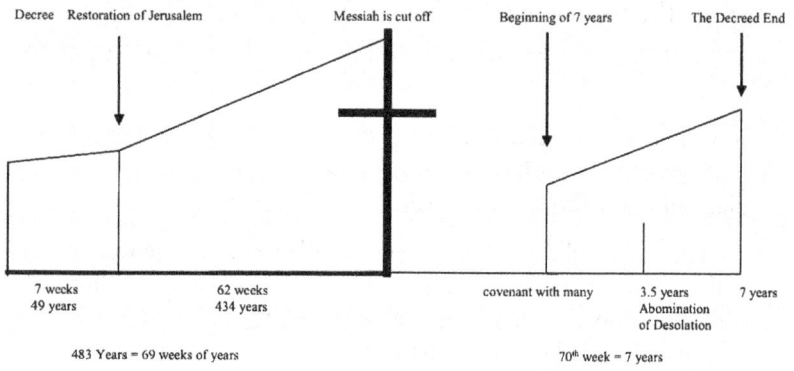

Decree Restoration of Jerusalem   Messiah is cut off   Beginning of 7 years   The Decreed End

| 7 weeks | 62 weeks | covenant with many | 3.5 years | 7 years |
| 49 years | 434 years | | Abomination of Desolation | |

483 Years = 69 weeks of years   70th week = 7 years

Chronological Problems

The inability of preterists to definitively identify this abomination of desolation *in history* is an oft-observed weakness of the entire system. DeMar admits that the preterist community lacks consensus about this identification.[7] Gentry concedes that some verses of the Olivet Discourse, beginning with the abomination

5   Wright 1996, p. 351
6   Gentry 2010c, loc. 1774; Ice and Gentry 1999, p.45
7   DeMar 1999, p. 109

in Matthew 24:15, "appear more difficult to assimilate into the preterist approach."[8]   However, their inability to conclusively identify the abomination has not deterred them from hunting feverishly through the annals of history to find it, a search forced upon them by their interpretation of the discourse. This weakness is especially troubling for the preterist system because the Lord taught that the abomination will be *the* climactic event that signifies the arrival of the unprecedented tribulation and the end of the age.

A variety of preterist opinions exist regarding the identity of the abomination of desolation (Matt. 24:15). Many preterists attach the label to the revolutionary actions of the Jewish Zealots against the Romans.[9] However, the actions associated with the Zealots, *as they pertained to the Second Temple,* occurred too late to allow for the specified period of at least 3.5 years of unprecedented tribulation. Chilton suggested that the abomination "seems to be the occasion when the Edomites (Idumeans), the agelong enemies of Israel, attacked Jerusalem. ... One evening in A.D. 68 the Edomites surrounded the holy city with 20,000 soldiers."[10] The problem with this view is that this event in AD 68 also took place *much too late* to allow for the specified 3.5 years of the unequaled tribulation. These events occurred only two years prior to the destruction of Jerusalem in AD 70. In addition, both of these preterist views are at odds with most other preterists, who see the abomination as referring to the actions of Vespasian and Titus and their Roman legions.[11]

J. Stuart Russell explained that, in his day, "most [preterist] expositors find an allusion to the standards of the Roman legions in the expression, 'the abomination of desolation,' and the explanation is highly probable."[12] This view suggests that the graven

---

8   Gentry 2010c, loc. 1710

9   Ice and Gentry 1999, p. 47

10 Chilton 2007, p. 92

11 E.g., Kik 1971, pp. 102, 110

12 Russell 2003, p. 73; Similarly Kik 1971, pp. 103-04

and molten images of Caesar and the legionary eagles atop the Roman standards constituted a desecration of Jerusalem's holiness. One weakness of this preterist position is that it removes the abomination from the temple complex, whereas the abomination in Daniel's prophecies is specifically concerned with the desecration of the temple sanctuary and the removal of the regular burnt offerings (Dan. 8:12-14; 9:27; 11:31; 12:11). This preterist view also places the abomination *far too late* chronologically. General Vespasian and his Roman armies arrived to begin their initial assault on Jerusalem in the late spring of AD 68, and General Titus resumed this assault in the spring of AD 69. General Titus and his Roman forces eventually entered the Jerusalem temple, but this occurred *even later* in the late summer of AD 70. N. T. Wright discusses several other pitfalls with this preterist interpretation of the abomination as described by Jesus:

> This is scarcely to be taken as a reference, after the event, to the actual happenings of AD 66-70. For a start, Titus and his legions were occupying the Mount of Olives and Mount Scopus, the two highest hills overlooking Jerusalem; fleeing to the hills would mean surrender and/or death. For another thing, by the time the Romans took the sanctuary itself it was too late to do anything about running away. Thirdly, the tradition of the Christians getting out of Jerusalem and going to Pella hardly counts as fleeing 'to the hills'; to get to Pella they would have had to descend 3,000 feet to the Jordan valley and then travel north for about thirty miles (Pella itself is about three miles east of the Jordan, and twenty miles south of the sea of Galilee). No one in their right mind would describe a flight to Pella as 'to the hills'.[13]

DeMar is aware of the difficulties with these preterist interpretations of the abomination of desolation. He points out that Luke's parallel account shows that Jerusalem would be "surrounded by armies" (Luke 21:20-21), which he believes is a reference to the saints fleeing the city after the invasion and subsequent withdrawal of the armies of Cestius Gallus. He explains that "escape

---

13 Wright 1996, p. 353

was made possible because Cestius and his armies suddenly and without warning withdrew from the temple area."[14] However, this position forces the preterist interpreter to locate the abomination at this particular time, specifically, in November AD 66. These events occurred *far too early* to fit the biblical chronology, as this would place the abomination almost a full four years before the destruction of Jerusalem.

DeMar then puts forth four different events as "possible" abominations of desolation with candidates including the Zealots, Idumeans, Romans, and Jews.[15] He scavenges for any historical occurrence that could possibly be identified as the abomination, but to no avail. He even considers the ongoing sacrifices that the high priests performed after the crucifixion of Jesus to be the "abomination, a rejection of the work of Christ."[16] This idea, which DeMar attributes to preterist James B. Jordan, reveals their desperation. By the time of the destruction of the Second Temple, the high priests had been offering sacrifices in the temple *for nearly three decades* following the crucifixion of Jesus. These sacrifices could not have constituted the particular sign that Jesus said will mark the beginning of the unequalled tribulation (cf. Matt. 24:14-19), especially since the priests had offered such sacrifices only a few days after he delivered the Olivet Discourse!

Preterists ignore the Lord's instruction to the reader that the abomination will be the very event that had been "spoken of by the prophet Daniel" (Matt. 24:15). They seek in vain to identify the primary sign that will signal the unprecedented tribulation because the historical events preceding the destruction of the Second Temple do not fit the details of Daniel's prophecies. It appears that DeMar attempts to avoid these chronological problems by arguing that the words of Jesus in Matthew 24:22 (i.e., "those days will be cut short") imply a foreshortening of the tribu-

---

14 DeMar 1999, p. 111
15 Ibid., pp. 104-109
16 Ibid., p. 108

lation period.[17] Nevertheless, the Lord did not teach a *premature* termination of the prophetic 3.5 years of the tribulation period; rather, he promised to return to save "the elect" and to preserve humanity ("no human being would be saved" in Matt. 24:22) by preventing the tribulation from continuing unabated *beyond* those appointed days.

Preterists also cast aspersion on the futurist interpretation of the abomination of desolation. Hanegraaff, for example, argues that Jesus could not have predicted a worldwide tribulation because no one could escape it simply by fleeing into the mountains outside Judea.[18] DeMar agrees: "People around the globe will have no such advantage [of seeing the abomination] if what Jesus is describing here refers to a worldwide tribulation period. The only ones who can benefit are those who can see the temple. The tribulation period cannot be global because all one has to do to escape is flee to the mountains."[19] Such musings betray an ignorance of the futurist position which sees an unprecedented worldwide tribulation *as only beginning at its epicenter*, the Jerusalem temple. Jesus commanded that only "those who are in Judea" flee to the hills (Matt. 24:16), a necessary exodus due to the invading armies of the Antichrist (Luke 21:20), and perhaps, the multinational invasion of Jerusalem (e.g., Zech. 14:1-5), in addition to the abomination standing in the place that it should not (Mark 13:14). Furthermore, the apostle Paul implied that those at least as far away as ancient Thessalonica should be able to identify "the man of lawlessness ... [who] takes his seat in the temple of God" (2 Thess. 2:3, 4).

Some preterists contend that the abomination of desolation must have been fulfilled in the first century AD because Jesus described first-century living conditions in this section of the Olivet Discourse (Matt. 24:17-20). DeMar explains, "Most roofs in Israel were flat with an outside staircase... In these verses, Jesus

17 Ibid., pp. 121-122
18 Hanegraaff 2007, p. 31
19 DeMar 1999, p. 121; cf. pp. 120, 122

refs to the strict Sabbath laws that were operating in first-century Israel".[20] This contention fails to consider that these architectural features still exist in modern Israel. Furthermore, based on rabbinic laws, the rebuilding of the Third Temple will undoubtedly be accompanied by the reinstatement of Sabbath requirements for all Jews, the same requirements that Orthodox Jews observe today. Many of these Sabbath laws have already been reinstated and are being enforced in the modern State of Israel.

DeMar also argues that Luke's parallel passage to the Olivet Discourse is concerned with the "days of vengeance" (Luke 21:22; cf. Isa. 61:2; 63:4), a period that DeMar identifies with Jerusalem's destruction in AD 70.[21] This portion of the discourse reads as follows:

> But when you see Jerusalem surrounded by armies, then know that its desolation has come near. Then let those who are in Judea flee to the mountains, and let those who are inside the city depart, and let not those who are out in the country enter it, for these are days of vengeance, to fulfill all that is written. Alas for women who are pregnant and for those who are nursing infants in those days! For there will be great distress upon the earth and wrath against this people. They will fall by the edge of the sword and be led captive among all nations, and Jerusalem will be trampled underfoot by the Gentiles, until the times of the Gentiles are fulfilled. (Luke 21:20-24)

Contrary to DeMar's claim, this passage does not describe the relatively-long period of exile that began with the destruction of Jerusalem in AD 70, but *the much shorter exile that will occur during the future tribulation period.* This is based on several lines of evidence. First, the period of unprecedented tribulation that will begin with the appearance of the abomination of desolation "in the holy place" (Matt. 24:15ff) tightly corresponds with the period when the nations will trample Jerusalem, after armies have surrounded the city, according to Luke's parallel account (Luke

20 Ibid., p. 111
21 Ibid., p.25

21:20-24). Second, the prophet Daniel consistently described this unprecedented tribulation as a period of 3.5 years that will begin with the setting up of the abomination of desolation and the removal of the daily burnt offering (Dan. 9:27; 12:1, 7, 11). Third, a corresponding passage in the Apocalypse demonstrates that the temple's outer court will be "given over to the nations, and they will trample the holy city for forty-two months. ... 1,260 days" (Rev. 11:2, 3). Fourth, Jesus equated the period when Jerusalem will be "trampled underfoot" by the nations with the time when the Jews will be sent into exile "among all nations" (Luke 21:24). The implication is that Jerusalem will no longer be trampled by the nations after this period of Gentile domination (i.e., "the times of the Gentiles" in Luke 21:24), presumably because the Jewish nation will be redeemed, or more to the point, the Lord will have installed his King on Zion and terrified the kings of the earth in his fury (Ps. 2) (see Chapter 17). Fifth, other prophetic texts demonstrate that the trampling of the sanctuary will occur *after a relatively recent return from exile* (Isa. 63:18; cf. 64:10-11; Ezek. 38:8; Zeph. 2:1-2), which does not fit the description of the destructions of the First or Second Temples.

The Great Tribulation

Their prophetic system pushes many preterists into interpreting the unprecedented tribulation that Jesus described as *mere hyperbole.* Hanegraaff represented the opinion of many preterists when he wrote that Jesus "was not literally predicting that the destruction of Jerusalem would be more cataclysmic than the catastrophe caused by Noah's flood" but was "clearly using prophetic hyperbole."[22] Preterists recognize that they cannot sustain their premise that the great tribulation ended with the destruction of the temple in AD 70 while taking the words of Jesus literally, when he described the tribulation with such particularity - "such as has not been from the beginning of the world until now, no, and never will be. And if those days had not been cut short, no human being

[22] Hanegraaff 2007, p. 30, 62

would be saved" (Matt. 24:21-22; cf. Dan. 12:1-2). Admittedly, it is challenging to imagine a time that exceeds the post-World War II, post-Holocaust devastation.

Some preterists teach that the Old Testament supports their thesis that Jesus used hyperbole to describe the *unprecedented* tribulation.[23] For example, Hanegraaff surmises that the prophet Jeremiah employed such hyperbolic language to describe the destruction of the First Temple in the sixth century BC. The prophet Jeremiah declared, "Ask now, and see, can a man bear a child? Why then do I see every man with his hands on his stomach like a woman in labor? Why has every face turned pale? That day is so great *there is none like it*; it is a time of distress for Jacob; yet he shall be saved out of it" (Jer. 30:6-7, emphasis added).[24]

However, the immediate context of this passage reveals that the prophet was not speaking of events in Jeremiah's day, but about the future unequalled tribulation. This is evident from the description of the messianic birth pains (v. 6), the ultimate restoration of Judah and Israel to the land in "quiet and ease . . . and none shall make him afraid" (vv. 3, 10), the nation serving the risen Davidic Messiah (v. 9), and the complete destruction of all wicked nations on the day of the Lord (vv. 7, 9).

Chilton objected to the futurist understanding of the great tribulation because it seemed to require a double fulfillment. He explains that the Olivet Discourse "cannot be made to fit into some 'double-fulfillment' scheme of interpretation; the Great Tribulation of A.D. 70 was an absolutely unique event, never to be repeated."[25] Most futurists agree with Chilton that the tribulation will be unprecedented, and hence *without duplication*, but disagree with his assessment that it refers to the period of the First Jewish-Roman War (AD 66-70). However, the futurist position allows that the Olivet Prophecy provides a certain *versatility of*

---

23 E.g., Gentry 2010c, loc. 1925; cf. loc. 1935
24 Hanegraaff 2007, p. 62
25 Chilton 2007, p. 93

application sufficient to prompt the first-century Jewish saints to flee Judea to escape the onslaught of the Roman armies.[26]

Jesus continued his discourse by warning about false christs ("anointed ones") and false prophets who will make false predictions about messianic appearances during the great tribulation:

> Then if anyone says to you, "Look, here is the Christ!" or "There he is!" do not believe it. For false christs and false prophets will arise and perform great signs and wonders, so as to lead astray, if possible, even the elect. See, I have told you beforehand. So, if they say to you, "Look, he is in the wilderness," do not go out. If they say, "Look, he is in the inner rooms," do not believe it. For as the lightning comes from the east and shines as far as the west, so will be the coming of the Son of Man. Wherever the corpse is, there the vultures will gather. (Matt. 24:23-28)

Some preterists agree with the traditional interpretation that Matthew 24:27 refers to the Lord's second advent. Gentry, for example, writes, "When he [Jesus] does return it will be visible and dramatic as lightning flashing."[27] Gentry then retreats into a diatribe about how Jesus was supposedly contrasting "his dramatic coming in the second advent with the metaphorical coming in AD 70", only to return in verse 28 to the topic of the "AD 70 judgment."[28] Apparently Gentry realizes that the Son of Man's coming (παρουσία) in verse 27 is concerned with *the personal presence of the Messiah* at his return, as also evidenced by the contrasted content in the previous verse ("Look, he is in the wilderness/inner rooms" in verse 26). As we will see in Chapter Seven, Gentry's futile attempt to disconnect the coming of Jesus from his *personal return* is not based on exegetical considerations but on concerns to protect his preterist position regarding the Olivet Discourse.

Preterist opinions differ as to whether Matthew 24:28 ("Wherever the corpse is, there the vultures will gather") envisions literal

---

26 Eusebius, *Ecclesiastical History* 3.5.3
27 Gentry 2010c, loc.1989; Similarly Kik 1971, p. 124
28 Ibid., loc. 1989-1994; Similarly Kik 1971, p. 124

vultures feasting on human corpses[29] or is a metaphor to illustrate the idea that Gentry puts forth: "Israel is judicially dead; the Roman armies will devour her carcass."[30] Gentry, following N. T. Wright and others, argues that the vultures, variously translated as eagles, refers to the Roman Eagles.[31] This interpretation is unlikely because the corresponding prophecy in the Apocalypse depicts birds feasting upon the carcasses of those slain in battle. The apostle John wrote, "Then I saw an angel standing in the sun, and with a loud voice he called to all the birds that fly directly overhead, 'Come, gather for the great supper of God, to eat the flesh of kings, the flesh of captains, the flesh of mighty men, the flesh of horses and their riders, and the flesh of all men, both free and slave, both small and great.'... And the rest were slain by the sword that came from the mouth of him who was sitting on the horse, and all the birds were gorged with their flesh" (Rev. 19:17-18, 21; cf. Ezek. 39:17-20).

We have seen that preterists are unable to identify the abomination of desolation in history. Their attempts to identify it fail to account for the prophetic expectations of the book of Daniel and the Olivet Discourse. The historical events of the first century AD do not provide for biblical expectations of an idol being set up in the Jerusalem temple that signals the beginning of a period of unprecedented tribulation lasting 3.5 years. Preterists have proposed several candidates for the abomination, including the actions of the Jewish Zealots, the Edomites, Cestius Gallus, General Vespasian, and General Titus, but none of the events associated with these historical players fit the prophetic details of the biblical prophecies.

29 Hanegraaff 2007, p. 33
30 Gentry 2010c, loc. 2019; cf. loc. 2045; cf. loc. 2004, 2024; Kik 1971, p. 110
31 Wright 1996, p. 360; Gentry 2010c, loc. 2024-2029

6

The Day of the Lord

The Lord Jesus Christ taught that specific cosmic phenomena will occur after the great tribulation. He stated, "Immediately after the tribulation of those days the sun will be darkened, and the moon will not give its light, and the stars will fall from heaven, and the powers of the heavens will be shaken" (Matt. 24:29). Gentry admits that a literal, straight-forward interpretation of this passage does not support preterism. He writes, "A quick reading of this statement seems to undermine the preterist approach I have been presenting....And certainly if we were to interpret this passage in a strictly literal sense, it would be difficult to associate these prophetic events with AD 70. But looks are deceiving."[1] Kik admits that this passage "employs such strong and vivid language that many think it can be descriptive of nothing else than the end of the world and the second coming of Christ. These descriptive terms would seem to indicate a catastrophic end of the earth."[2] In this chapter, we will examine preterist claims about this passage and the reasons why this verse does not favor a preterist interpretation.

The language of cosmic phenomena in Matthew 24:29 pertains to the eschatological day of YHVH (הָוֹהְי סוֹי)—the day of the LORD. In this passage, Jesus taught that the darkening of the Sun, moon, and stars will occur "immediately after" the unprecedented tribulation. Equally true, such cosmic phenomena will signal the onset of the day of the Lord, as God said through the prophet Joel: "And I will show wonders in the heavens and on the earth, blood and fire and columns of smoke. The sun shall be turned to darkness, and the moon to blood, *before the great and*

---

1 Gentry 2010c, loc. 2055-2061; Similarly Kik 1971, pp. 31-32
2 Kik 1971, p. 127

awesome day of the Lord comes" (Joel 2:30-31, emphasis added; cf. Acts 2:20-21). These prophecies provide the reader with a sequence of events regarding the day of the Lord.

Figure 3: The Tribulation and the Day of the Lord

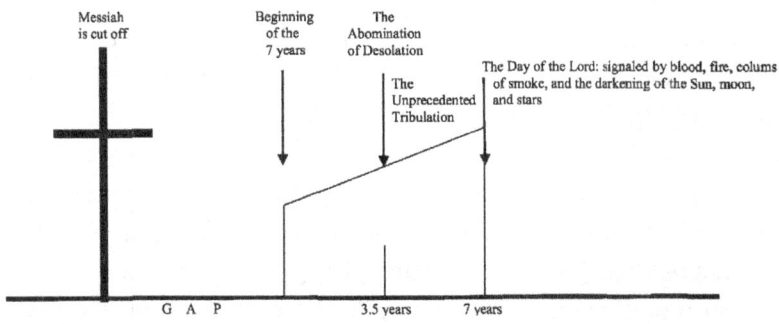

Preterists and futurists generally agree that Matthew 24:29 is not a quotation of a single text but represents a general theme found in multiple Old Testament passages (e.g., Isa. 13:10; 34:4; Ezek. 32:7; Joel 2:10, 31; 3:15; Amos 8:9).[3] The New Testament scholar, Craig L. Blomberg, explains, "[The lines of Matt. 24:29] allude to Isa. 13:10, with echoes of 34:4. ...The closest thing to an actual quotation that we find in Matthew is 'the moon will not give its light,' with a different Greek word used for 'light' than in the LXX. It is Isa. 34:4, though, that actually has the stars being dissolved and falling. ...A constellation of allusions rather than an actual quotation seems to be a more accurate description of Matthew's form."[4]

These Old Testament prophets depicted the darkening of the Sun, moon, and stars at the day of the Lord (Isa. 13:10; 24:23; 50:3; Joel 2:10; 3:15; Amos 8:9; cf. Rev. 6:12-14). They taught that the heavenly bodies will become darkened so that they no longer shine (Joel 2:10; 3:15; cf. Ezek. 32:7-8). The luminaries will no

---

3 Chilton 2007, pp. 99, 133; DeMar 1999, p. 150; Gentry 2010c, loc. 2009-2121; Hanegraaff 2007, pp. 31, 89; Mathison 2004, p. 159; Sproul 1998, p. 52

4 Blomberg, Craig L. in Beale and Carson 2007, p. 87

longer provide light although they will continue to operate within their orbits (Isa. 13:10; cf. 24:23). The prophet Joel declared, "Let all the inhabitants of the land tremble, for the day of the Lord is coming; it is near, a day of darkness and gloom, a day of clouds and thick darkness!" (Joel 2:2-3; cf. Zeph. 1:15-16) The day of the Lord will be characterized by darkness because God will "make the sun go down at noon" so that the earth will be darkened during the time of "broad daylight" (Isa. 59:9-10; Ezek. 30:3; Amos 5:19-20; 8:9). People will walk "like the blind" so that they stumble (Isa. 59:9-10; Zeph. 1:17).

Consistent with the Old Testament prophets, the apostle John connected the timing of the day of the Lord with four observable phenomena: (1) a great earthquake, (2) the darkening of the Sun and moon, (3) the stars falling to the earth, and (4) the sky vanishing "like a scroll that is being rolled up." He wrote, "When [the Lamb of God] opened the sixth seal, I looked, and behold, there was a great earthquake, and the sun became black as sackcloth, the full moon became like blood, and the stars of the sky fell to the earth as the fig tree sheds its winter fruit when shaken by a gale. The sky vanished like a scroll that is being rolled up, and every mountain and island was removed from its place" (Rev. 6:12-14). John saw that the Sun will become "black as sackcloth" and the moon will appear crimson "like blood" (Rev. 6:12; cf. Joel 2:30-31), similar to Isaiah's prophecy that God will clothe the heavens with black sackcloth, reminiscent of an ancient mourning practice (Isa. 50:3).

In particular, the earthquake will cause every mountain and island to be moved from its geographical location. It should be noted that the atmospheric dust and debris from such an earthquake would be sufficient to darken the daytime sky and create the perception of a blood-red moon, an appropriate heavenly symbol corresponding to the blood spilled on earth at that time (c.f., Joel 2:30). In addition, a massive earthquake is associated with other passages regarding the day of the Lord (Isa. 2:13-16; 30:25; 40:4; Ezek. 38:18-20; Amos 8:8; Zech. 14:4-5; Rev. 11:13; 16:18-21).

The language of Revelation 6:12-14 and related passages strongly favors a literal interpretation.

Revelation 6:13-14 also depicts the "stars" falling to the earth "as the fig tree sheds its winter fruit when shaken by a gale" and the sky vanishing "like a scroll that is being rolled up." This is an allusion to Isaiah's prophecy that "all the host of heaven shall rot away, and the skies roll up like a scroll. All their host shall fall, as leaves fall from the vine, like leaves falling from the fig tree" (Isa. 34:4). However, John's passage also appeals to the statement of the Lord Jesus that "the stars will fall from heaven, and the powers of the heavens will be shaken" (Matt. 24:29). This motif is consistent with Luke's unambiguous parallel account of *literal* cosmic and oceanic phenomena ("signs in the sun and moon and stars, and on the earth distress of nations in perplexity because of the roaring of the sea and the waves" in Luke 21:25). This also strongly argues against any *symbolic* interpretation of the cosmic phenomena depicted in Jesus' statement in Matthew 24:29.

Preterist N. T. Wright explains that the various descriptions of the day of the Lord "have regularly been seen as predictions of the end of the space-time universe,"[5] and he contends that they do not refer to the end of the universe or the final judgment.[6] Hanegraaff chides, "To suppose that stars are literally going to fall from the sky is nonsense. One star alone would obliterate the earth—let alone a hundred billion stars."[7] Such statements contain at least two fallacies. First, the biblical word ἀστέρες ("stars") often does not refer to stars in the modern, limited sense of distant suns from other galaxies. This Greek term can refer to any fiery objects in the sky such as meteors, asteroids, and burning debris. Therefore, it seems reasonable, even preferable, to understand the falling "stars" (whatever they consist of) as the *cause* of the great earthquake and massive atmospheric conditions such as "blood and fire and columns of smoke" (Joel 2:30; variously "vapor of smoke" in

5   Wright 1996, pp. 320, 362

6   Ibid., p. 325 using material from Caird & Hurst 1994, 361ff

7   Hanegraaff 2007, p. 136; cf. DeMar 1999, p. 142

Acts 2:19). Consequently, such passages can be rendered literally without creating a scenario where the planet is vaporized. Second, the traditional futurist position does *not* advance the idea that the universe will be completely destroyed on the day of the Lord, but that the present cosmos will experience massive atmospheric changes. Nonetheless, the planet will continue to exist until after the millennium (thus pre-millennialism).

Preterists sometimes obscure the fact that the Apocalypse variously portrays "stars" as literal (e.g., Rev. 6:13; 8:10-12) and figurative (e.g., Rev. 1:20; 2:28; 12:1; 22:6). Many futurist commentators understand the casting down of "a third of the stars of heaven" to the earth (Rev. 12:4) as symbolic, as evidenced by the allusion to the metaphor of Daniel 8:10. Nevertheless, while critiquing futurism, DeMar finds it necessary to point out that the fall of "'a third of the *meteorites* of heaven' would have a devastating effect on our planet."[8] DeMar fails to regard the fact that the surrounding context of each individual use of the word "stars" ought to guide our interpretation. As a general rule, any biblical text should be understood literally unless the historical or linguistic context makes such an interpretation unlikely or impossible.

The majority of preterists argue that the language of cosmic destruction in Matthew 24:29 symbolizes the end of the nation of Israel in AD 70.[9] For example, Leithart claims that this language is "obviously used to describe an historical event, the collapse of a political-religious order" by which he means "the end of the Old Covenant order or Judaism by using language of cosmic collapse."[10] Kik agrees, "In the light of prophetic language and pronouncements, this verse is descriptive of the passing away of Judaism. It describes the eclipse of the Old Testament dispensation. It describes the passing away of Jewish privileges and

---

8   DeMar 1999, p. 143; cf. pp. 143, 146
9   Ibid., pp. 144, 147; Gentry 2010c, loc. 2066; Kik 1971, p. 32; Leithart 2004; Wright 1996, p. 362
10 Leithart 2004, pp. 5, 2

glories."[11] He also writes, "The sun of Judaism has been darkened; as the moon it no longer reflects the light of God; bright stars, as the list of heroes in Hebrews 11, no longer shine in the Israel of the flesh."[12] Gentry explains, "When a national government collapses in war and upheaval, Scripture often poetically portrays it 'as a cosmic catastrophe – an undoing of Creation.' ...And in a sense it is 'the end of the world' for those nations God judges. So is it with Israel in AD 70."[13] Preterists reason that Jesus employed this cosmic language to speak about the destruction of Israel, since similar prophetic passages depict the downfall of ancient geopolitical civilizations such as Egypt, Babylon, and Edom. The following quotes illustrate this view:

> David Chilton: There was a "language" of prophecy, instantly recognizable to those familiar with the Old Testament ... As Jesus foretold the complete end of the Old Covenant System – which was, in a sense, the end of the whole world – He spoke of it as any of the prophets would have, in the stirring language of covenantal judgment. ...these heavenly lights are used to speak of earthly authorities and governors ... It must be stressed that none of these events literally took place. God did not intend anyone to place a literalist construction on these statements. Poetically, however, all these things did happen: as far as these wicked nations were concerned, "the lights went out." This is simply figurative language, which would not surprise us at all if we were more familiar with the Bible and appreciative of its literary character. ...that the light of Israel is going to be extinguished; the covenant nation will cease to exist. When the Tribulation is over, old Israel will be gone.[14]

> Hank Hanegraaff: Jesus is not predicting the eradication of the cosmos. Nor is he prophesying the end of civilization... Rather, Jesus is employing hyperbolic language that is deeply rooted in Old Testament history.[15]

---

11 Kik 1971, p. 32, cf. pp. 128, 132, 136-37

12 Ibid., pp. 128-29

13 Gentry 2010c, loc. 2121-2127

14 Chilton 2007, pp. 98, 99

15 Hanegraaff 2007, p. 31

J. Marcellus Kik: A study of the Old Testament Scriptures discloses to us the fact that there is an apocalyptic language which describes great national disasters. Familiar symbols are used to articulate the destruction of nations.[16]

Keith Mathison: Over and over, the prophets describe the catastrophes that are about to befall Israel and her enemies in terms of the earth being shaken, the stars falling, and the sun and moon being darkened. ...Many of these prophecies describe judgments that occurred centuries ago. This 'cosmic judgment language' is a metaphorical way of describing important events surrounding the fall of earthly kingdoms.[17]

James Stuart Russell: It will at once be seen that the imagery employed in this passage [Isaiah 13] is almost identical with that of our Lord. If these symbols therefore were proper to represent the fall of Babylon, why should they be improper to set forth a still greater catastrophe—the destruction of Jerusalem?[18]

R. C. Sproul: The graphic language used by Jesus to describe the attending events is metaphorical and consistent with the poetry of fervor used by Old Testament prophets.[19]

N. T. Wright: They [i.e., the day of the Lord passages] ... are, as we have seen from the passages in Isaiah and Jeremiah ... , typical Jewish imagery for events within the present order that are felt and perceived as 'cosmic' or, as we should say, as 'earth-shattering'. More particularly, they are regular Jewish imagery for events that bring the story of Israel to its appointed climax. The days of Jerusalem's destruction would be looked upon as days of cosmic catastrophe.[20]

This preterist argument that the Old Testament prophecies about the day of the Lord pointed to national judgments *in history* simply begs the question. One reason for this is that the downfall of historical civilizations did *not* exhaustively fulfill the prophetic expectations regarding the day of the Lord. Rather, the

16 Kik 1971, p. 129
17 Mathison 2004, p. 162
18 Russell 2003, p. 80
19 Sproul 1998, p. 56
20 Wright 1996, p. 362

prophets warned their immediate audience of coming judgment by employing language that was readily understood as pointing to the eschatological day of the Lord. Furthermore, only futurism accounts for the prophetic expectations of a multinational military invasion of the land of Israel that will occur prior to the day of the Lord (Ezek. 38:1-39:24; Joel 3:1-16; Zeph. 1:15-16; Zech. 14:1-5; 12-15; Rev. 16:12-16; cf. Isa. 13:4-6). Finally, the prophecies reveal that Judah and Jerusalem will be delivered while the nations who invade them will be destroyed on that day (Ezek. 38:21-23; 39:3-20; Joel 3:1-16; Zech. 14:3, 11-19; cf. Isa. 13:14-16). The exact opposite scenario played itself out during the First Jewish-Roman War, that is, Judea and Jerusalem were *destroyed* while the invading armies, the Roman troops, were *victorious* in AD 70! Preterists attempt in vain to explain away this historical fact. For example, James Jordan desperately argues that the Roman Empire "did not cease to exist in AD 70" but ceased to be "a spiritual power energized by the full power of Satan."[21]

The Already and Not Yet

The Old Testament prophecies concerning the day of the Lord sometimes pointed to localized, historical judgments that were fulfilled *in part* during the lifetimes of their original audience. Nevertheless, these prophecies collectively form a larger patchwork motif that awaits *plenary* fulfillment at the ultimate day of the Lord (i.e., judgment day). As mentioned in Chapter Two, the terminology of such passages conveyed a firm expectation of judgment for the hearers and urged immediate repentance. In this manner, eschatological prophecies allowed for contemporary application while holding out until the end of the age for their exhaustive fulfillment. This is an example of inaugurated eschatology, otherwise known as the "already and not yet" principle of biblical interpretation.

A detailed and comprehensive analysis of this "already and not yet" pattern regarding the day of the Lord (and other eschato-

---

21 Jordan 2014, loc. 508

logical events) is beyond the scope of this work. However, suffice it to say that this pattern is conceded by many partial preterists. For example, Gentry expounds, "This is akin to there being several historical episodes of 'the day of the Lord' in the Old Testament ...Each of these anticipate the final 'day of the Lord' event at the end of history (2 Pet 3:10)."[22] Gentry provides the example of the day of the Lord in Hebrews 10:25, which he believes was prophetically foreshadowed by "the day of Israel's judgment in AD 70"[23]. Mathison similarly elucidates, "All of these different events that are referred to as 'the day of the Lord' are types of the final day of the Lord—the day on which God will lead his armies into battle, utterly and completely defeating all his enemies."[24] Hanegraaff approves of this evaluation:

> While the near-future catastrophe (demotion of Babylon and destruction of Jerusalem) fulfills the cosmic language, it does not exhaust its meaning... While Peter's prophecy [2 Peter 3:10-13] was fulfilled in the destruction of Jerusalem, the events of AD 70 and the cosmic language Peter used to describe them point forward to an even greater day of judgment when the problem of sin and Satan will be full and finally resolved! ... In sum, then, John [in Revelation], like Jesus and the prophets before him, uses the imagery of sun, moon, and stars to refer to the near-future judgment of Jerusalem. While the language finds ultimate fulfillment in the second coming of Christ, it is inaugurated in the Jewish holocaust of AD 70.[25]

Full preterists and many partial preterists teach that the prophecy given by the apostle Peter concerning the day of the Lord (2 Peter 3:4-13) was fulfilled in AD 70. Leithart represents the sentiments of many preterists that the collapsing-universe language in Matthew 24:29 and elsewhere points to the destruction of the temple in AD 70, which "marked the end of the Old

---

22 Gentry 2010c, loc. 1009; Similarly Kik 1971, pp. 68-69
23 Gentry 2010c, loc. 2405
24 Mathison 2004, p. 159
25 Hanegraaff 2007, pp. 135-136

Creation and brought in a New Creation."[26] He then provided a detailed "preterist reading of 2 Peter,"[27] as did John Owen[28] and Chilton.[29] He explains his reason for regarding Peter's prophecy as having been fulfilled in the first century AD. He wrote, "If 1 Peter is about a revelation that is 'ready' to come, about an 'end of all things' that is 'at hand,' about a judgment that is 'ready to begin' at the house of God, then 2 Peter, which is a reminder of things taught in the previous letter, must be about the same topic.... Peter wrote his second letter on the theme of the coming of Jesus, which he says was also a theme of his first letter, which is 1 Peter. Since 1 Peter's teaching about the 'coming' of Jesus highlights its imminence, 2 Peter must be dealing with the same looming events."[30]

We will now examine the apostle's prophecy in 2 Peter 3 and explore some of the dangerous implications of a preterist interpretation of the passage.

> They [scoffers] will say, "Where is the promise of his coming? For ever since the fathers fell asleep, all things are continuing as they were from the beginning of creation." For they deliberately overlook this fact, that the heavens existed long ago, and the earth was formed out of water and through water by the word of God, and that by means of these the world that then existed was deluged with water and perished. But by the same word the heavens and earth that now exist are stored up for fire, being kept until the day of judgment and destruction of the ungodly. But do not overlook this one fact, beloved, that with the Lord one day is as a thousand years, and a thousand years as one day. The Lord is not slow to fulfill his promise as some count slowness, but is patient toward you, not wishing that any should perish, but that all should reach repentance. But the day of the Lord will come like a thief, and then the heavens will pass away with a roar, and the heavenly bodies will be burned up and dissolved, and the earth and the works

26 Leithart 2004, p. 25
27 Ibid., p. 1
28 Owen 1965-68, 9:134-135
29 Chilton 2006
30 Leithart 2004, pp. 13-14; cf. DeMar 1999, p. 30

that are done on it will be exposed. Since all these things are thus to be dissolved, what sort of people ought you to be in lives of holiness and godliness, waiting for and hastening the coming of the day of God, because of which the heavens will be set on fire and dissolved, and the heavenly bodies will melt as they burn! But according to his promise we are waiting for new heavens and a new earth in which righteousness dwells. (2 Peter 3:4-13; cf. 1 Peter 1:8, 13)

In this passage, the apostle Peter foresaw the *literal* destruction of "the heavens and earth." He appealed to the themes of creation (Gen. 1-2) and the flood (Gen. 6-9) to argue against the uniformitarianism of the scoffers who deny that God will fullfill his promise to return and bring a cataclysmic judgment against the world (2 Peter 3:4; cf. Isa. 24). Peter explained that God will destroy the present heavens and earth "by the same word" that he created the world and later destroyed it by the flood (vv. 5-7). The "heavens" are reserved for a fiery dissolution that will be revealed on the day of the Lord (v. 10), variously called "the day of judgment" (v. 7) and "the day of God" (v. 12). The apostle confirmed that the created order will *literally* be destroyed by fire by finding a parallel in its *literal* destruction with water. It should not escape the reader's attention that the planet continued to exist after it was destroyed by the flood.

Peter reminded his readers, based on the promises in Isaiah 65:17-25 and 66:22, that the Lord will create "new heavens and a new earth" (2 Peter 3:13). The New Testament scholar, D. A. Carson, points out a practical implication of this new creation:

The Isaianic promise of "a new heaven and a new earth" (LXX) is also picked up by Revelation's final vision: Rev. 21:1, with its promise of a new heaven and a new earth, introduces the glorious description of the final state that follows the millennium and the judgment of God. The same vision can be cast without using the same words that Peter uses: the apostle Paul talks about the anticipated liberation of the entire creation from its bondage to decay (Rom. 8:18-25). *It is doubtful that either Christian steadfastness or Christian morality, let alone Christian spirituality and Christian eschatology, can long be maintained without the dominance of this vision.*[31]

In addition to compromising Christian ethics and eschatology, many preterists surrender other important doctrines in order to maintain a consistent hermeneutic. For example, they superimpose their preterist interpretation of Matthew 24:29 onto related passages concerning the day of the Lord such as 2 Peter 3:4-13. They teach that these passages were fulfilled in the destruction of Jerusalem and its temple in AD 70. Consequently, they *necessarily* deny that the themes of old creation-new creation are concerned with the destruction and renewal of the literal cosmos. They surmise that the *totality* of the new creation is the Christian church, the new covenant, or the like. This creates uncertainty in the minds of many preterists about the historic interpretation of other new creation passages such as Romans 8:18-25 and Revelation 21. The preterist must then consider whether Christians will be resurrected to enter the heavenly Jerusalem, a city that they suppose has already descended in a metaphorical or relational-covenantal fashion in AD 70. This brings up the consideration of whether sin, sorrow, pain, and death will be fully abolished in the new creation (as per Rev. 21:4) since it supposedly arrived in AD 70.

The apostle Paul warned about preterist teachers who advance the idea that the day of the Lord has already occurred (2 Thess. 2:1-8; cf. 2 Tim. 2:17-18). Some preterists have heeded Paul's warning and do not adhere to a fully-realized interpretation of the day of the Lord. For example, Chilton, Gentry, James Jordan, and others teach that the new creation is being manifested progressively, having arrived only in a nascent sense in the first century.[32] Regarding Revelation 21:1, Chilton wrote, *"salvation is a re-creation ...* 'a new heaven and earth,' ... the *primary* significance of that phrase is symbolic, and has to do with the blessings of salvation. John next saw 'the Holy City, New Jerusalem ... *it is*

---

31 Carson, D. A. in Beale and Carson 2007, p. 1061, emphasis added
32 E.g., Jordan 2014, loc. 604

the Church. ... We are in the New Jerusalem now. Proof? ...(Heb. 12:22-23) ... The highest fulfillment will take place in heaven for eternity. But, *definitively* and *progressively*, it is true now. We are living in the new heaven and the new earth; we are citizens of the New Jerusalem."[33]

While futurists disagree with the preterist view that the dissolution of the old creation is about the destruction of Jerusalem in AD 70, they generally agree that the new creation exhibits an "already and not yet" aspect of fulfillment. Jesus Christ was resurrected from the dead to be a firstfruits' offering to God (1 Cor. 15:23), and the regenerating power of the Holy Spirit is a firstfruits' work of our own resurrection (Rom. 8:23). As such, we who belong to Christ also belong to the new creation (2 Cor. 5:17) and to the heavenly Jerusalem that he has prepared for us to receive (Heb. 11:10, 16; 12:22; Rev. 21:1ff). God's new creation has *begun* in the person of Jesus and in his firstfruits church but this does not mean that it has completely and *consummately* arrived. Consequently, some partial preterists, those who advocate an "already and not yet" approach to the new creation, correctly teach that its arrival awaits a future fulfillment at the return of Jesus Christ.

---

33 Chilton 2007, pp. 203-204

7

Coming on the Clouds

The cosmic events of the day of the Lord will culminate in the glorious appearing of Jesus Christ from heaven. In the Olivet Discourse, the Master promised, "Then will appear in heaven the sign of the Son of Man, and then all the tribes of the earth will mourn, and they will see the Son of Man coming on the clouds of heaven with power and great glory" (Matt. 24:30). This verse is a conflation of Daniel 7:13 ("behold, with the clouds of heaven there came one like a son of man"), Zechariah 12:10 LXX ("they will weep"; "all the tribes"), and possibly Isaiah 11:12 and others. The historic church has taught that Matthew 24:30 is an unambiguous reference to the glorious *return* of Jesus.[1]

Matthew 24:30 presents a dilemma for preterists, since they teach that it does not refer to the second coming of Jesus, but to first-century events. Chilton explains: "What appears to pose a problem for this interpretation, however, is what Jesus says ... Jesus seems to be saying that the Second Coming will occur immediately after the Tribulation. Did the Second Coming occur in A.D. 70? Have we missed it?"[2] Sproul frames the problem for preterism:

> This passage describes the parousia in vivid and graphic images of astronomical perturbations. It speaks of signs in the sky that will be visible and the sound of a trumpet that will be audible. Perhaps no portion of the Olivet Discourse provides more difficulties to the preterist view than this one. This portion leads many interpreters to see a clear historical division between references to the destruction of Jerusalem and references to the parousia of Christ. These interpreters grant that the destruction of the temple and Jerusalem took

---

1 Wright 1996, p. 342
2 Chilton 2007, p. 97

place within the time-frame of one generation, but insist that Christ has yet to appear in clouds of glory. This is true of interpreters from both the liberal and the conservative ends of the theological spectrum.[3]

Some preterists chide that the futurist position erroneously conceives of Jesus as engaging in "a primitive form of space travel."[4] Wright claims that the coming of the Son of Man on clouds in this verse has *nothing* to do with his return but is "a symbol for a mighty reversal of fortunes within history and at the national level."[5] The idea behind the verse, then, would be that the destruction of Jerusalem and the temple in AD 70 was the "sign" proving that Jesus had been vindicated, exalted, and enthroned as Israel's Messiah![6] (an amazing counter-intuitive assertion) Hanegraaff expounds, "It is important to note that 'the sign' is what 'shall appear.' It is misleading to understand the phrase as meaning 'then shall appear the Son of Man in the sky.' The Son of Man does not appear; the sign appears. Then Christ defines what the sign signifies: it is the sign that the Son of Man is now in heaven."[7]

Most partial preterists teach that the Son of Man's coming in Matthew 24:30 refers to the post-resurrection ascension of Jesus.[8] Hanegraaff claims that Jesus is "clearly not *descending* to earth in his second coming but rather *ascending* to the throne of the Almighty in vindication and exaltation."[9] As N. T. Wright points out, the Greek word ἐρχόμενον (translated "coming") in this verse could be rendered "going."[10] The idea is that Jesus ascended to

3 Sproul 1998, p. 49

4 E.g., Wright 1996, p. 341 using material from Caird 1965, 20-22

5 Ibid.

6 Chilton 2007, pp. 100, 103; DeMar 1999, p. 165; Gentry 2010c, loc. 2156, 2161, 2187, 2192-2202; Hanegraaff 2007, pp. 26-27, 84; Kik 1971, pp. 137, 138; Mathison 2004, p. 201; Wright 1996, p. 362

7 Gentry 2010c, loc. 2138-2145; Similarly Kik 1971, p. 137

8 E.g., DeMar 1999, p. 163; Mathison 2004, pp. 164-65, 181, 182, 201

9 Hanegraaff 2007, p. 83; Similarly Adams and Fisher 2000, pp. 23-24; France 1985, pp. 343-44; Jordan 2014, loc. 215; Kik 1971, p. 37

10 Wright 1996, p. 361

receive his kingdom and to sit at the Father's right hand until the destruction of "his enemies" occurred in AD 70. Chilton explains that the directionality of Jesus "going" away to the Father finds its basis in the prophecy of Daniel 7:13-14:

> But notice exactly what Daniel says: Christ is seen going *up*, not *down*! The Son of Man is going to the Ancient of Days, not coming *from* Him! He is not descending in clouds to the earth, but ascending in clouds to His Father! Daniel was not predicting the Second Coming of Christ, but rather the climax of the First Advent, in which, after atoning for sins and defeating death and Satan, the Lord ascended on the clouds of heaven to be seated on His glorious throne at His Father's right hand.[11]

This preterist interpretation of Matthew 24:30 is counter-intuitive and fraught with several difficulties. Perhaps the most troublesome is that it requires multiple "comings" of Jesus. As DeMar admits, this view requires that preterists differentiate "the coming [παρουσία] of the Son of Man" in verse 27 from "the Son of Man coming [ἐρχόμενον] on the clouds of heaven" only a few verses later (v. 30). They interpret the former event as a judgment "coming" of Jesus in AD 70 and the latter as his ascension.[12] This interpretation is unlikely and forced, being necessary only to preserve a commitment to a preterist hermeneutic. In addition, the subject of the Son of Man with ἔρχομαι ("coming") also appears throughout the book of Revelation, where it refers to a *future* event and not to the ascension of Jesus; this argument will be presented in more depth later in this chapter. Furthermore, many preterists teach that "the coming of the Son of Man" in the Olivet Discourse points to a *third* "coming" of Jesus (i.e., his reigning presence). Specifically, N. T. Wright develops the view that the disciples were interested in Christ's arrival in Jerusalem to reign as King and that these verses represent, in some spiritual or figurative sense, his "'coming' to Jerusalem as *the vindicated,*

---

11 Chilton 2007, p. 69; also DeMar 1999, pp. 161, 164-65 and Wright 1996, p. 361
12 DeMar 1999, p. 71

rightful king."[13] Ironically, interpreters such as Wright put forth three very different "comings" of Jesus, yet leave no room in the Olivet Prophecy for his "coming" to refer to his glorious return, as the historic church has always taught!

One appealing motive for preterists to interpret the Lord's coming in Matthew 24:30 as his ascension is to avoid what they deem to be a necessary admission of prophetic failure as put forth by higher critics and skeptics.[14] Wright elaborates: "As we have seen, neither the godly traditions of the church nor the (sometimes) less godly traditions of scholarship are used to reading the passage in this way. The godly are less likely to accuse me of scholarly trickery, designed to get around what to them seems a clear statement of the future second coming of the Lord. The scholarly are likely to accuse me of pious trickery, getting round the problem that Jesus seems to have been mistaken."[15] Wright's solution is neither a comfort to the skeptics nor to the godly.

Hanegraaff, perhaps uniquely among preterists, claims to recognize some "already and not yet" aspects of Matthew 24:30. He suggests that Jesus was "using final consummation language to characterize a near-future event."[16] Hanegraaff's admission regarding the Lord's coming with clouds shows a willingness to understand this passage as a statement regarding the *return* of Jesus Christ. Yet, as we will see, Hanegraaff misses the manner in which Jesus used the language of the Old Testament to describe his glorious return.

Daniel 7 in the New Testament

Contrary to preterist claims, the prophecy of Daniel 7 does *not* prove that Jesus in Matthew 24:30 spoke about his ascension to the Father. The careful reader should notice that the prophecy does not indicate a clear *temporal* connection between the Son of

---

13 Wright 1996, p. 342; cf. p. 345

14 E.g., Sproul 1998, pp. 12-16

15 Wright 1996, p. 342

16 Hanegraaff 2007, p.26

Man's coming in the clouds and his ascension—his presentation before the Ancient of Days. The prophet Daniel wrote, "I saw in the night visions, and behold, with the clouds of heaven there came one like a son of man, and he came to the Ancient of Days and was presented before him. And to him was given dominion and glory and a kingdom, that all peoples, nations, and languages should serve him; his dominion is an everlasting dominion, which shall not pass away, and his kingdom one that shall not be destroyed" (Dan. 7:13-14). In light of the revealed "mystery" of the twofold advent of the Messiah, this temporal ambiguity is divinely intended. As we will see, the divine Son of Man will ascend to his Father in clouds and later return with the clouds in the same glory of his Father.

The book of Revelation provides clues about the temporal relationship between these two prophetic events. The apostle John described Jesus as having the title "one like a son of man" (Rev. 1:13, quoting Dan. 7:13) and displaying features reminiscent of Daniel's Ancient of Days ("The hairs of his head were white, like white wool, like snow. His eyes were like a flame of fire" Rev. 1:14; cf. Dan. 7:9-12; 10:6 LXX). Elsewhere in the book, the apostle presented Jesus as having *already* received "glory and dominion" (Rev. 1:6) and having ransomed people "from every tribe and language and people and nation, and you have made them a kingdom and priests to our God" (Rev. 5:9-10; cf. Dan. 7:14; Matt. 28:18-20). Yet Jesus promised to later give his people "authority over the nations ... even as I myself have received authority from my Father" (Rev. 2:26-27; cf. 3:21). The international kingdom that Jesus, the Son of Man, has already received, he will give in *totality* to his people in the future.

The apostle then presented the reader with a throne-room judgment scene in Revelation 4-5 that serves *as a detailed retelling of the courtroom scene of Daniel 7:13-14.*[17] A comparative chart in Appendix A of this book compares these two courtroom scenes

---

17 Beale, G. K., and Sean M. McDonough in Beale and Carson 1996; p. 1098; cf. Dan. 7:9; cf. 7:2, 6-7 in Rev. 4:1-3, 5

and demonstrates John's dependence upon Daniel 7. The court-room scene in the Apocalypse provides the backdrop of the Lion of Judah (i.e., Jesus) being presented before his Father with the angels to receive a sealed inheritance scroll (Rev. 5:6-9). The text reveals that Jesus had previously redeemed his saints through his death and that he will give the full inheritance of God's kingdom to them only *after* he breaks the seventh seal of the scroll (Rev. 8:1-2; cf. 6:1-17; 11:16). John later sees a vision of the Son of Man coming on a cloud of heaven (Rev. 14:14; cf. 1:7; 19:11-16).

The apostle John combined Daniel 7:13 and Zechariah 12:10, *in the exact manner of Matthew 24:30*, in order to present the Son of Man's advent as a *future* event.[18] He wrote, "Behold, he is coming [ἔρχεται] with the clouds, and every eye will see him, even those who pierced him, and all the tribes of the earth will wail on account of him" (Rev. 1:7). The next verse shows that this coming is in the future ("who is and who was and *who is to come*" in v. 8, emphasis added). The apostle elsewhere in the book presented the coming of Jesus as a *future* event, using such phrases as "I will come" (2:5), "I will come to you soon" (2:16), "until I come" (2:25), "I will come like a thief ... I will come" (3:3); "I am coming soon" (3:11), and "Behold, I am coming" (16:15). The climactic event of the book of Revelation that answers to Revelation 1:7 is the return of Jesus: "one like a son of man" who is seated on a white cloud (Rev. 14:14) and will come with a train of holy angels to slay the Beast, throwing him into fiery judgment (Rev. 19:11-21; cf. Dan. 7:11). In the language of Matthew 24:30, John's overall descriptions of the cloud-riding advent of the Son of Man is decidedly future and cannot describe the ascension.

The overall message of the Apocalypse demonstrates that Jesus first ascended to receive the kingdom and will *later* appear on clouds of glory for judgment (cf. Luke 19:12ff). As Craig L. Blomberg points out, this observation accords with the words of Jesus, when he quoted Daniel 7:13 (in Matt. 26:64; Mark 14:62; Luke 22:69) to reveal this two-stage process of redemption. He

18 Beale 1999, p. 197

wrote, "Jesus will shortly quote this passage from Daniel again, adding the phrase about 'seated at the right hand of power' (i.e., God), in a different position than in the OT text, so that Christ is *first* in God's presence and *then* coming on the clouds, presumably therefore coming from heaven to earth. The picture is one of a theophany, 'which is always from heaven to the world of humankind'."[19]

The claim that the Messiah will arrive bodily with clouds, based on the prophecy of Daniel 7:13, is not unique to Christianity; it was explicitly taught within Judaism. The Babylonian Talmud (*Sanhedrin 98a*) explains Daniel's reference to the advent of "one like the son of man . . . with the clouds of heaven" in order to describe his actual arrival to the Jewish nation:

> R' Yehoshua ben Levi noted a contradiction: On the one hand it is written: And behold! With the clouds of Heaven, one like a man came, which implies that the Messiah will come swiftly. But on the other hand it is written: a humble man, riding on a donkey, which implies that the Messiah will come sluggishly.... If [the Jews] are deserving, the Messiah will arrive with the clouds of Heaven. If they are not deserving, he will come as a humble man, riding on a donkey.[20]

The traditional Jewish expectation has always been that the Messiah will arrive bodily to Jerusalem at the end of the age.

Some preterists recognize that the language of the Son of Man's coming in Revelation 1:7 pertains to the second coming of Jesus. For example, Gentry betrays his apprehension about the preterist interpretation of this verse, as he explains that "the initial impression this verse leaves on us today is that John is speaking of the Second Advent. It certainly does involve language quite applicable to the future, glorious, history-ending Second Coming of Christ. The Scriptures speak often of his Second Coming, and even with this sort of cloud-coming judgment language (cp.

---

19 Blomberg, Craig L. in Beale and Carson 1996, pp. 87-88
20 *Talmud Bavli*. 2014, *Sanhedrin* 98a4.

Acts 1:9-11; 1 Thess. 4:16-17; 2 Thess. 1:7-10)...Yet looks are deceiving."[21]

A Literal, Visible Return

Many preterists argue that the Lord's phrase "every eye will see him" in Matthew 24:30 and Revelation 1:7 is a metaphor for comprehension or insight and does not refer to actually seeing the glorified Jesus.[22] This interpretation says that those who witnessed the destruction of the Second Temple came to understand through this event that Jesus is on his heavenly throne. Gentry explains, "They [those who saw the temple burning] 'see' it in the sense we 'see' how a math problem works: with the 'eye of understanding' rather than the organ of vision."[23] He continues, "First, *every eye* shall see him' simply means that this will be a public event, not hidden in a corner. The bible frequently uses 'all' or 'every' in a limited sense far short of global universality."[24] Nevertheless, the hesitancy of other preterists to deny the universal scope of this language is evident in their suggestions that this language alludes to a recognition after the destruction *of the Roman Empire* and not simply to the destruction of Judea and Jerusalem.[25]

The statement of Jesus found in Matthew 24:30 and Revelation 1:7 is a partial quote of Zechariah 12:10. A straightforward reading of this Old Testament text reveals that the people of Judea and Jerusalem will gaze at the pierced Lord. The prophecy reads, "And I [the LORD] will pour out on the house of David and the inhabitants of Jerusalem a spirit of grace and pleas for mercy, so that, *when they look on me, on him whom they have pierced*, they shall mourn for him" (Zech. 12:10, emphasis added). Significantly, the apostle John quoted this passage elsewhere with reference to those who visually looked at Jesus' pierced body (John 19:37), and he echoed it again in the account of Thomas, who saw and believed

---

21 Gentry 2010b, p. 34
22 DeMar 1999, p. 168; Hanegraaff 2007, p.27; Jordan 2014, loc. 215
23 Gentry 2010b, p. 45
24 Ibid.
25 Kik 1971, p. 39

in the glorified Jesus after touching his pierced hands and feet (John 20:25-29). In every occurrence of this phrase, people look upon the actual crucified, "flesh-and-bone" body of Christ.

Jesus added specific qualifiers to the prophecy of Zechariah that provide the reader with additional details regarding his return. The New Testament scholar, G. K. Beale, explains how these qualifiers function:

> The Zechariah [12:10] text has been altered in two significant ways. The phrases "every eye" and "of the earth" (cf. Zech. 14:17) have been added to universalize its original meaning. ...The word ge ("earth, land") cannot be a limited reference to the land of Israel; rather, it is a universal denotation, since this is the only meaning that the phrase pasai hai phylai tes ges ("all the tribes of the earth") has in the OT (LXX: Gen. 12:3; 28:14; Ps. 71:17; Zech. 14:17). The phrase "all the tribes of Israel" occurs repeatedly in the OT (approximately twenty-five times), which highlights the different wording of Rev. 1:7b.[26]

As Beale shows, the first qualifier ("all the tribes of the earth" in Matt. 24:30; Rev. 1:7) is *a technical expression found throughout the Old Testament that specifies the peoples or nations of the world*. Consequently, this phrase should not be restricted to the twelve tribes of Israel as preterists often argue.[27] The second qualifier, "every eye will see him" (Rev. 1:7), strongly indicates an optical visualization of the risen Lord, especially against the backdrop of Zechariah 12:10 (as argued above). All or nearly all the men *directly* responsible for the crucifixion of Jesus had died long before AD 70, most especially the elders of the Sanhedrin present at the trial of Jesus (cf. Matt. 26:64). Consequently, the qualifier "even those who pierced him" (Rev. 1:7) extends more universally, beyond the scope of the actual "executioners" of Jesus. This fact militates against the preterist view that John was referring to merely those directly involved with the Lord's cruci-

---

26 Beale, G. K., and Sean M. McDonough in Beale and Carson 1996, p. 1090
27 Chilton 2007, p. 101; Gentry 1998, pp. 127-28; Gentry 2010c, loc. 2208-2225; Gentry 2010b, pp. 39-40; Russell 2003, pp. 77, 380

fixion.[28] The context indicates a future, post-mortem setting on the day of the Lord.[29]

DeMar admits that the standard translation "all the tribes of the earth [γῆς]" (Matt. 24:30 and Rev. 1:7) is correct only *if* the larger statement found in these verses refers to the second coming of Jesus.[30] Notwithstanding, the assumption that the context of this verse is limited to first-century Jerusalem forces the preterist to revise the translation to "tribes of the *land*," meaning the twelve tribes of Israel.[31] This rendering heavily shapes their "translation" of the word γῆς ("earth/land") in other passages of Scripture, most commonly in the book of Revelation. For example, Russell translates this word as "land" instead of accepting the traditional rendering "earth" in such passages as Revelation 6:3-4, 7-8, 9-11, 15; 8:7.[32] He even argued that the phrase "all the nations" found later in the Olivet Discourse (Matt. 25:32) should with "great probability" be equated with the tribes of Israel! He wrote, "There is no impropriety in designating the *tribes as nations*. The promise of God to Abraham was that he should be the father of many nations".[33] Apparently Russell was ignorant of the fact that "many nations" (Gen. 17:5) was not limited to Jacob's offspring, and that Abraham sired other gentile nations, including Moab, Ammon, Edom, and the Ishmaelites.

Another objection to the preterist view of Zechariah 12:10 is that the overwhelming majority of Judean Jews did not receive "a spirit of grace and pleas for mercy" at the destruction of Jerusalem in AD 70. While the context includes a military invasion of the land (vv. 2-6, 11), it also contains the promise that God will "give salvation to the tents of Judah" (v. 7), "protect the inhabitants of Jerusalem" (v. 8), and "destroy all the nations that come against Jerusalem" (v. 9; cf. vv. 3-9). These prophetic events did

28 DeMar 1999, p. 168; Gentry 1998, p. 142; Gentry 2010b, p. 39
29 Contra Kik 1971, p. 39
30 DeMar 1999, p. 166
31 Kik 1971, p. 139
32 Russell 2003, pp. 390, 392, 394, 399, 407; Similarly Jordan 2014, loc. 191
33 Russell 2003, p. 104

not occur at Jerusalem's destruction in AD 70, despite preterists' desperate attempts to allegorize the Scriptures to suggest otherwise. The weeping and "pleas of mercy" in Zechariah 12:10, and hence Matthew 24:30, should be understood as the humble pleading of national repentance in the presence of the Lord "whom they have pierced"—the glorified Jesus. This exact vocabulary is found in Jeremiah's passage about God's new covenant promise to regather the people of Israel back to their homeland; he states, "with *weeping* they shall come, and *with pleas for mercy* I will lead them back" (Jer. 31:9, emphasis added; cf. Jer. 50:4).

Partial preterism's critique of the futurist view that Christ's return on clouds (Matt. 24:30) is "a primitive form of space travel" is a double-edged sword for partial preterism because these preterists *also* teach that Jesus will return in the future *in the exact manner that they criticize*, that is, descending with the clouds of heaven! The apostle Paul taught, "For the Lord himself will descend from heaven... Then we who are alive ... will be caught up together with them [the resurrected believers] in the clouds to meet the Lord in the air" (1 Thess. 4:16, 17; cf. 1 Cor. 15:23).

Some preterists have attempted to allegorize the meaning of Paul's words; however, the book of Acts also teaches that the Master will return *literally* and *bodily* by descending from heaven. Luke wrote, "And when he had said these things, as they were *looking* on, he was lifted up, and *a cloud* took him out of their sight. And while they were *gazing* into heaven as he went, behold, two men stood by them in white robes, and said, 'Men of Galilee, why do you stand *looking* into heaven? This Jesus, who was taken up from you into heaven, will come *in the same way as you saw him go* into heaven'" (Acts 1:9-11, emphasis added). This passage shows that the Lord's *descent* will take place in the exact manner that the disciples had seen him *ascending* into heaven. Unsurprisingly for the futurist, the text highlights two facts concerning his ascension: (1) it was optically visualized by human observers and (2) it was accompanied by a visible cloud.

Cloud Theophanies in the Old Testament

Preterists appeal to multiple Old Testament passages, in addition to Daniel 7:13-14, to support their view that Matthew 24:30 is *not* about the future return of Christ. They argue that a theophany (i.e., a visual manifestation of God) consisting of a cloud coming is a common Old Testament *metaphor* or *symbol* for God's "presence, judgment, and salvation."[34] They put forth many biblical texts as supposed proof of this *symbolic* phenomenon of God "riding on clouds" in judgment upon nations.[35] Mathison expresses the common preterist sentiment that "none of these texts is intended to communicate the idea that God is literally going to ride on a cloud into one of these nations."[36] Yet an evaluation of these passages reveals that this contention is misleading, and at times, blatantly false.

The phenomena of Yahweh *visually* appearing with a *literal* cloud originates in the Pentateuch. The book of Exodus relates multiple accounts of the LORD's glory cloud appearing to Moses and the Israelites. His divine presence descended in a thick cloud of darkness ("the pillar of cloud by day and the pillar of fire by night") to protect and accompany the Israelites at the Red Sea (Ex. 13:21-22; 14:19-20, 24; II Sam. 22:10). The cloud *visually* appeared atop Mount Sinai, led the Israelites through their desert journeys, and "dwelt among them" in the tabernacle (Ex. 19:9, 11; 20:21; 24:15-18; 33:2, 9-10; 34:5; Num. 11:25; Deut. 33:2). The cloud also filled the First Temple at its dedication by King Solomon (I Kings 8:11-13).

Preterists generally accept the concept that God manifested his glory with a visible cloud during the Old Testament period.[37] DeMar and others object, saying that this evidence is insufficient

---

34 Chilton 2007, p. 102; cf. Hanegraaff 2007, pp. 26, 83-84, 106

35 DeMar 1999, pp. 72, 124, 160-61; Gentry 1998, p. 123; Gentry 2010b, pp. 35, 36; Hanegraaff 2007, pp. 26, 83-84; Kik 1971, p. 38; Mathison 2004, pp. 162-163

36 Mathison 2004, pp. 162-163; Similarly Kik 1971, p. 141

37 E.g., DeMar 1999, p. 160

to support the futurist interpretation of Matthew 24:30 because God was not seen as *physically present* in those encounters.[38] This is an odd objection for a variety of reasons. For example, as argued above, these passages portray the presence and glory of God as having been accompanied by *a literal cloud* that was *optically visible* to observers. Many of these theophanies portray the Lord in human form, presumably as pre-incarnate appearances of Jesus Christ (e.g., Ex. 24:10; Isa. 6:1-5, 8; Ezek. 1:26-28; 10:1; Dan. 7:13; 8:15). In addition, as argued above, passages such as Acts 1:9-11 and 1 Thessalonians 4:16-17 predict that Jesus will *literally* and *visibly* descend from heaven when he returns. Consequently, it is highly unlikely that Jesus had in mind anything other than his literal arrival as the incarnate, resurrected Son of Man when he prophesied that *he* will be *seen* "coming on the clouds of heaven" (Matt. 24:30).

Preterists point to a variety of other Old Testament passages to support their allegorical interpretation of Matthew 24:30. Some of these passages do *not* describe cloud-coming theophanies but the clouds of darkness that will be visible on the day of the Lord (e.g., Ezek. 30:3; Joel 2:1-2; Zeph. 1:14-15). Other passages are found in the Psalms and *poetic* sections of the Prophets, and they *recast the Exodus narrative* along with its cloud theophanies. For example, the psalmist poetically described God as coming with the glory cloud to deliver David from the hands of King Saul (Ps. 18:6-17). Similarly, the prophet Nahum warned of divine judgment against Nineveh by quoting and alluding to the Exodus narrative (Ex. 20:5 in Nah. 1:2 and Ex. 34:6-7 in Nah. 1:3). He presented the Lord as having clouds under his feet and "rebuking the sea" so as to make it dry land (Nah. 1:3-4), reminiscent of the Red Sea crossing (Ex. 14:21-22). The prophet Micah utilized themes of the day of the Lord to warn of Samaria's looming destruction (Mic. 1:3-5; cf. Ps. 97:1-6); he saw God descending "out of his place" to "tread upon the high places of the earth" so that mountains melt before his divine presence (Mic. 1:3-4). Unlike Jesus' prophecy

38 DeMar 1999, pp. 124, 160

in Matthew 24:30, these passages are found in *poetic* portions of Scripture. In addition, they function to reinforce the *literal* glory cloud that *visibly* appeared during Israel's exodus from Egypt.

The classic example cited by preterists of cloud-coming language is Isaiah 19:1-4.[39] The passage begins "Behold, the LORD is riding on a swift cloud and comes to Egypt" (Isa. 19:1) and continues with a prophecy concerning Egypt's destruction by civil war, harsh servitude, and drought. Preterists and many futurists interpret this passage as referring to the imminent Assyrian invasion of Egypt in the late-seventh century BC.[40] Gentry contends that it contains "apocalyptic language" and that "no interpreter believes the Egyptians saw God Almighty sitting on a cloud and descending among them in judgment."[41] However, the background of this passage calls to mind the Exodus narrative, where God *literally* appeared in a *visible* glory cloud to destroy Pharaoh's Egypt. Furthermore, the surrounding context shows that this passage is ultimately eschatological and finds its culmination in the future day of the Lord, when Egypt and Assyria will join Israel in the worship of the one true God (vv. 23-25). The cumulative evidence from the passage does not deny a literal cloud coming, but affirms it from history and predicts it in eschatology.

The Gathering of the Elect

The Lord continued the Olivet Discourse, saying, "And he [the Son of Man] will send out his angels with a loud trumpet call, and they will gather his elect from the four winds, from one end of heaven to the other" (Matt. 24:31). Preterists consistently put forth the notion that the angels (ἀγγέλους) are human "messengers" (c.f. Luke 7:24; 9:52) who would preach "the trumpet call" of the gospel throughout the nations *after* the destruction of Jerusalem in AD 70.[42] Some preterists, such as Gentry, do not appear to

---

39 DeMar 1999, p. 161; Gentry 2010b, pp. 35, 36; Kik 1971, p. 38

40 Mathison 2004, pp. 162-163

41 Gentry 2010b, pp. 35, 36

42 Chilton 2007, p. 103; DeMar 1999, pp. 174, 278; Gentry 2010c, loc. Gentry 2010c, loc. 2313-2318, 2363; Kik 1971, p. 148

be entirely comfortable with their reinterpretation of this passage and admit that it could refer to angelic "supernatural power which lies behind such preaching."[43] According to the preterist interpretation, the gathering of the elect (Matt. 24:31) means that Jesus would *spiritually* bring the elect gentiles into the church (e.g., John 11:52). R. T. France argues that the destruction of Jerusalem was "the cue for the establishment of the universal reign of the Son of Man and the gathering of a new people of God from the ends of the earth."[44] According to Chilton and others, the desolation of Jerusalem made the church the "New Synagogue" and "the true, the super-Synagogue."[45]

One difficulty of the preterist interpretation of this verse is that Jesus had previously taught in the Olivet Discourse that the worldwide preaching of the gospel must occur *before* the end of the age (Matt. 24:14). This anachronism is seen most clearly in the preterist claim that the gospel had already gone to "the entire world" prior to AD 70 (see Chapter Four). One wonders, then, how the gospel went to all the nations before AD 70 while the destruction of Jerusalem signaled the beginning of this same event! Gentry, perceiving this weakness in the preterist argument, suggests that the language of Jesus "highlights AD 70 as the ultimate spark to the worldwide mission. Indeed, the events of AD 70 finally separate Christianity from Judaism."[46] He remarks that the worldwide gathering of the nations "begins in earnest" at AD 70.[47] Similarly, DeMar attempts to qualify Jesus' statement by positing that the gospel went "to the Jew first" prior to AD 70 and thereafter went "to the Gentiles in new fullness and with the expectation that the *nations*—Gentiles—would be discipled (Matt. 28:18-20)."[48] However, such elastic use of words does not avoid the anachronism.

43 Gentry 2010c, loc. 2363
44 France 2007, p. 911
45 Chilton 2007, pp. 104-05
46 Gentry 2010c, loc. 2374
47 Ibid., loc. 1697
48 DeMar 1999, p. 176

Preterist attempts to explain away the clear meaning of Matthew 24:31 also gloss over well-attested supporting passages of Scripture that clearly describe the Lord's return. Kik admits, "This [Matt. 24:31], some maintain, is a description of the final resurrection at the second coming of the Lord. That there is some ground for such an interpretation one cannot deny. The trumpet is associated with the resurrection of the dead in several passages."[49] One passage that exemplifies this is the apostle Paul's teaching that the descent of Jesus from heaven will be accompanied by at least one angel, the sound of a trumpet call, and the gathering of his elect "in the clouds" (1 Thess. 4:16-17). In his correspondence with the Corinthians, Paul also connected the return of Jesus with the last trumpet and the resurrection of the righteous dead (1 Cor. 15:20-23, 50-54; cf. Rev. 11:15-18). Other passages describe the revealing of the Lord Jesus from heaven, with the accompaniment of mighty angels, to render judgment (Matt. 13:41; 16:27; 2 Thess. 1:8).

Table 1: Common Elements of Matthew 24, 1 Thessalonians 4, and 1 Corinthians 15

	Matthew 24:30-31	1 Thessalonians 4:16-17	1 Corinthians 15:22-23, 51-53
Jesus Christ Appearing in/ from Heaven	"Then will appear in heaven the sign of the Son of Man... and they will see the Son of Man coming"	"For the Lord himself will descend from heaven... "	"in Christ shall all be made alive.... at his coming those who belong to Christ.... "
Clouds	"on the clouds of heaven ... "	"in the clouds ...the Lord in the air ... "	----
Angel(s)	"And he will send out his angels ... "	"with the voice of an archangel ... "	----

49 Kik 1971, p. 145

	Matthew 24:30-31	1 Thessalonians 4:16-17	1 Corinthians 15:22-23, 51-53
A Trumpet	"with a loud trumpet call and…"	"with the sound of the trumpet of God…."	"in a moment, in the twinkling of an eye, at the last trumpet. For the trumpet will sound…"
Gathering of the Righteous	"they will gather his elect from the four winds, from one end of heaven to the other." (cf. "from the ends of the earth to the ends of heaven" Mark 13:27)	"And the dead in Christ will rise first. Then we who are alive, who are left, will be caught up together with them in the clouds to meet the Lord in the air."	"Behold! I tell you a mystery. We shall not all sleep, but we shall all be changed …and the dead will be raised imperishable, and we shall be changed."

Jesus provided the interpretation of a parable about the angelic end-time gathering in the Synoptic Gospels. These words clarify the meaning of Matthew 24:31 by identifying the angels and their role in the harvest gathering. The Lord taught, "The harvest is the end of the age, and the reapers are angels. Just as the weeds are gathered and burned with fire, so will it be at the end of the age. The Son of Man will send his angels, and they will gather out of his kingdom all causes of sin and all law-breakers, and throw them into the fiery furnace. In that place there will be weeping and gnashing of teeth. Then the righteous will shine like the sun in the kingdom of their Father. He who has ears, let him hear" (Matt. 13:39-43). The *heavenly* origin of the angels is seen in their role of separating out the evildoers and throwing them into "the fiery furnace" (i.e., hell), hardly the function of earthly preachers of the gospel! Jesus did not formally depict the gathering of the saints here, yet he mentioned in the original parable that he will "gather the wheat [the righteous]" into his barn (Matt. 13:30). In addition, he mentioned that "the righteous will shine like the sun in the kingdom," an allusion to the resurrection verse of Daniel 12:3 ("many of those who sleep in the dust of the earth shall awake ... and those who are wise shall shine like the brightness of the sky above; and those who turn many to righteousness, like the stars forever and ever."). The Lord's parable directly connects this harvest gathering with the resurrection of the dead and the end of the age.

In his "little apocalypse," the prophet Isaiah connected several eschatological events, including the tribulation, the day of the Lord, the "great trumpet" blast, the LORD's arrival, the resurrection of the dead, and the gathering of Israel's elect (Isa. 24-27). Isaiah depicted the coming day of the Lord (Isa. 24) and prophesied that the Lord will provide a luxurious feast in Jerusalem, when he will "swallow up death forever" and "wipe away tears from all faces" (Isa. 25:6-8; cf. 1 Cor. 15:54; Rev. 7:17). This language describes the resurrection from the dead, and the national birth pains will end with the resurrection of the earth's dead after God's "fury has passed by" (Isa. 26:17-20). This event will correspond with the time that the Lord comes "out from his place to punish the inhabitants of the earth" and to raise the dead (Isa. 26:21). He will then ("in that day") "glean" the people of Israel by gathering them back to the land when the "great trumpet" is blown, as he prophesied: "In that day from the river Euphrates to the Brook of Egypt the LORD will thresh out the grain, and you will be gleaned one by one, O people of Israel. And in that day *a great trumpet will be blown*, and those who were lost in the land of Assyria and those who were driven out to the land of Egypt will come and worship the LORD on the holy mountain at Jerusalem" (Isa. 27:12-13). Isaiah's "little apocalypse", like several New Testament passages, connect the same events described by Jesus in Matthew 24:31.

8

This Generation Will Not Pass Away

The Lord Jesus continued the Olivet Discourse by utilizing an allegory. He taught, "From the fig tree learn its lesson: as soon as its branch becomes tender and puts out its leaves, you know that summer is near. So also, when you see *all these things*, you know that he is near, at the very gates" (Matt. 24:33, emphasis added). The idea is that the arrival of specific prophetic events (i.e., "all these things") will signal the nearness of the Lord's return like the budding leaves of a fig tree signal the nearness of summer. As explained in previous chapters of this book, the abomination of desolation is the primary sign signaling the 3.5-year unprecedented tribulation that will end with the day of the Lord, the glorious return of Jesus, and the angelic gathering of God's elect. Jesus then declared, "Truly, I say to you, this generation will not pass away until *all these things* take place" (Matt. 24:34, emphasis added). It is important to clarify at this point that the phrase "all these things" includes the unprecedented tribulation (vv. 15-28) and the subsequent return of the Son of Man to *gather* his saints (vv. 29-31).

Preterists such as J. Marcellus Kik and Kenneth Gentry consider the statement of Jesus in Matthew 24:34 "the key" for properly interpreting the Olivet Prophecy.[1] Gentry considers it a "confident, clear, and compelling pronouncement regarding the time of the events" described in the verses preceding it.[2] Chilton summarizes the preterist interpretation of this verse: "This means that everything Jesus spoke of in this passage, at least up to verse 34, *took place before the generation then living passed away....*

---

1 Gentry 2010c, loc. 1311; Kik 1971, pp. 30, 59, 60
2 Gentry 2010c, loc. 1072

The question is, do you believe Him?"[3] Preterists argue that "this generation" in this verse refers to the contemporary generation alive when Jesus delivered his discourse.[4] Gentry considers this an "inescapable conclusion," and he confidently proclaims, "Thus, we may say (as strange as it may seem) that 'this generation means this generation.'"[5] DeMar provides a glimpse into the rationale for understanding the verse in this manner:

> At first reading one gets the distinct impression that Jesus is saying that the people with whom He was speaking would live to see and experience the events described in Matthew 24. This seemed impossible! And yet, there it was. I looked up every other occurrence of the phrase "this generation," and each time I came up with the same answer: Jesus was referring to *His* generation, the generation of people alive when He uttered the words. Every Bible commentator danced around the text. "It means the generation alive when the events described in the previous verses begin to manifest themselves," one respected commentator wrote. If that's true, I thought, then this is the only place where "this generation" means a future generation. That's not sound Bible interpretation. ... My discontent grew. I was struck with the obvious, straightforward, literal, plain interpretation.[6]

DeMar and his colleagues reason that the expression ἡ γενεὰ αὕτη ("this generation") in Matthew 24:34 *must* refer to Jesus' contemporary generation because it *always* carries this meaning when it appears throughout the Synoptic Gospels.[7] As we will soon see, this reasoning is incorrect and betrays an ignorance of how Jesus employed the phrase throughout the Gospels. Preterists also contend that it is "grammatically impossible" for Jesus in Matthew 24:34 to have meant anything other than his contem-

---

3 Chilton 2007, p. 86; Similarly Adams and Fisher 2000, p. 108; Sproul 1998, pp. 18, 72.

4 DeMar 1999, pp. 159, 184; Gentry 2010c, loc. 1150; Hanegraaff 2007, p. 75; Kik 1971, p. 63; Mathison 2004, p. 179; Sproul 1998, p. 18

5 Gentry 2010c, loc. 1204; cf. loc. 1150; Similarly DeMar 1999, pp. 26, 55

6 DeMar 1999, p.15

7 Ibid., pp. 56, 344; Gentry 2010c, loc. 1111; Hanegraaff 2007, p. 77; Kik 1971, pp. 30, 31, 61

porary generation, because "*this* generation" does not mean "*that* generation."[8] Hanegraaff posits that skeptics such as Bertrand Russell and Albert Schweitzer were correct in dismissing the supposed "grammatical gyrations" of futurists who argue that "this generation" refers to another generation.[9] However, R. C. Sproul correctly identifies a fallacy with this critique of futurism; he writes, "I think DeMar commits a basic error at this point. Futurists do not tend to argue that Jesus was not speaking to that generation of his contemporaries. Rather they argue that the term *generation* here refers not to a specific time-frame of forty years, but to a 'kind' or 'sort' of people. Some of these interpreters see 'this generation' as a description of believers, while others see it as a description of the wicked." In other words, Sproul concedes that most futurists teach that the phrase "this generation" *includes* the contemporaries of Jesus but is not *restricted* to them, as preterists insist.[10] Before we examine the meaning of the expression "this generation," we will digress for a moment to evaluate the meaning of the phrase "all these things."

The Meaning of "All These Things"

Jesus borrowed the phrase "all these things" (Matt. 24:33-34) from a series of Old Testament eschatological passages regarding (1) the unprecedented tribulation and (2) the subsequent salvation of the nation of Israel. The primary source for this phrase is found in the covenantal "blessings and curses" listed in the book of Deuteronomy. In these prophetic portions of Scripture, Moses warned that the covenantal curses would ravage the nation (Deut. 32:21-30), most particularly at its "latter end" (Deut. 32:29; cf. 31:17-18; 32:20) and "in the latter days" (Deut. 31:29). The prophet connected this time period with Israel's tribulation and national repentance. Moses prophesied, "When you [Israel] are in tribulation, and *all these things* come upon you in the latter days, you will

---

8   Hanegraaff 2007, pp. 79, 83, 94; Similarly DeMar 1999, p. 58
9   Ibid., p. 83
10 Sproul 1998, p. 65

return to the LORD your God and obey his voice. For the LORD your God is a merciful God. He will not leave you or destroy you or forget the covenant with your fathers" (Deut. 4:30-31, emphasis added; cf. Jer. 5:19).

This new covenant promise is that the nation will return to God to mercifully receive a spiritual "circumcision", an event that will occur "when *all these things* come upon you [Israel], the blessing and the curse" (Deut. 30:1ff, emphasis added; cf. Ezek. 37:21-28; Jer. 31:33-40). The promise to Israel is that the Lord "will restore your fortunes and have mercy on you, and he will gather you again from all the peoples where the LORD your God has scattered you ... into the land that your fathers possessed" (Deut. 30:3-5). God will "have compassion on his servants, when he sees that their power is gone and there is none remaining, bond or free" (Deut. 32:36; cf. Isa. 6:11-12). This motif appears again in the angel's oath that the prophetic vision will continue "for a time, times, and half a time [i.e., 3.5 years], and that when the shattering of the power of the holy people comes to an end, *all these things* would be finished" (Dan. 12:7, emphasis added). The "all these things" in the immediate context of the prophecy includes the previous material of Jacob's unprecedented tribulation and subsequent resurrection from the dead (Dan. 12:1-3). The repeated theme in both passages is that God will accomplish the salvation blessings of national Israel after the judgments of the tribulation.

The Meaning of "This Generation"

By examining the Synoptics, we get the picture that the expression "this generation" functions as a *technical* term in Matthew 24:34 and throughout the New Testament. When we compare the adjectives that Jesus and his apostles affixed to the word "generation" with the same expressions as they appear in the book of Deuteronomy, the specific and technical meaning of this term is most evident. The New Testament contains the following *modifications* to the word γενεὰ ("generation"):

"O faithless generation ... " (Mark 9:19)

"O faithless and twisted generation … " (Matt. 17:17; Luke 9:41)

" … an evil and adulterous generation… " (Matt. 12:39; 16:4)

" … an evil generation … " (Luke 11:29)

" … this adulteress and sinful generation …" (Mark 8:38)

" … this crooked generation …" (Acts 2:40)

" … a crooked and twisted generation … " (Phil. 2:15)

These expressions first appear in the book of Deuteronomy. Before examining these occurrences, the reader should understand that the Greek word γενεά ("generation") often refers to offspring and not only to a group of individuals living during a limited time frame. Sproul admits, "The entry on *genea* in Gerhard Kittel's *Theological Dictionary of the New Testament* says that in general usage *genea* means 'birth' or 'descent,' but that it can also mean 'generation.'"[11] The word γενεά ("generation") is roughly equivalent to the Hebrew word רוד ("generation") which came over into the Septuagint (LXX) as γενεά. This Hebrew word רוד is found throughout the Old Testament and often has a *qualitative* meaning. In other words, the word describes a general quality or character of people and is not primarily concerned with a specific time period. Evald Lövestam explains as follows:

> The word רוד shows considerable variation in its purport. It can have varied references. In the Old Testament it is mostly used of 'generation' in the true sense. But it is also used of רוד צידק, the *dor* of the righteous (in contrast to the evildoers, Ps 14:5), of רוד ויתובא, his fathers' *dor* (i.e. the dead, Ps 49:20), of דינב רוד, that is the *dor* of God's children (Ps 73:15), of רוד מירשי, the *dor* of the upright (Ps 112:2), of וושיר רד, the former *dor* (generally seen, Job 8:8), etc.[12]

New Testament scholars generally agree that Jesus' frequent use of ἡ γενεά αὕτη ("this generation") is part of a larger thematic

11 Sproul 1998, p. 71
12 Lövestam 1995, p. 8

interweaving of three Deuteronomic expressions. We can discover how Jesus and the apostles made use of these expressions once we properly understand what the phraseology meant in its original context. The first expression, "this evil generation" (Deut. 1:35), refers to the Israelites who died because of their unbelief during the forty years of wandering in the desert (Deut. 1:34-39; cf. Heb. 3:7-19). The expression, "this evil generation", can be understood quantitatively (i.e., as a limited period of time), but also as containing a significant *qualitative* element ("evil"). For example, two other expressions in the Song of Moses in which "generation" is used are primarily qualitative, not quantitative, referring to the rebellious nation as a *collective whole*.

In the preamble to this song, Moses rebuked the "offspring" of Israel for their evil inclination to rebellion and stubbornness (Deut. 31:21, 27). In the song itself, the prophet labeled the children of Israel as wicked offspring: "They have dealt corruptly with him [God]; they are no longer his children because they are blemished; they are a *crooked and twisted generation*" (Deut. 32:5, emphasis added). Then God himself warned, "I will see what their end will be, for they *are a perverse generation*, children in whom is *no faithfulness*" (Deut. 32:20, emphasis added; cf. 31:17). The idea is that the nation of Israel is a corporate offspring of "blemished" children who perpetually engage in idolatry and rejection of the Lord. The generation in question does not refer to a specific time period but to a *trans-historical phenomenon of a type of people*. It does not refer to the ethnicity of the Israelites but to the nation's *spiritual* condition, its degenerate disposition towards iniquity.

We must conclude, then, that the New Testament motif of ἡ γενεὰ αὕτη ("this generation") is faithful to its Old Testament usage as a *qualitative* description of the general character of the Israelite nation. This evil inclination was not a unique feature of Jesus' first-century audience, but one that had always existed, and will *continue* to exist until their national repentance at the return of Jesus Christ. As we will see, the faithful remnant of righteous

Israelites is *not* included in this qualitative expression "this generation."

In his seminal work, *Jesus and 'this Generation'*, Evald Lövestam painstakingly demonstrates that the concept of ἡ γενεὰ αὕτη ("this generation") should be understood qualitatively as referring to a *character* of people.[13] He shows that several *repeated elements* appear in the biblical record as they relate to "this generation": First, the expression *always* has a negative tone and refers to people characterized by moral wickedness. In other words, "this generation" is decisively an evil and perverse generation. Consequently, the Lord Jesus and his apostles (post-Pentecost) were *not* part of the evil generation. Second, God repeatedly sends preachers to this generation to proclaim a message of repentance. Third, this message is accompanied by miraculous signs, yet this generation reacts with doubt and disbelief. Fourth, this generation persecutes and often kills God's righteous messengers. Fifth, this generation will be condemned on judgment day, but the righteous messengers and those who are "saved from" it (e.g. Acts 2:4) will be vindicated and receive rewards. Sixth, the New Testament links this pattern of rejecting "the sent ones" with similar narratives in the Old Testament. The constellation of teachings surrounding "this generation" consistently draws the readers' attention to the *perpetual, consistent nature* of those who reject God's message of salvation.

As Lövestam demonstrates, this salvific-historical pattern for "this generation" is evident in every pericope (section of material) where the expression appears. The repeated elements discussed above appear in the pericopes regarding the demand for a sign (Matt. 12:38-42; 16:1-4; Mark 8:11-13; Luke 11:16, 29-32), the parable of the playing children (Matt. 11:16-19; Luke 7:31-35), the epileptic boy (Matt. 17:14-20; Mark 9:14-29; Luke 9:37-43a), the eschatological sayings about "this generation" (Mark 8:38; Luke 17:22-37), the judgment on "this generation" (Matt. 23:34-36; Luke 11:49-51), the Olivet Discourse (Matt. 24; Luke 13; Luke 21),

---

13 Lövestam 1995

Peter's appeal on the day of Pentecost (Acts 2:40), and the epistolary references (Phil. 2:12-16; Heb. 3:7-4:11). This is conclusive evidence that the phrase "this generation" conveys a technical meaning referring to the trans-historical *offspring* of wickedness, as it does in the Song of Moses (Deut. 32:5, 20).

Clearly then, τὴν γενεὰν ταύτην ("this generation") in Matthew 23:36 continues the divine testimony concerning this historic *qualitative and corporate* "perverse generation, sons in whom is no faithfulness" (Deut. 32:20). However, contrary to the preterist position as articulated by Gentry, the similar use of the expression in Matthew 24:34 does not *prove* that both expressions are quantitative and "must mean that [same] first century generation".[14] Seeing both passages as describing the contemporaries of Jesus, DeMar states that both appearances of the phrase, in Matthew 23:36 and 24:34, "form eschatological bookends for determining when the predicted events that occur between these two time markers are to be fulfilled."[15] Matthew 23:32-36 reads as follows:

> Fill up, then, the measure of your fathers. You serpents, you brood of vipers, how are you to escape being sentenced to hell? Therefore, I send you prophets and wise men and scribes, some of whom you will kill and crucify, and some you will flog in your synagogues and persecute from town to town, so that on you may come all the righteous blood shed on earth, from the blood of righteous Abel to the blood of Zechariah the son of Barachiah, whom you murdered between the sanctuary and the altar. Truly, I say to you, *all these things will come upon this generation.* (Matt. 23:32-36, emphasis added)

The Lord's expression "this generation" in Matthew 23:36 could convey, at least at face value, a quantitative meaning, that is, all people living at about the same time, a specific time period such as forty years. Yet significantly, the passage hints that the expression carries a qualitative and trans-historical meaning.

---

14 Gentry 2010c, loc. 1111; cf. loc. 573, 695, 1161, 1210; Similarly DeMar 1999, pp. 52, 55-56 and Kik 1971, p. 64
15 DeMar 1999, p. 55

Jesus' immediate audience, identified as scribes and Pharisees (Matt. 23:29), undoubtedly belonged to the generation in question; however, the astonishing feature is that they will be held responsible for the spilled blood of *all* the martyrs going back to *the beginning of human history* (Gen. 4:8-11). The coming judgment on "this generation" presumably included the desolation of the Jerusalem temple (Matt. 23:38), yet the meaning conveyed is that this chronological bracket of people will be held responsible for the heinous sins of *the entirety* of biblical history, as if it were preeminently wicked. But this contention is not supported by the Scriptures. More reasonable and biblical is the concept of a transhistorical phenomenon, a generation that encompasses *all* generations and *transcends* the quantitative definition of a restricted, contemporary time period.

The scribes and Pharisees in Matthew 23 should be understood as belonging to the larger generation of evildoers. They would be held responsible for the rejection of all God's people "from the blood of righteous Abel to the blood of Zechariah the son of Barachiah" (Matt. 23:35). Lövestam provides the following explanation:

> This [phrase] then means that the reference is to a period long since over. There is substantial time between the death of the last prophetic martyr in the OT and the era of "this genea". How can that be? If it was a matter of a general accumulation of guilt as is often assumed, the sense would seem to require that the speaker covered the whole period up to the time of speaking, the time of "this genea". It would have been natural to mention John the Baptist or Jesus or the messengers who according to the logion were going to be killed, instead of mentioning Zechariah. But this is not the case.[16]

Jesus explained that the scribes and Pharisees of "this generation" maintained a *corporate solidarity* with those who had persecuted and rejected "all the prophets" of the Old Testament era, a solidarity evidenced by their continued ancestral pattern of wickedness (Matt. 23:34-35; cf. 5:12; 21:33-41). It should not be lost on

16 Lövestam 1995, p. 76

the reader that the covenant nation soon murdered the Son of God and persecuted his apostles (Acts 2:23; 5:30; 1 Thess. 2:14-15). The apostle Peter also labeled them "this crooked generation" (Acts 2:40).

The reason for the scribes and Pharisees' culpability in these heinous crimes is that they too were part of the *offspring* with evil inclinations. Jesus called them "children of hell" (Matt. 23:15), "sons of those who murdered the prophets" (v. 31), and "serpents, you brood of vipers" (v. 33; cf. Matt. 3:7; 12:34; John 8:44). Consequently, they deserved God's covenantal wrath including eternal damnation (i.e., "being sentenced to hell" in Matt. 23:33). They "filled up ... the measure of their fathers" by rejecting and murdering the apostles as their ancestors had rejected and murdered the prophets (Matt. 23:29-36). The Judean Jews as a collective whole deserved divine retribution, as seen in the Pauline phrase "as always to fill up the measure of their sins" (1 Thess. 2:16, emphasis added; cf. Matt. 23:32). They were *perpetually* ("as always") deserving divine wrath because they had not changed in their disposition towards the Lord's messengers.

The first Christian martyr, Stephen, spoke about this *persistent* pattern of rejecting God's messengers. In his remarks to the religious leaders of the Jewish nation, he proclaimed, "You stiff-necked people, uncircumcised in heart and ears, you *always* resist the Holy Spirit. *As your fathers did, so did you.* Which of the prophets did your fathers not persecute? And they killed those who announced beforehand the coming of the Righteous One, whom you have now betrayed and murdered, you who received the law as delivered by angels and did not keep it" (Acts 7:51-53, emphasis added). This perpetual pattern of wickedness had continued unabated since the nation's inception, but not merely among the leaders: "And now, brethren, I know that you acted in ignorance, just as your rulers did also" (Acts 3:17).

The trans-historical nature of the generation in question is also seen in Christ's indication that it would remain until his glorious return. His diatribe against the scribes and Pharisees in

95

Matthew 23 ends with the statement, "See, your house is left to *you* desolate. For I tell *you, you* will not see me again, until *you* say, 'Blessed is he who comes in the name of the Lord'" (Matt. 23:38-39, emphasis added). J. Stuart Russell pointed to the appearance of the second person plural ("you") to argue that Jesus was promising to return to his contemporaries in Matthew 23:39.[17]

Partial preterists, however, do not eagerly adopt this interpretation. Gentry creatively, although unconvincingly, argues that this passage does not refer to a future hope for Israel but speaks of "a condition of indefinite possibility" (borrowing from R. T. France) that was fulfilled in their "constrained admission of Jesus' blessedness" which they made in their destruction in AD 70.[18] However, the antecedent for the representative "you" being addressed in this verse is Jerusalem (v. 37) that stands as a metonymy for the people of the city (Matt. 23:1). Jesus prophesied here that the people of Jerusalem would make the statement of Psalm 118:26. This statement is from *a psalm of thanksgiving that speaks of the LORD returning to Jerusalem to deliver Israel* from their distress. This theme of the psalm fits the national salvation of Israel at the Lord's return but is not consistent with the events of Jerusalem's demise in AD 70. Kik admits that this passage refers to the day when the Jews will be "included amongst the chosen."[19]

The appearance of the expression "this generation" in Philippians 2:15 sheds additional light on the scope of this generation's corruption. The apostle Paul wrote, "Do all things without grumbling or disputing, that you may be blameless and innocent, *children* of God *without blemish in the midst of a crooked and twisted generation*, among whom you shine as lights in the world, holding fast to the word of life, so that in the day of Christ I may be proud that I did not run in vain or labor in vain" (Phil. 2:14-16, emphasis added). Paul alluded to Deuteronomy 32:5 ("they are no longer

---

17 Russell 2003, p. 52
18 Gentry 2010c, loc. 826-842; cf. France 1985, p. 332
19 Kik 1971, p. 81

his children because they are blemished; they are a crooked and twisted generation") in this passage to exhort the Christians at Philippi to live as blameless children of God. The unique feature of this passage is that the inhabitants of Philippi "among whom" these Christians lived were predominantly gentiles! This provides evidence that "this generation" is a qualitative term that crosses epochs and ethnic boundaries. For Paul, the corruption of sin is foundational and ubiquitous (Rom. 3:9) and "this generation" describes Jews and gentiles alike.

The preterist arguments regarding "this generation" (Matt. 24:34) fall apart *even if the phrase is understood quantitatively*. A few examples will demonstrate the falsity of their contention that Jesus would have used "that" (ἐκεῖνος) instead of "this" (οὗτος/ταύτῃ) if he had wanted to speak of events in our future. First, the New Testament writers used the proximal demonstrative (οὗτος/ταύτῃ, usually translated "this") to describe events that occurred in a distant time from the speaker (e.g., Luke 23:7). In the Olivet Discourse, for example, Jesus used the proximal demonstrative to speak of an event in the distant future (Luke 17:34). Many modern translations render the phrase "that night" instead of "this night" for clarity, but the Greek text clearly supports the latter. Second, the writer of the book of Hebrews employed the proximal demonstrative "this" (οὗτος/ταύτῃ) with the noun "generation" (γενεᾷ) to describe a context distant to the writer by thousands of years! The text of Hebrews 3:10 reads, "Therefore I [God] was provoked with that [literally 'this'] generation." Third, Koine Greek has three distinct demonstratives, ὅδε meaning "this here", οὗτος meaning "this", and ἐκεῖνος meaning "that", so one could use preterist logic to argue that Jesus would have used ὅδε in Matthew 24:34 if he had wanted to refer to his contemporaries only.

Preterists often wonder why Jesus appears to have predicted ultimate eschatological events in the near future of his original hearers.[20] By itself, the grammatical construction of the expression "this generation" (Matt. 24:34) could convey three different

20 E.g., Gentry 2010c, loc. 122

meanings. First, it could carry a restricted, temporal force that referred only to the contemporary audience of Jesus that was alive in the first century. Second, the expression could, albeit with greater difficulty, refer to those alive at the great tribulation in their distant future. Yet, as demonstrated above, these two meanings are prohibited by the immediate context of the Olivet Discourse and by the technical use of this phrase throughout the Synoptics and the Bible. The overwhelming biblical evidence regarding the phrase "this generation" shows that it refers to the qualitative, age-enduring offspring of the Serpent (Gen. 3:15). We should conclude that the inherent *ambiguity* of this expression's meaning is *intentional* on the part of Jesus. This ambiguity, coupled with Jesus' statements that the exact timing of his return is unknowable (Matt. 24:36, 44), leaves open the *possibility* that his original audience could have lived to see his glorious return. This semantic versatility allows the reader to understand the events surrounding the desolation of Jerusalem and the temple in AD 70 as a *partial and typological* fulfillment that ultimately points to the complete, *plenary* fulfillment at the end of the age. This must be the case because "all these things" did *not* take place in the first century.

Jesus has given the church an enigma in Matthew 24:34. The interpreter who embraces the inerrancy of Scripture is divinely "hedged in" by the biblical evidence so as to be left with only one conclusion. That conclusion is that the expression "this generation" points to the qualitative, trans-historical offspring of evil-doers described throughout the Bible. This people are "the generation" of the wicked (Ps. 14:2-5) and "the children of the evil one" (Matt. 13:38) who are under the domain of Satan, the ruler and god of "this world" (John 12:31; 14:30; 16:11, 2 Cor. 4:4), during the period of "the present evil age" (Gal. 1:4). The generation in question consists of all Jews and gentiles who have not escaped the corruption of this age by believing in our Lord Jesus Christ. Our Master taught that this present evil age and this wicked generation will not "pass away" until all the eschatological events he had spoken about have taken place (Matt. 24:4-33). The death knell for preterism is that the destruction of Jerusalem and the temple came and went in AD 70 *without so much as a hint of Jesus' return.* This caused significant doubts in the minds of many Christians regarding the promises of Jesus to return soon, as evidenced in the statement about the scoffers in 2 Peter 3 (see Chapter Two). The Lord addressed this issue in the Olivet Discourse by teaching that even the dissolution of the cosmos will not detract from the certainty of his covenantal promises, as he promised: "Heaven and earth will pass away, but my words will not pass away" (Matt. 24:35).

9

Why Jesus Did Not Transition to the Distant Future in Matthew 24:36

Many preterists see a break in the Olivet Discourse, beginning in Matthew 24:36 (cf. Mark 13:32), that shifts from first-century events to events in our future.[1] This verse reads, "But concerning that day and hour no one knows, not even the angels of heaven, nor the Son, but the Father only." Preterist J. Marcellus Kik explains that the earlier portion of the discourse is about "the subject of the destruction of Jerusalem, or his judgment against the Jewish nation" while the latter portion relates to events of "his second coming at the end of the age when he would judge the world."[2] This approach is appealing because it seeks to find linguistic and syntactical evidence for dividing the discourse. However, it crumbles upon critical examination.

R. T. France, the foremost champion of this position, posits five exegetical reasons for dividing the Olivet Discourse beginning at Matthew 24:36.[3] His reasons for division are summarized as follows: First, this verse begins with "but about" (περὶ δὲ), a phrase that was used earlier (Matt 22:31) to denote a subject change. The apostle Paul also employed this phrase as a "rhetorical formula" to change subjects. Second, Jesus suddenly shifts from describing the plural "those days" (Matt. 24:19, 22, 29) to the singular "that day and hour" (Matt. 24:42, 44, 50; 25:13). Third, the timing of the events prior to verse 36 can be predicted based on signs (Matt.

---

1   Kik 1971, p. 158; Similarly, R. T. France, Kenneth Gentry, and Alistair I. Wilson.
2   Kik 1971, p.69; cf. pp. 60, 67
3   France 2007, pp. 340-41, 936-38

24:15, 34), but the timing of the latter event is "unknown and unknowable" and will occur "without prior warning." Fourth, prior to verse 36, the participle "coming" (ἐρχόμενον) was employed to predict the "coming of the Son of Man" as described in Daniel 7:13-14, whereas the latter verses look forward to Christ's future "coming" (παρουσία) (Matt. 24:37, 39) and do not reflect any elements from Daniel's vision. Fifth, the earlier verses contain temporal indicators whereas the latter verses do not. We will now examine each of these arguments in detail.

The Meaning of "But Concerning"

France's first contention that the phrase "now/but concerning" (περὶ δὲ) always introduces a new topic is verifiably false. The phrase occurs 14 times in the New Testament outside the Olivet Discourse, nine of which occur in the writings of the apostle Paul (Acts 21:25; 1 Cor. 7:1, 25; 8:1; 12:1; 16:1, 12; 1 Thess. 4:9; 5:1). In addition to occurring three times in the Septuagint (Gen. 15:12; 17:20; 41:32 LXX), the phrase is found three times in the Gospel of Matthew (20:6; 22:30; 27:46), once in Mark (12:26), and once in John (16:11). Paul employed the phrase throughout 1 Corinthians, and possibly in Acts 21:25 and 1 Thessalonians 4:9, as a literary device that functions to introduce a new topic. However, outside of Pauline literature, the biblical writers *never* used περὶ δὲ to introduce a new topic. Rather, the phrase typically has a resumptive force: it emphasizes the fact that the speaker is returning to a point that he presented previously.

The phrase "now/but concerning" (περὶ δὲ) in Matthew's Gospel is *always* resumptive and never introduces a new subject. It first appears in Jesus' Parable of the Workers of the Vineyard (Matt. 20:1-16). The parable is about a "master of the house" who hired workers to tend his vineyard at various hours of the day (vv. 2-6). The phrase περὶ δὲ (v. 6) *concludes* an unbroken series of chronological events. It functions to emphasize that the master hired certain workers late in the day (i.e., the eleventh hour) and scandalously paid them the same amount as the other workers (cf.

v. 12). The expression περὶ δὲ occurs again in Matthew 22:30 (cf. Mark 12:26) where it transitions from Jesus' specific statement about certain individuals receiving the resurrection of the dead (Matt. 22:29-30; Mark 12:24-25) to a general statement about the resurrection (Matt. 22:31-32; Mark 12:26); the same eschatological theme occurs before and after the phrase. The phrase περὶ δὲ also appears in Matthew 27:46. Matthew explained that the sky was darkened from the sixth hour to the ninth hour during Jesus' crucifixion, and he included the phrase to highlight the final hour (Matt. 27:45-46). The subject before and after the expression is the same, and it functions to consummate an uninterrupted sequence of actions.

Gentry surmises that "but concerning" (περὶ δὲ) in Matthew 24:36 is resumptive and that Jesus used it to cue his disciples that he was answering their second question concerning "the sign of your coming [παρουσίας] and of the close of the age?" (v. 3).[4] This argument is problematic because Jesus had already begun answering their second question concerning "the sign of his coming" in the preceding verses (vv. 27-35). Furthermore, the argument creates an artificial distinction between "the close of the age" (v. 3) and the period of the destruction of Jerusalem and its temple. Although Gentry interprets "the end" in verse six as referring to the destruction of the temple, he fails to recognize that its antecedent is "the close [συντελείας] of the age" in verse three. The prophet Daniel also spoke about the end (συντελείας), the period of the unprecedented tribulation and resurrection from the dead (Dan. 12:1-7, 13 LXX).

"Those Days" and "The Day"

France again overplays his hand with his second proposal that a subject change occurs in Matthew 24:36, as evidenced by the switch from the plural "those days" to the singular "the day" and "the hour." This red herring becomes apparent upon close examination of the analogy that follows in Matthew 24:37-39.

4   Gentry 2010c, loc. 2480, 2490, chapter eight.

Jesus compared the flood in Noah's day to the day of his return, stating, "For as were the days of Noah, so will be the coming of the Son of Man" (Matt. 24:37; cf. Luke 17:26; Isa. 54:9). The period of "those days" of Noah were characterized by an unsuspecting populace who engaged in normal daily activities until "the day" when he and his family entered the ark and the flood came upon the remainder of the world (Matt. 24:38). The period of "those days" were contiguous with and culminated in "the day" that the flood arrived. The force of this statement is easily overlooked, but it is prima facie evidence that no gap will separate "those days" of the unprecedented tribulation from "the day" of the Lord's return. In addition, "those days" of Noah and "the day" of the flood all transpired in Noah's days, suggesting that those who endure the tribulation period will witness the return of Jesus.

France encounters further difficulties when the evidence from Luke's parallel account is considered. In Luke's Gospel, the analogy of Noah (Luke 17:26-27) is immediately followed by the analogy of Lot (Luke 17:28), both of which contain several of the same elements. The passage reads as follows: "Likewise, just as it was in the days of Lot—they were eating and drinking, buying and selling, planting and building, but on *the day* when Lot went out from Sodom, fire and sulfur rained from heaven and destroyed them all—so will it be on *the day* when the Son of Man is revealed. On *that day*, let the one who is on the housetop, with his goods in the house, not come down to take them away, and likewise let the one who is in the field not turn back. Remember Lot's wife" (Luke 17:28-32, emphasis added). Several observations reveal the fallacy of France's argument. First, the narrative does not allow for a gap between "the days" of the peoples' daily activities and "the day" that Lot fled Sodom prior to the city's fiery destruction. Second, these events all transpired within Lot's lifetime. Third, the city was burned up on "the day" when Lot fled, which is analogous to the fiery destruction on the day of the Lord (c.f. 2 Peter 3:7, 10, 12-13; Rev. 18:8-10). Fourth, Jesus used "the day" to indicate the coming of the Son of Man (Luke 17:24, 29), the exact phrase that France correctly maintains must refer to the future return of Jesus. These parallels demonstrate that "the day" of his return will conclude immediately after the "those days" of the unequaled tribulation. The biblical text does not allow for an intervening time gap here.

Figure 4: Two Models of "Those Days" and the Day of the Lord

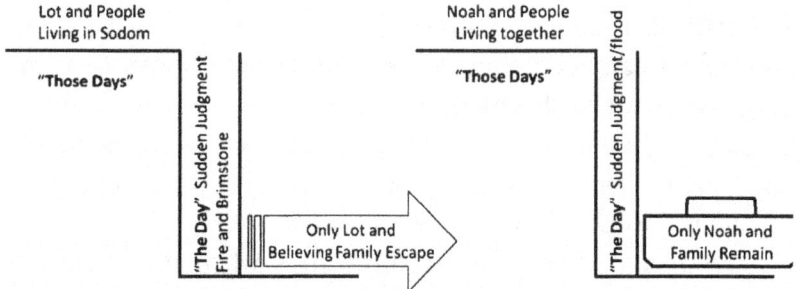

The Model Based on the Analogies of Lot and Noah

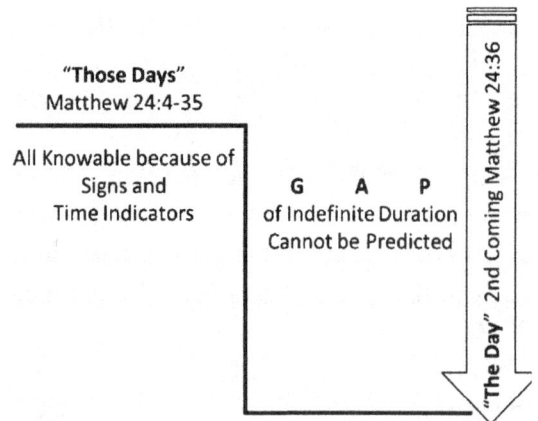

The Model of R. T. France

France's third and fifth reasons for dividing the Olivet Discourse beginning at Matthew 24:36 are similar because they both suggest that the timing of the earlier events can be predicted by signs and time indicators, whereas the timing of the return of

Jesus cannot be predicted (Matt. 24:36ff). This is a non sequitur for at least two reasons. First, while the signs in Matthew 24:4-14 demonstrate that the end of the age has not yet arrived (vv. 6, 8, 13), the specific sign of the abomination of desolation and the subsequent unprecedented tribulation (vv. 15-29) show that the Lord's coming is "near, at the very gates" (v. 33). The necessity of paying attention to this specific sign proves that the *precise* timing (i.e., the exact "day and hour" v. 36) of his return is unknown. Second, the statement "that day and hour no one knows" (v. 36) modifies the previous statement that "this generation" would remain until the end (vv. 34-35). The antecedent for "that day and hour" (v. 36) is undoubtedly the coming of the Son of Man of the preceding verses (vv. 29-35). The absence of any other referent also strongly suggests that Jesus did not switch topics in verse 36.

Different Words for the Lord's Coming?

France's fourth reason for dividing the Olivet Prophecy is that the participle "coming" (ερχομενον) occurs prior to Matthew 24:36 and "coming" (παρουσία) occurs afterward. This is demonstrably false. The disciples' original inquiry pertained to the sign of his "coming" (παρουσία) (v. 3), and Jesus answered in verse 27 with an explanation about "the coming [παρουσία] of the Son of Man." In addition, several cognates of the verb "to come" (ερχομαι) appear after verse 36 where the subject is the Lord's return (Matt. 24:42, 43, 44; 25:6, 13, 19, 31; cf. Mark 13:36), but France attempts to maneuver around this by demanding that the specific participle ερχομενον appears. This hardly suffices, especially since the participial form occurs only once in the entire discourse (Matt. 24:30). Furthermore, the early disciples employed the word "coming" (παρουσία) elsewhere to refer to the Lord's coming that most preterists teach occurred in AD 70. For example, James declared that "the coming [παρουσία] of the Lord is at hand" (James 5:7-8), and Paul reminded the saints in Thessalonica that the Man of Lawlessness will be destroyed at Jesus' "coming" (παρουσία) (2 Thess. 2:1, 8).

France's claim that the details of the Lord's coming (παρουσία) after Matthew 24:36 "do not reflect any elements from Daniel's vision" in Daniel 7 is also false. In the vision of Daniel 7 and the latter part of the Olivet Discourse, the Son of Man appears in heavenly glory with the angels (Dan. 7:10, 13-14; Matt. 25:31), the Lord sits on the throne as judge (Dan 7:9, 26; Matt. 25:31), the everlasting kingdom is given to all nations (Dan. 7:14, 22, 27; Matt. 25:32, 34, 46), and the wicked are punished by fire (Dan 7:11; Matt. 25:41-46; cf. Ezek. 34:17, 20). A detailed comparison of these similarities is provided in Appendix B.

Gentry's Arguments for Division

Gentry provides additional arguments in favor of dividing the Olivet Prophecy beginning with Matthew 24:36. He contends that verses 4-31 answered the first of the disciples' questions concerning when "these things" (i.e., the destruction of the temple) would occur but verses 36-46 answered the second question of the sign of Jesus' coming (παρουσία).[5] In contrast to Gentry's argument, Jesus focused on the *sign* of his coming (παρουσία) prior to verse 36 (specifically vv. 27-30) and concentrated more on the *timing* of this coming in the latter portion of the discourse. This is further supported by the fact that Mark combined the disciples' two questions into one question ("Tell us, when will these things be, and what will be the sign when all these things are about to be accomplished?" Mark 13:4), suggesting that the disciples did not ask two temporally-distinct questions but connected the destruction of the temple with the glorious arrival of Christ.

Gentry also argues that Jesus' statement in Matthew 24:34 concerning "this generation" serves as a concluding statement.

> Why would such a statement be inserted one-fourth of the way through the discourse if it were dealing in its entirety with events that were to occur in "this generation"? Such would not make sense. That would be like someone giving

5 Ibid., chapter eight.

a speech, and after fifteen minutes saying, "In conclusion," then continuing the speech for another forty-five minutes.[6]

While verse 34 functions as a kind of concluding statement, this does not mean that Jesus introduced an *entirely new topic* in verse 36. One reason for this is that Matthew combined two different source materials at this point in the Olivet Discourse, which is seen by the fact that this material is divided into two sections in Luke's Gospel (Luke 21:25-33; 17:26-37; See Table 2). Matthew included the latter material (Matt 24:36-25:46) to explain the timing of the Lord's "coming" ($\pi\alpha\rhoο\upsilon\sigma\iota\alpha$) that he had already introduced in Matthew 24:27-30.

Gentry argues that temporal progress indicators, such as "then" and "immediately after," do not appear after Matthew 24:35, which suggests that the latter portion of the discourse is not part of the historical sequence described in verses 4-35.[7] However, it is more favorable to view the temporal indicators as connecting the specific signs with the Lord's return *with a shift in emphasis*, beginning in verse 36, to the hiddenness of the timing of his return. In addition, the absence of clear temporal indicators argues in favor of the temporal continuity of the latter portion of the discourse with the preceding material.

Other Problems with Dividing the Olivet Discourse

Many preterists equivocate on the meaning of Jesus' teaching that the wicked will be thrown into the fiery furnace or outer darkness, and "in that place there will be weeping and gnashing of teeth" (Matt. 8:12; 13:42, 50; 22:13; 24:51; 25:30; Luke 13:28; cf. Matt. 21:33-43). This phrase appears throughout the Synoptic Gospels in passages that preterists believe predicted the destruction of Jerusalem in AD 70. For example, it appears in the Parable of the Great Banquet, a parable that Jesus taught about a king who prepared a wedding for his son (Matt. 22:1-14; cf. Luke 14:16-24). In the parable, the king sent his servants to invite guests to the

---

6 Ibid., loc. 2460, chapter eight

7 Ibid., loc. 2504, chapter eight

wedding feast, but those who had been invited abused and killed the servants (Matt. 22:3-6). This made the king angry, so he "sent his troops and destroyed those murderers and burned their city" (Matt. 22:7; cf. 8:12). Preterists interpret this verse as referring to the Roman invasion of Judah and the subsequent burning of Jerusalem's temple in AD 70.[8]

However, Jesus employed this phrase elsewhere, when he explicitly stated that this event will take place at "the end of the age" (Matt. 13:39-40, 49). This is problematic for preterists who insist on dividing the Olivet Prophecy, because they teach (correctly!) that this "end" refers to the future return of Jesus and *not* to AD 70. Furthermore, the phrase also appears twice *after* the supposed division at Matthew 24:36, in the section of the discourse that these preterists teach as referring to the future return of Jesus (Matt. 24:51; 25:30; cf. Luke 19:27). It is unlikely that Jesus used this same expression to refer to both the destruction of Jerusalem in AD 70 *and* to the judgment of hell at the future day of Jesus Christ.

Preterists encounter another significant difficulty while attempting to divide the Olivet Discourse beginning with Matthew 24:36. Jesus mentioned at least two specific prophetic events that appear in the text before this supposed transition verse *and* in the pericope (the section of material) of Luke 17:26-37. The two expressions read as follows:

> Let the one who is on the housetop not go down to take what is in his house, and let the one who is in the field not turn back to take his cloak. (Matt. 24:17-18; Luke 17:31)

> Wherever the corpse is, there the vultures will gather. (Matt. 24:28; Luke 17:37)

Preterists dig themselves into a hole by arguing that the events described in the early portion of the discourse (Matt. 24:15-35) were fulfilled in the First Jewish-Roman War in AD 66-70, while maintaining that the latter portion of the discourse (Matt.

---

8 E.g., Kik 1971, p. 77

24:36-41), *a section of text that shares common source material with the pericope of Luke 17:26-37*, will occur at the future return of Jesus. Preterists who argue that Luke 17:26-37 was fulfilled in AD 66-70 must also admit that Jesus predicted these same events in a passage that they believe is about our future (Matt. 24:37-41). Both passages include the detailed comparison between "the days of Noah" and "the days of the Son of Man" (Matt. 24:37-39; Luke 17:26-30), as well as the statement "one will be taken and the other left" (Matt. 24:40-42; Luke 17:35-37). On the other hand, those who try to escape this problem by arguing that Luke 17:26-37 is about our future must allow for a future Jewish flight from Judea and banquet for vultures, as futurism maintains.

It is highly unlikely that Jesus used the same descriptions to depict two distinct events, which are separated by thousands of years, without giving clear temporal indications in the text to warrant such an approach. The only real solution is to understand the entire Olivet Discourse, along with Luke's parallel material, as predicting events within one specific time frame.

The following table shows the common source material for the Olivet Discourse in the Gospels of Matthew and Luke. The overlapping material is in **bold print** for easy comparison. These verses in **bold** precede the supposed division of Matthew 24:36 and are considered by preterists to describe events that occurred in AD 66-70. However, they also appear after the division in Luke's parallel account and are considered by many preterists to depict future events.

Table 2: Parallels Between Matthew 24 and Luke's Gospel

Matthew 24	Luke 21, 17, 12
Matthew 24:1-14	Luke 21:5-19
24:15 "So when you see the abomination of desolation spoken of by the prophet Daniel, standing in the holy place (let the reader understand),..."	21:20 "But when you see Jerusalem surrounded by armies, then know that its desolation has come near."
24:16 "...then let those who are in Judea flee to the mountains."	21:21 "Then let those who are in Judea flee to the mountains, and let those who are inside the city depart, and let not those who are out in the country enter it,..."
24:17-18 "Let the one who is on the housetop not go down to take what is in his house, and let the one who is in the field not turn back to take his cloak."	*See below for the parallel account.*
24:19-22	21:22-24
24:23, 27	17:22-25
24:28 "Wherever the corpse is, there the vultures will gather."	*See below for the parallel account.*
24:29 "Immediately after the tribulation of those days the sun will be darkened, and the moon will not give its light, and the stars will fall from heaven,..."	21:25-26 "And there will be signs in sun and moon and stars, and on the earth distress of nations in perplexity because of the roaring of the sea and the waves, people fainting with fear and with foreboding of what is coming on the world. For the powers of the heavens will be shaken."
"...and the powers of the heavens will be shaken."	
24:30 "Then will appear in heaven the sign of the Son of Man, and then all the tribes of the earth will mourn, and they will see the Son of Man coming on the clouds of heaven with power and great glory."	21:27 And then they will see the Son of Man coming in a cloud with power and great glory
24:31-35	21:29-33

110

24:36 "But concerning that day and hour no one knows, not even the angels of heaven, nor the Son, but the Father only."

24:37 "For as were the days of Noah, so will be the coming of the Son of Man."

17:26 "Just as it was in the days of Noah, so will it be in the days of the Son of Man."

24:38 "For as in those days before the flood they were eating and drinking, marrying and giving in marriage, until the day when Noah entered the ark,..."

17:27 "They were eating and drinking and marrying and being given in marriage, until the day when Noah entered the ark,..." and the flood came and destroyed them all

24:39 "...and they were unaware until the flood came and swept them all away, so will be the coming of the Son of Man."

17:30 "...so will it be on the day when the Son of Man is revealed."

See above for the parallel account.

17:31 "On that day, let the one who is on the housetop, with his goods in the house, not come down to take them away, and likewise let the one who is in the field not turn back..."

24:40 "Then two men will be in the field; one will be taken and one left."

24:41 "Two women will be grinding at the mill; one will be taken and one left."

17:35 "There will be two women grinding together. One will be taken and the other left."

See above for the parallel account.

17:37 "And they said to him, 'Where, Lord?' **"He said to them," 'Where the corpse is, there the vultures will gather.'**

24:42 "Therefore, stay awake, for you do not know on what day your Lord is coming."

24:43-51

12:39-46

111

As we have seen, the inseparability of the Olivet Discourse is based upon the internal consistency of its contents, the weaknesses of the arguments for dividing it, and the appearance of common source material before and after Matthew 24:36. The late-eighteenth century preterist Nehemiah Nisbett sounded the alarm against those seeking to divide the discourse:

> Some men of great learning and eminence have thought that our Lord is here [Matt. 24:36] speaking, not of the destruction of Jerusalem, but of that more solemn and awful one of the day of judgment. But I can by no means think that the Evangelists are such loose, inaccurate writers, as to make so sudden and abrupt a transition, as they are here supposed to do; much less to break through the fundamental rules of good writing, by apparently referring to something which they had said before; when in reality they were beginning a new subject, and the absurdity of the supposition will appear more strongly, if it is recollected that the question of the disciples was, "When shall these things be?"[9]

---

9 Nisbett 1787, pp. 38-39

10

The Olivet Discourse in 1 Thessalonians 4-5

This chapter will demonstrate that the apostle Paul derived his material for 1 Thessalonians 4:13 to 5:11 from the Olivet Discourse. The following excerpt contains Paul's encouraging instruction for the Thessalonian saints:

> 4:13 But we do not want you to be uninformed, brothers, about those who are asleep, that you may not grieve as others do who have no hope. 14 For since we believe that Jesus died and rose again, even so, through Jesus, God will bring with him those who have fallen asleep. 15 For this we declare to you by a word from the Lord, that we who are alive, who are left until the coming of the Lord, will not precede those who have fallen asleep. 16 For the Lord himself will descend from heaven with a cry of command, with the voice of an archangel, and with the sound of the trumpet of God. And the dead in Christ will rise first. 17 Then we who are alive, who are left, will be caught up together with them in the clouds to meet the Lord in the air, and so we will always be with the Lord. 18 Therefore encourage one another with these words.
>
> 5:1 Now concerning the times and the seasons, brothers, you have no need to have anything written to you. 2 For you yourselves are fully aware that the day of the Lord will come like a thief in the night. 3 While people are saying, "There is peace and security," then sudden destruction will come upon them as labor pains come upon a pregnant woman, and they will not escape.
>
> 4 But you are not in darkness, brothers, for that day to surprise you like a thief. 5 For you are all children of light, children of the day. We are not of the night or of the darkness. 6 So then let us not sleep, as others do, but let us keep awake and be sober. 7 For those who sleep, sleep at night, and those who get drunk, are drunk at night. 8 But since we belong to the day,

let us be sober, having put on the breastplate of faith and love, and for a helmet the hope of salvation. [9] For God has not destined us for wrath, but to obtain salvation through our Lord Jesus Christ, [10] who died for us so that whether we are awake or asleep we might live with him. [11] Therefore encourage one another and build one another up, just as you are doing. (1 Thess. 4:13-5:11)

The statement "For we declare to you by a word from the Lord" (1 Thess. 4:15) requires some consideration of the syntax. Gordon Fee explains, "Almost everyone considers all of [1 Thess. 4] verses 15b-17b to be a recital of what Paul here calls 'the Lord's word.' Thus he begins, 'for *this* we tell you with/by a/the word of the Lord, namely *that* ...' The slashes indicate areas of considerable debate in terms of understanding what Paul is referring to."[1] Due to these difficulties, the reader must consider other factors in order to determine the meaning of the apostle's statement. The idea that "the word [λόγῳ] of the Lord" (v. 15) refers to a *logion*, an authentic saying from the mouth of Jesus of Nazareth, has much to commend it. As noteworthy supporting evidence for this claim, the apostle Paul *always* referred to the historical Jesus when he used the title "the Lord" (κύριος), except when quoting the Old Testament (LXX). In addition, the apostle habitually identified the source of his teaching when he spoke by direct revelation from the Holy Spirit and was not quoting Jesus (1 Cor. 2:12-16; 7:40; 2 Cor. 13:3; Gal. 4:12; 1 Thess. 2:13). Finally, when the apostle identified "the Lord" (κύριος) as the source of his teachings, the *content* of the teaching also appeared in statements spoken by Jesus (e.g., 1 Cor. 7:10-11, 25; 9:14; 11:23-25). As we will soon see, this is also the case in 1 Thessalonians 4:13-5:11.

Several biblical scholars teach that the Olivet Discourse is "the word" of the historical Jesus referred to in 1 Thessalonians 4:15.[2] Charles Wanamaker sees this portion of the apostle Paul's teaching as representing a Jewish *midrash* of the discourse.[3]

---

1   Fee 2009, pp. 182-84
2   Rigaux 1968, p. 539; Hartman 1966, pp. 187-90; Hyldahl 1980, p. 130; Seyoon 2002, pp. 231-42
3   Wanamaker 1990, pp. 171-77

Several observations from the Olivet Prophecy and 1 Thessalonian 4-5 reveal the likelihood of this assertion. For example, many scholars have argued for the thematic unity of 1 Thessalonians 4:13-18 with 5:1-11.[4] Gordon Fee notes that the eschatological content of 1 Thessalonians 5:1-11 is "quite closely related to what preceded" and that verses 10-11 summarize important ideas from 1 Thessalonians 4:13-18. He explains that Paul did not mention the return of Jesus again in 1 Thessalonians 5:10-11 because he was relating how the disciples should live prior to his return.[5] Similarly, G. K. Beale justifies a thematic unity between these two chapters:

> The probability is that [the verses of 1 Thess.] 4:15-17 describe generally the same end-time scenario as 5:1-11. Specifically, Paul narrates the resurrection at the end of the age and then recapitulates in chapter 5 by speaking about the timing of this event and about the judgment on unbelievers, which will also happen at the same time. That both 4:15-18 and 5:1-11 explain the same events is discernible from observing that both passages actually form one continuous depiction of the same narrative in Matthew 24.[6]

Beale, following J. Bernard Orchard and others, contends that the apostle Paul likely paraphrased the Olivet Discourse in 1 Thessalonian 4:13-5:11.[7] Beale demonstrates this dependency in a comparison chart that provides numerous parallels between the two passages,[8] and many other scholars have noted the literary parallels between the two passages.[9] Undoubtedly, the linguistic signature of the Olivet Discourse finds duplication in 1 Thessalonians 4:16-5:9. The power of this argument rests in the thematic parallels, a similar sequence of events, and the appearance of "now concerning" (περὶ δὲ) at the same point within the sequence. The following comparative chart demonstrates these features, proving

4   Howard 1988, pp. 163-90; Beale 2003, pp. 130, 142-43; Fee 2009, pp. 182-84
5   Fee 2009, pp. 182-84
6   Beale 2003, pp. 136-38.
7   Ibid., pp. 130, 142-43; Orchard 1938, pp. 19-42; Bell 1967, pp. 249-50
8   Beale 2003, p.137
9   Waterman 1975, pp. 105-13; Marshall 1983, p. 126

beyond a reasonable doubt that Paul borrowed heavily from the Olivet Discourse for his teaching in 1 Thessalonians 4:16-5:9.

Table 3: Parallels Between the Olivet Discourse and 1 Thessalonians 4:16-5:

Matthew 24	1 Thessalonians 4:16-5:9
24:30 "...they will see the Son of Man coming on the clouds of heaven..."	4:16, 17 "For the Lord himself will descend from heaven ...in the clouds..."
24:31 "... his angels with a loud trumpet call and they will gather his elect from the four winds, from one end of heaven to the other." (cf. Mark 13:27: "...from the ends of the earth to the ends of heaven")	4:16-17 "...with the voice of an archangel, and with the sound of the trumpet of God. And the dead in Christ will rise first. Then we who are alive, who are left, will be caught up together with them in the clouds to meet the Lord in the air."
24:36 "But concerning [περὶ δὲ] that day and hour no one knows..."	5:1-2 "Now concerning [περὶ δὲ] the times and the seasons, brothers, you have no need to have anything written to you."
24:39 "...and they were unaware until the flood came and swept them all away, so will be the coming of the Son of Man. (cf. Luke 21:34, 36: "suddenly ...praying that you may have strength to escape")	5:3 "While people are saying, "There is peace and security," then sudden destruction will come upon them . . . and they will not escape."
24:8 "...birth pains [ὠδίν]..."	5:3 "...labor pains [ὠδίν]..."
24:42-44 "Therefore, stay awake, for you do not know on what day your Lord is coming. But know this, that if the master of the house had known in what part of the night the thief was coming, he would have stayed awake and would not have let his house be broken into. Therefore, you also must be ready, for the Son of Man is coming at an hour you do not expect."	5:2, 4-7, 8, 10 "For you yourselves are fully aware that the day of the Lord will come like a thief in the night . . . But you are not in darkness, brothers, for that day to surprise you like a thief. For you are all children of light, children of the day. We are not of the night or of the darkness. So then let us not sleep, as others do, but let us keep awake and be sober. For those who sleep, sleep at night ...But since we belong to the day ... whether we are awake or asleep..."

117

Matthew 24	1 Thessalonians 4:16-5:9
24:49 "…drinks with drunkards…"	5:7-8 "…those who get drunk . . . let us be sober…"
24:13 "But the one who endures to the end will be saved."	5:9 "For God has not destined us for wrath, but to obtain salvation (cf. 2:16: "wrath")…"
25:6 "…there was a cry …"Come out to meet [εἰς ἀπάντησιν] him."	4:16-17 "…with a cry of command . . . to meet [εἰς ἀπάντησιν] the Lord."

This comparative chart provides persuasive evidence that Paul appealed to the Olivet Discourse for his material in 1 Thessalonians 4:16-5:9. He followed the discourse in a sequential manner and alluded to Jesus' teachings in the Olivet Discourse that appear *before and after the supposed transition verse of Matthew 24:36.* This further militates against dividing the discourse at this verse, as many preterists do. This same argument prohibits anyone from dividing the Discourse anywhere after Matthew 24:29. As the following syllogism shows, Paul's use of the Olivet Discourse at this point demonstrates that Matthew 24:30-31 is concerned with the resurrection of the righteous dead, an event that severely undermines preterism.

Major Premise: 1 Thessalonians 4:16-17 describes the same events as Matthew 24:30-31 (as shown in Table 3).
Minor Premise: 1 Thessalonians 4:16-17 is about the return of Jesus and the resurrection of the righteous dead.
Conclusion: Matthew 24:30-31 is about the return of Jesus and the resurrection of the righteous dead.

R. T. France and N. T. Wright object to the argument that Paul borrowed from the Olivet Discourse in 1 Thessalonians 4-5 on the grounds that it is eisegesis.[10] Their concern that such an interpretation prohibits Matthew and Mark from "having their own voices" sounds reasonable, but evades a more important consideration--that the striking parallels between these passages increase

10 France 2002, p. 503; Wright, N. T. as quoted in in Newman 1999, pp. 244-77

the likelihood that they describe the same prophetic events. The 1 Thessalonians passage provides definitive answers as to the identity of "the elect" and the exact manner of the *mystery* of their "gathering together", as mentioned in Matthew 24:31 (cf. 1 Cor. 15:51; 2 Thess. 2:1). Kim Seyoon effectively argues that Paul's purpose for addressing the topic of the resurrection of the dead at this point was to clarify the Lord's statement in Matthew 24:30.[11] Furthermore, since "the coming of the Son of Man" accompanied by angels (ἀγγέλους) (Matt. 24:30-31) is an allusion to Daniel 7:13-14, as both France and Wright acknowledge, it follows that these angels in the Olivet Discourse are *heavenly beings*, as in Daniel's vision, and not human "messengers" of the gospel, as France posits (see Chapter Seven). The Lord's angelic entourage in both passages is consistent with the presence of the archangel at the glorious return of Christ in 1 Thessalonians 4:16 (cf. "angels" 2 Thess. 1:8).

Jesus' expectation that the resurrection of the righteous dead would occur "immediately after the [unprecedented] tribulation" (Matt. 24:29-30) is the logical antecedent to Paul's equation of Matthew 24:30-31 with his own teaching in 1 Thessalonians 4:16-17. This is also consistent with Daniel's vision, which includes the concept that the resurrection of the dead will occur at the time of the unprecedented tribulation (Dan. 12:1-3); this is argued more fully in Chapter 14. Despite the futile attempts of DeMar and others to deny a literal rapture,[12] Paul's rapture passage explains that the living saints will experience a mysterious transformation when the Lord returns (1 Thess. 4:13-18), by which the dead and living saints will receive glorified, incorruptible bodies. Neither group need wait any longer for kingdom glory, so that "what is mortal may be swallowed up by life" (2 Cor. 5:4, 1 Thess. 4:13-18; cf. 1 Cor. 15:50-57). The apostle called this translation of the living "a mystery" (1 Cor. 15:51; cf. Rev. 10:7).

---

11 Seyoon 2002, pp. 231-42

12 DeMar 1999, p.159; DeMar later admits that the passage does "indicate the rapture" (p. 277).

Double Vision

In the Olivet Discourse, the Lord Jesus taught that he will gloriously appear at the end of the age and will send his angels, who "with a loud trumpet call . . . will gather his elect from the four winds" (Matt. 24:6, 13-14, 31, 34). The Lukan version of the discourse presents this as the time when God's kingdom will arrive (Luke 21:31-32). Similarly, the apostle John connected the final angelic trumpet blast with the "mystery of God," the consummate arrival of God's kingdom, and the time for judging and rewarding the dead:

> In the days of the trumpet call to be sounded by the seventh angel, the mystery of God would be fulfilled, just as he announced to his servants the prophets. ... Then the seventh angel blew his trumpet, and there were loud voices in heaven, saying, "The kingdom of the world has become the kingdom of our Lord and his Christ, and he shall reign forever and ever." ..."you [Lord] have taken your great power and begun to reign. The nations raged, but your wrath came, and the time for the dead to be judged, and for rewarding your servants, the prophets and saints, and those who fear your name, both small and great, and for destroying the destroyers of the earth." (Rev. 10:7; 11: 15, 17-18)

Partial preterists teach that all these events occurred in AD 70, a view that ultimately requires *two* last trumpets signaling *two* consummate arrivals of the kingdom of God, because the apostle Paul explicitly connected the Lord's glorious return from heaven with the time of "the end," the sounding of the final trumpet, the resurrection of the righteous dead, and the arrival of God's kingdom (1 Cor. 15:23-26, 50-55). He elsewhere associated the timing of Christ's return from heaven with an angelic command, the sounding of "the trumpet of God," and the resurrection/rapture of the saints (1 Thess. 4:16). In addition, partial preterists teach that God's kingdom arrived in AD 70 (cf. Luke 21:31-32; Rev. 11:15). This paradigm requires God's kingdom, recently inaugurated in the early Christian church, to have arrived in some consummated sense in AD 70, only to await another consummate arrival at the Lord's return!

Partial preterists also paint themselves into a corner by contending that the biblical period of "the last days" does not end with "the last day." They insist that "the last days" refers to the period that ended the Jewish kingdom in AD 70. However, they agree with the futurist position that the resurrection of the dead will occur in our future on "the last day" (John 6:39-40, 44, 54; 11:24; 12:48). This preterist framework *implicitly* requires *two* days called "the last day," one in AD 70 that ended "the last-days" period of the first century AD and another "last day" at the return of Jesus, when the dead will be resurrected.[13] This logic can be taken a step further. Partial preterists must necessarily allow for an additional period of "last days" leading up to this future "last day," which is, at best, confusing. They also argue that pre-millennialism shares the same problem because it accepts that the end of the age will take place more than 1,000 years prior to the final resurrection of the dead (Rev. 20:5, 11-15). However, futurism does *not* claim that Scripture calls the millennium "the last days" or its end "the last day."

Partial preterists also unwittingly create two periods of the end times. The prophet Daniel prophesied that the unprecedented tribulation will occur at the divinely-appointed "time of the end" (Dan. 8:17-19; 11:27, 35, 40; 12:1- 9). Preterists teach that this appointed time refers to the destruction of Jerusalem and the temple in AD 70. However, many preterists also believe that planet Earth will be dissolved or destroyed in our future. One wonders how these preterists can escape the conclusion that such an event would not constitute the time of the end.

---

13 See admission in Sproul 1998, pp. 168, 170, 183

Figure 5: Two Models for the Last Days and the Last Day

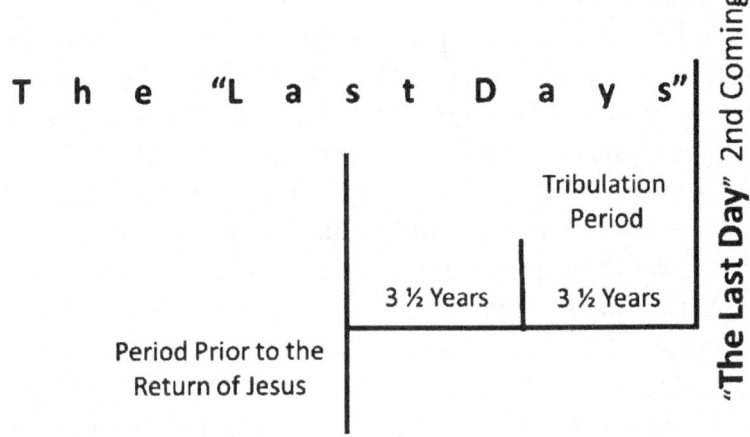

The Futurist Model

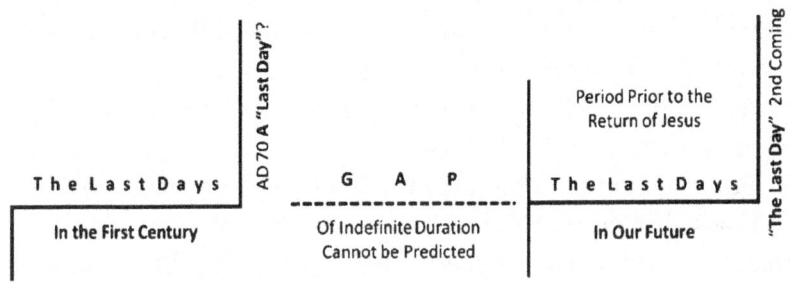

The Partial Preterist Model

Preterists correctly criticize dispensationalism for positing a secret rapture "coming" of Jesus followed by a third coming, his glorious return. However, the partial preterist paradigm requires a spiritual or judgment "coming" of Jesus in AD 70 followed by a third coming in our future![14] Many preterists postulate three distinct "comings" of Jesus in addition to the "coming of the Son of Man" in Matthew 24:30, which they interpret as his ascension. Therefore, they need at least three to five eschatological "comings" of Jesus Christ: (1) his "coming" to earth in the first advent, (2)

---

14 See Sproul 1998, p. 169 for an admission of two parousias.

his "coming/going" to the Father at his ascension (based on their interpretation of Matt. 24:30), (3) his judgment "coming" against the Jewish kingdom in AD 70, (4) his spiritual "coming," that is, the arrival of his reigning presence at Jerusalem in AD 70, as taught by N. T. Wright and others, and (5) his glorious return in our future.

Partial preterism requires at least *two* distinct last trumpets, which signal *two* distinct "comings" of Jesus on *two* distinct judgment days, at two distinct times of the end, which result in two distinct gatherings of God's elect, two distinct arrivals of God's kingdom, and two distinct dissolutions of two distinct heavens and earths. This "double vision" transforms the power and plainness of biblical eschatology into a maze of confusion.

The biblical evidence demonstrates that partial preterists have invented artificial divisions within the eschatological framework of the Bible. Essentially, this model of eschatology demands that the Scriptures conform to preterist prophetic presuppositions about the historic past. In a word, they "force fit" the historical events of the first century into the biblical prophecies, thereby obscuring and betraying the plain meaning of the Scriptures.

11

Nero and the Mark of the Beast

The apostle John provided the reader with an important clue to identify the person known as the Beast in the book of Revelation. He prophesied, "This calls for wisdom: let the one who has understanding calculate the number of the beast, for it is the number of a man, and his number is 666" (Rev. 13:18). Most preterists argue that the Jewish practice of gematria demonstrates that the apostle had Emperor Nero in view.[1] *Gematria* is a Jewish alphanumeric code in which Hebrew (or Aramaic) letters and words are assigned specific numerical values.[2] Gentry explains how *gematria* could be used to identify Nero as 666. He explains, "When Nero Caesar's name is transliterated into Hebrew, we get *Neron Kesar* (*nrwn qsr*: Hebrew has no letters to represent vowels). It has been documented by archaeological finds that a first century Hebrew spelling of Nero's name provides us with precisely the value of 666. Jastrow's lexicon of the Talmud contains this very spelling."[3]

Chilton believed that John's original readers would have immediately guessed the identification of Nero and "those who understood Hebrew probably grasped it instantly."[4] DeMar teaches that John's readers would have decoded this enigmatic number "with relative ease."[5] Hanegraaff insists that John's original audience would have been "absolutely certain" that their calculations

---

1 Adams and Fisher 2000, pp. 55-56; Chilton 2007, p. 181; DeMar 1999, p. 257; Hanegraaff 2007, p. 146; Russell 2003, pp. 462-65; Sproul 1998, p. 203
2 "Gematria," *Wikipedia*, on May 23, 2017. https://en.wikipedia.org/wiki/Gematria .
3 Gentry as quoted in DeMar 1999, p. 258
4 Chilton 2007, p. 181
5 DeMar 1999, p. 257

identified Nero as the Beast.[6] Hanegraaff concludes, "Obviously no amount of wisdom would have enabled a first-century audience to figure out the number of a twenty-first-century Beast."[7] Other preterists disagree. James Jordan declares, "666 does *not* have anything to do with Nero Caesar."[8]

The preterist contention that the number 666 should be identified with Nero is rife with difficulties. Gentry admits that the preterist view requires a rare spelling of Nero Caesar that is decidedly "not the most common one" and that it must include an additional Hebrew letter נ (transliterated nun).[9] Hanegraaff points out that the calculation only fits Νερων Καισαρ (Greek for Nero Caesar) if it is first transliterated into Hebrew.[10] Simon Kistemaker summarizes the many fallacies with the preterist calculation of 666:

> A popular interpretation of many scholars is that the number 666 has the numerical value of the name Nero Caesar. We should keep in mind, however, that it was not until the 1830s that four German scholars proposed the name Nero for the number 666. But the choice of Nero's name creates many difficulties. First, to arrive at the number 666 as the numerical value of Nero's name, one has to add the name Caesar. But even then, the expanded name Nero Caesar has the numerical value of only 616. Only when one adds an extra letter *n* to the name Nero, resulting in Neron Caesar, is the full number 666 achieved. But then one has to resort to the Hebrew spelling of Neron Caesar, which is *nun* = 50, *resh* = 200, *waw* = 6, *nun* = 50, *qoph* = 100, *samech* = 60, *resh* = 200, for a total of 666. But the normal spelling of the transliterated Hebrew word for "Caesar" is *qysr*, which includes the letter *yodh*. This letter, with the numerical value of 10, makes the total 676; therefore, proponents of this numerical scheme have searched for a manuscript that lacks the extra letter *yodh*. Among the literature of the Dead Sea Scrolls, archaeologists have discovered a

6   Hanegraaff 2007, p. 144

7   Ibid., p.8

8   Jordan 2014, loc. 427

9   Gentry 1998, p. 199

10 Hanegraaff 2007, p. 146

fragment that has the Hebraic (Aramaic) spelling of the name Neron. The next word *qysr* has two damaged consonants after the letter *q*, but there is no room for a vowel. Nevertheless, the questions must be asked, "Why would the author not use a Greek form instead of a Hebrew form?"[11]

While it is possible that the apostle John intended a calculation using gematria in Revelation 13:18, it is more likely that he had the Greek method of isopsephy in mind. The widespread use of isopsephy throughout the Roman Empire is well attested in first-century Greek manuscripts, and the practice would have been understood by John's original audience, the seven churches of Asia that were comprised predominantly of gentiles and Hellenized, Greek-speaking Jews. Obviously, this is a problem for the preterist interpretation because isopsephy does not fit the view, as Hanegraaff notes. He explains that the Greek isopsephism for Nero totals 1,005 instead of the 666 required by Revelation 13:18.[12]

The discerning Christian should understand that the calculation of the Beast's number 666, using either gematria or isopsephy, does not result in the name *Nero Claudius Caesar Augustus Germanicus* or any of its derivatives. As many preterist teachers admit, they must reject the usual spelling for Nero and choose an extremely rare form of his name, which has been reconstituted from a damaged manuscript that may have originally included an extra Hebrew letter. This is nothing short of exercising selection bias and conforming data to fit a predetermined conclusion.

A Confused Chronology

Most preterists teach that Emperor Nero was the Beast who would speak blasphemies, "make war on the saints and . . . conquer them" for 42 months (Rev. 13:5-10).[13] The passage reads as follows:

11 Kistemaker in Mathison 2004, pp. 228-29
12 Hanegraaff 2007, p. 146
13 Adams and Fisher 2000, p. 55; Chilton 2007, p. 179; Hanegraaff 2007, p. 148; Jordan 2014, loc. 324; Russell 2003, p. 512

And the beast was given a mouth uttering haughty and blasphemous words, and it was allowed to exercise authority for forty-two months. It opened its mouth to utter blasphemies against God, blaspheming his name and his dwelling, that is, those who dwell in heaven. Also it was allowed to make war on the saints and to conquer them. And authority was given it over every tribe and people and language and nation, and all who dwell on earth will worship it, everyone whose name has not been written before the foundation of the world in the book of life of the Lamb who was slain. If anyone has an ear, let him hear: If anyone is to be taken captive, to captivity he goes; if anyone is to be slain with the sword, with the sword must he be slain. Here is a call for the endurance and faith of the saints. (Rev. 13:5-10)

Preterists interpret this 42-month period of the Beast as the Neronian persecution that began with the emperor's persecution of Christians in Rome, from approximately November AD 64 until his suicide in June AD 68. Gentry comments, "The fit [with Nero] is both relevant and remarkable."[14] However, the proposed chronology of Nero cannot account for the prophecy that the Son of Man will appear and subsequently kill the Beast and his armies (Rev. 19:19-21; cf. 2 Thess. 2:8). Preterists teach that "the coming of the Son of Man" occurred in conjunction with Jerusalem's destruction in AD 70; however, the fall of Jerusalem took place more than two years after Nero's death! This may explain why Hanegraaff erroneously places the Year of the Four Emperors (AD 69) and the destruction of Jerusalem during the Neronian persecution.[15] J. Stuart Russell recognized the anachronism regarding Nero's death:

No doubt there is here something of an anachronism. The death of Nero is placed in the vision subsequent to the judgment of Jerusalem, whereas it actually preceded that event by two years or more. As we have before remarked, something must be conceded to poetic license. In an epic, a drama, or a vision, it is unreasonable to require strict chronological

14 Gentry 2010b, pp. 68, 69; Hanegraaff 2007, p. 144; Russell 2003, p. 460
15 Hanegraaff 2007, p. 144

sequence. ... There is, however, another answer to the charge of anachronism. It deserves consideration whether this whole scene of the great battle and victory of Christ the King, and the punishment of the beast and his armies, may not be properly conceived as taking place in the spirit, not in the flesh? That is, whether it may not be the representation of transactions in the unseen state; the judgment of the dead, and not of the living.[16]

Russell's proposals that this anachronism can be explained as "poetic license" or as taking place in the unseen realm are hardly satisfying. Gentry opts for the explanation that the 1,260 days is a symbolic figure.[17] The preterist evasion of the *literalness* of this time period is problematic. Preterists generally acknowledge that the Bible equates the various references to "time, times, and half a time" (Dan. 7:25; 12:7; Rev. 12:14), "half of the week" (Dan. 9:27), "forty-two months" (Rev. 11:2; 13:5), and "1,260 days" (Rev. 11:3; 12:6).[18] The angel provided the prophet Daniel with a mysterious extension of this 3.5-year period that nearly every commentator regards as *literal*. It reads, "And from the time that the regular burnt offering is taken away and the abomination that makes desolate is set up, there shall be 1,290 days. Blessed is he who waits and arrives at the 1,335 days" (Dan. 12:11-12; cf. 8:3). A symbolic interpretation hardly suits the *precision* of the specific designations 1,260 days, 1,290 days, and 1,335 days. The specificity of these numbers demonstrates the *literalness* of the angel's intended meaning.

No preterist proposal for the abomination of desolation fits the prophetic timeline of events as found in the books of Daniel and Revelation. Preterists often point out that the First Jewish-Roman War broke out approximately 42 months before Jerusalem's destruction,[19] and many preterists begin their calculation

16 Russell 2003, p. 512; cf. Kistemaker in Mathison 2004, p. 224
17 Chilton 2007, p. 179
18 Gentry 1998, p. 253; Russell 2003, pg. 429, 453
19 Gentry 1998, p. 250, 252; Hanegraaff 2007, pg. 61; Russell 2003, p. 429, 453

with Emperor Nero's commission of Vespasian to squash the Jewish rebellion in the winter of AD 66-67. Gentry supposes that this 42-month calculation should begin with the time that Rome began "to get into a position to destroy the Temple."[20] Nevertheless, it took Vespasian's legions months to arrive in Palestine (circa February-March AD 67), and their first assault on Jerusalem began several months later. The holy temple was not destroyed until July or August AD 70. None of these events in Judea and Jerusalem occurred early enough to allow for 42 months, and no other proposed *terminius ad quem* for any action of Nero, Vespasian, or Titus in "the holy place" (cf. Matt. 24:15) allows for a period of at least 42 months.

As demonstrated in Chapter Five, the 42-month unprecedented tribulation will begin when those residing in Judea see "the abomination of desolation ... standing in the holy place" as foretold in the prophecies of Daniel (Matt. 24:15). In the book of Daniel, each of the references to the abomination contains the theme of *an individual putting an end to the daily sacrifice in the Jerusalem temple*. For example, the prophet Daniel saw that the little horn will become great so that "the regular burnt offering was taken away from him, and the place of his sanctuary was overthrown" (Dan. 8:11). Similarly, an angel foretold about a prince who "for half of the week shall put an end to sacrifice and offering. And on the wing of abomination shall come one who makes desolate" (Dan. 9:27). Daniel was also told that a king will use his military to "appear and profane the temple and fortress, and shall take away the regular burnt offering. And they shall set up the abomination that makes desolate" (Dan. 11:31). Elsewhere, the angel explained to the prophet that 1,290 days will elapse "from the time that the regular burnt offering is taken away and the abomination that makes desolate is set up" (Dan. 12:11). Consistent with this motif, the apostle Paul spoke of a Man of Lawlessness who "takes his seat in the temple of God, proclaiming himself to be God" (2 Thess. 2:4; cf. Dan. 11:36-37),

20 Gentry 1998, pp. 250, 252-53

and the apostle John foresaw that the temple's outer courtyard will be "given over to the nations, and they will trample the holy city for forty-two months" (Rev. 11:2).

Many preterists recognize that the abomination must include the desecration of the holy temple, so they argue that these prophecies must refer to the invasion of the temple by the Zealots and Idumeans.[21] This invasion took place in the early winter of AD 68 which is *much too late* to allow for a period of 42 months prior to the destruction of Jerusalem in AD 70. In addition, this interpretation does not adequately account for the role of an individual who is variously called a former "little horn" (Dan. 8:11), the prince (Dan. 9:26), the king (Dan. 11:36), and the Man of Lawlessness (2 Thess. 2:3). No individual proudly exalted himself above all gods and sat in the temple, only to be killed by the Son of Man at his glorious appearance (2 Thess. 2:4, 8; cf. Isa. 11:4 LXX; Dan. 7:11; 11:36; Rev. 19:20-21). As well, they speculate that this event must have occurred during the First Jewish-Roman War, but the historian Josephus recorded that the perpetual daily sacrifice (i.e., *tamid* offering) continued in the Jerusalem temple until the summer of AD 70.[22] This removal of the daily sacrifice took place only one or two months before the temple was destroyed, thus not permitting the full 42 months required by the biblical prophecies.

Seven Heads and Ten Horns

Many of the same difficulties plague the preterist interpretation of the seven heads and ten horns of the apostle John's Beast. The passage reads as follows:

> But the angel said to me, "Why do you marvel? I will tell you the mystery of the woman, and of the beast with seven heads and ten horns that carries her. The beast that you saw was, and is not, and is about to rise from the bottomless pit and go to destruction. And the dwellers on earth whose names have not been written in the book of life from the foundation of the world will marvel to see the beast, because it was and is not

---

21 Russell 2003, p. 427

22 Josephus, *War of the Jews* 6.2.1; 6.94

and is to come. This calls for a mind with wisdom: the seven heads are seven mountains on which the woman is seated; they are also seven kings, five of whom have fallen, one is, the other has not yet come, and when he does come he must remain only a little while. As for the beast that was and is not, it is an eighth but it belongs to the seven, and it goes to destruction." (Rev. 17:7-11)

Almost universally, preterists identify the seven mountains of this passage as Rome, the City of Seven Hills,[23] and classify the seven kings as consecutive Caesars of the Roman Empire.[24] Many preterists offer the explanation that the fatal head wound refers to Nero's suicide in AD 68 that effectively ended the Julio-Claudian dynasty and the healing of the wound as Vespasian's rise to power to "resurrect" the destabilized Empire (cf. Rev. 13:3, 12-15; 17:8).[25] Some view the eighth king as Emperor Otho who was thought by some contemporaries to be the revived Nero,[26] a theory consistent with the Nero Redivivus myth.[27] Nevertheless, Otho had a relatively uneventful and short-lived reign. He did not persecute Christians in the manner of Nero, and he died long before the destruction of Jerusalem. Chilton, along with some other preterists, avoid the problems with this theory by suggesting the unlikely notion that the Roman Empire was fatally wounded with "the sword of the gospel."[28] Kik posits the idea that the healed head wound refers to the supposed death of the Roman Empire in AD 476 and its revival under Charlemagne in AD 800.[29]

Kistemaker summarizes the chronological problems with preterist attempts to identify the eight kings as Roman Caesars: "Although Julius Caesar was the first emperor, he is not part of New Testament history. If we begin with Augustus (Luke 2:1),

---

23 Chilton 2007, p. 188; Gentry 1998, p. 149; Gentry 2010b, p. 59; Hane-graaff 2007, p. 113; Sproul 1998, p. 159; Contra Jordan 2014, loc. 535

24 Chilton 2007, p. 188; Hanegraaff 2007, p. 114

25 Gentry 1998, p. 144; Gentry 2010b, p. 71; Hanegraaff 2007, pp. 149, 150

26 Gentry 1998, p. 308; Gentry 2010b, p. 71

27 Gentry 1998, Chapter 18

28 Chilton 2007, p. 178

29 Kik 1971, p. 250

then Nero is number five on the list. But where do we place Galba, Otho, and Vitellius? Are they excluded because of their short-lived reigns? And if we eliminate them, is Vespasian number six, Titus seven, and Domitian eight? There are at least nine different ways of counting these Roman emperors, and a lack of consensus is evident. It is impossible to declare with any degree of certainty that John had in mind either Nero or Vespasian as the ruling king when Revelation was composed."[30]

Figure 6: One Preterist Interpretation of the Roman Emperors	
1. Julius	July 100 BC - March 44 BC
2. Augustus	January 27 BC - August 14 AD
3. Tiberius	September 14 AD - March 37 AD
4. Caligula	March 37 AD - January 41 AD
5. Claudius	January 41 AD - October 54 AD
"five of whom have fallen" (Rev. 17:10)	
6. Nero	October 54 AD - June 68 AD
"one is" (Rev. 17:10)	
7. Galba	June 68 AD - January 69 AD
"he must remain only a little while" (Rev. 17:10)	
8. Otho	January 69 AD - April 69 AD
9. Vitellius	April 69 AD - December 69 AD
10. Vespasian	July 69 AD - June 79 AD
11. Titus	June 79 AD - September AD 81

Gentry, like many preterists, begins his count with Julius Caesar and claims that Galba, Otho, and Vitellius are the three kings subdued by the little horn of Daniel 7 (cf. Dan. 7:8, 20, 24).[31] He then critiques a common preterist explanation for why most omit Galba, Otho, and Vitellius from the list of emperors. He explains, "To find the objectors citing Suetonius as evidence that

30 Kistemaker as quoted in Mathison 2004, p. 231
31 Gentry 1998, p. 157

the three emperors of Rome's Civil War were not really considered emperors is somewhat surprising. After all, Suetonius does include them in his book *Lives of the Twelve Caesars*! Furthermore, these three are considered emperors by Tacitus, Josephus, Sibylline Oracles, and 4 Ezra, as well."[32] Gentry posits that the apostle John deliberately skipped Otho and Vitellius (but not Galba!) in his enumerated list of eight kings (cf. Rev. 17:10-11). He reasons that the indefinite article ("*an* eighth") appears in verse 11 to show that Vespasian was not the immediate successor of Galba, but simply reigned sometime after Galba's reign. He claims that Vespasian "is not in the specified enumeration, but possesses the quality of an eighth, a resurrection."[33] The careful reader must wonder if Gentry has an ulterior motive for regarding Galba as the seventh king instead of skipping him, as he does the other two deposed kings. This motive is seen in his admission that the seventh king would reign for "only a little while" (Rev. 17:10) and therefore could not refer to Vespasian, who reigned as emperor for more than a decade.[34] In fact, Vespasian's reign continued nine years beyond the destruction of Jerusalem.

Another significant difficulty for preterists is identifying the ten horns or kings. The passage reads as follows: "And the ten horns that you saw are ten kings who have not yet received royal power, but they are to receive authority as kings for one hour, together with the beast. These are of one mind, and they hand over their power and authority to the beast. They will make war on the Lamb, and the Lamb will conquer them, for he is Lord of lords and King of kings, and those with him are called and chosen and faithful" (Rev. 17:12-14). J. Stuart Russell correctly recognized that the ten kings must rule contemporaneously in the future ("who have not yet received royal power, but they are to receive authority as kings for one hour, together with the beast"

---

32 Ibid., p. 161

33 Ibid., pp. xxx, xxxi

34 Ibid., p. 161

Rev. 17:12).[35] Consequently, Russell rejected the common preterist notion that these kings were from the Herodian Dynasty, rulers who reigned over Judea from 47 BC to 100 AD, with only Agrippa II reigning during the First Jewish-Roman War.[36] He favored the view that the ten kings were the Roman procurators of Judea during the periods of Claudius and Nero.[37] Similarly, DeMar has suggested that they refer to monarchs who ruled Rome's first-century imperial provinces.[38] However, these suggestions fail to account for the fact that *more than twenty* provinces existed at the outbreak of the war. This means that preterists must omit most of the provincial governors to make the data fit their theory of only ten kings.

The Man of Lawlessness

Just as preterists divorce the resurrection of the saints from the day of the Lord, the Son of Man's glorious appearance, and the gathering of the elect in the Olivet Discourse (Matt. 24:29-31), they attempt the same estrangement in 2 Thessalonians 1 and 2. The text reads as follows:

> Now concerning the coming of our Lord Jesus Christ and our being gathered together to him, we ask you, brothers, not to be quickly shaken in mind or alarmed, either by a spirit or a spoken word, or a letter seeming to be from us, to the effect that the day of the Lord has come. Let no one deceive you in any way. For that day will not come, unless the rebellion comes first, and the man of lawlessness is revealed, the son of destruction, who opposes and exalts himself against every so-called god or object of worship, so that he takes his seat in the temple of God, proclaiming himself to be God. Do you not remember that when I was still with you I told you these things? And you know what is restraining him now so that he may be revealed in his time. For the mystery of lawlessness is already at work. Only he who now restrains it will do so until he is out of the way. And then the lawless one will be

35 Russell 2003, pp. 500, 502
36 Jordon 2014, loc. 535
37 Russell 2003, p. 500
38 DeMar 1999, pp. 370, 372

revealed, whom the Lord Jesus will kill with the breath of his mouth and bring to nothing by the appearance of his coming. The coming of the lawless one is by the activity of Satan with all power and false signs and wonders, and with all wicked deception for those who are perishing, because they refused to love the truth and so be saved. Therefore, God sends them a strong delusion, so that they may believe what is false, in order that all may be condemned who did not believe the truth but had pleasure in unrighteousness. (2 Thess. 2:1-12)

Preterists attack the futurist interpretation of this passage in various ways. For example, DeMar declares, "There is no doubt that Jesus' 'coming' in 2 Thessalonians 2:1 should be attributed to the first century since the time indicators ('has come,' 'now,' 'already') leave no room in this passage for a coming in the distant future."[39] DeMar fails to understand that the apostle Paul used the term "has come" (2 Thess. 2:2) to warn the Thessalonian saints that they should reject the *faulty* notion that the day of the Lord had already arrived. In addition, most futurists view "the restrainer" as a spiritual or angelic power that prevented this man from being revealed in the first century (2 Thess. 2:6-7). Futurists agree with DeMar that this "mystery of iniquity" was *already* working among the disobedient when Paul wrote his letter (2 Thess. 2:6-7; cf. 1 Tim. 3:16; 1 John 4:3). However, futurists also maintain that the restrainer will prevent the human incarnation of his demonic presence (i.e., the Antichrist) until "his [appointed] time" (2 Thess. 2:6), that is, when Satan is cast out of heaven 42 months before Christ's return (Rev. 12:6, 9-17).

Due to the close proximity and thematic relationship with 2 Thessalonians 2:1-12, preterists predictably deny that 2 Thessalonians 1:5-10 is about the return of Jesus Christ. The passage reads as follows:

This is evidence of the righteous judgment of God, that you may be considered worthy of the kingdom of God, for which you are also suffering—since indeed God considers it just to repay with affliction those who afflict you, and to grant relief

39 Ibid., pp. 277, 278

135

to you who are afflicted as well as to us, when the Lord Jesus is revealed from heaven with his mighty angels in flaming fire, inflicting vengeance on those who do not know God and on those who do not obey the gospel of our Lord Jesus. They will suffer the punishment of eternal destruction, away from the presence of the Lord and from the glory of his might, when he comes on that day to be glorified in his saints, and to be marveled at among all who have believed, because our testimony to you was believed. (2 Thess. 1:5-10)

Chilton argues that the *revealing* and *coming* of Jesus in this passage cannot refer to Christ's *return* because those who had been persecuting the Thessalonian saints were to be the recipients of God's retributive wrath at this time.[40] This position is also taken by other preterists, but it is an unnecessary contrivance because the righteous *dead* are often described as patiently waiting until they receive vindication and their persecutors receive condemnation (e.g., Rev. 6:9-11; 14:13). Consequently, these prophetic events do not require the persecuted saints to remain alive until the time of their vindication.

DeMar also claims that the gathering of the saints in 2 Thessalonians 2:1 cannot refer to the rapture because the Greek *episunagogue* (translated "gather") is not the same word that the apostle used for the rapture in 1 Thessalonians 4.[41] However, the verb is closely related to the verb ἐπισυνάγω ("to gather") that Jesus employed in Matthew 24:31, a verse that we demonstrated in Chapters 7 and 10 speaks about the literal gathering of the saints at the return of Christ. The most satisfying option is to understand the two Thessalonian passages as connected thematically, especially given the fact that the apostle used the introductory formula "now concerning" (2 Thess. 2:1) that he often used to alert the reader that he was expounding on previous teachings (e.g., 1 Cor. 7:1, 25; 8:1; 12:1; 16:1, 12).

J. Stuart Russell demonstrates the parallels between John's Beast and Paul's Man of Lawlessness so as to leave no doubt that

---

40 Chilton 2007, p. 120
41 DeMar 1999, pp. 277, 278

their identity is one and the same.[42] He does not hesitate to identify Nero, whom he believes was the Beast of the book of Revelation, as the Man of Lawlessness.[43] Those who take this approach typically see Emperor Claudius as the restrainer of 2 Thessalonians 2:6-7, whose reign temporarily kept Nero from obtaining the throne.[44] As DeMar correctly points out, this interpretation contains an obvious error, since Nero "never sat in the temple" as the prophecy requires (2 Thess. 2:4).[45] Chilton simply glosses over this requirement and implies that Nero took his seat in *pagan* temples![46] Gentry interprets the phrase figuratively and quotes Scullard: "[A] statue [of Julius Caesar] was placed in the temple of Quirinus (deified Romulus), another near those of the kings of Rome, and yet another showed him with a globe beneath his feet; his chariot was set up opposite the temple of Juppiter [sic]. As a *triumphator* he was granted the right to a gilded chair."[47] These interpretive options are illegitimate because several eschatological prophecies connect the evil ruler with bringing desolation upon the *Jerusalem* temple (Dan. 8:11-14; 9:27; 11:31; 12:11; Matt. 24:15-21, Mark 13:14-19, Luke 21:20-24; cf. Rev. 11:2).

Table 4: Comparison of Paul's Man of Lawlessness and John's Beast

	The Man of Lawlessness in 2 Thessalonians 2	The Beast in the Book of Revelation
Destined for Destruction	"...the son of destruction..." (2 Thess. 2:3)	"...and go to destruction ... it goes to destruction." (Rev. 17:8, 11)

42 Russell 2003, p. 505

43 Ibid., p. 182

44 Ibid., p. 182

45 DeMar 1999, p. 291

46 Chilton 2007, p. 177

47 Scullard as quoted in Gentry 1998, p. 265

	The Man of Lawlessness in 2 Thessalonians 2	The Beast in the Book of Revelation
Speaks Blasphemies Against God and the Worship of God	"...who opposes and exalts himself against every so-called god or object of worship,..."	"...they worshipped the beast... And the beast was given a mouth uttering haughty and blasphemous words, and it was allowed to exercise authority for forty-two months. It opened its mouth to utter blasphemies against God, blaspheming his name and his dwelling... and all who dwell on earth will worship it..." (Rev. 13:4, 5-6, 8; cf. Dan. 7:25)
Entering and Profaning the Temple of God	"...so that he takes his seat in the temple of God, proclaiming himself to be God." (2 Thess. 2:4; cf. Dan. 11:36-37)	"...the temple of God.... do not measure the court outside the temple; leave that out for it is given over to the nations, and they will trample the holy city for forty-two months." (Rev. 11:1, 2)
Called the Mystery	"...the mystery of lawlessness is already at work..." (2 Thess. 2:7)	"...the mystery ... of the beast..." (Rev. 13:7)

138

	The Man of Lawlessness in 2 Thessalonians 2	The Beast in the Book of Revelation
Accompanied by Satanic Signs and Wonders	"The coming of the lawless one is by the activity of Satan with all power and false signs and wonders, and with all wicked deception for those who are perishing, because they refused to love the truth and so be saved. Therefore God sends them a strong delusion, so that they may believe what is false..." (2 Thess. 2:9-11)	"And to it the dragon gave his power ... It performs great signs, even making fire come down from heaven to earth in front of people, and by the signs that it was allowed to work in the presence of the beast it deceives those who dwell on the earth..." (Rev. 13:2, 13-14; cf. 19:20)
Killed by Jesus at His Appearance by the Sword/Breath of His Mouth and Thrown Into Fire	"And then the lawless one will be revealed, whom the Lord Jesus will kill with the breath of his mouth and bring to nothing by the appearance of his coming..." (2 Thess. 2:8; cf. Isa. 11:4) *For eternal destruction in flaming fire (2 Thess. 1:6-10; cf. Dan. 7:11)*	"From his mouth comes a sharp sword with which to strike down the nations . . . And the beast was captured, and with it the false prophet . . . These two were thrown alive into the lake of fire that burns with sulfur. And the rest were slain by the sword that came from the mouth of him who was sitting on the horse." (Rev. 19:15, 20a, 20b-21; cf. 17:14)
Condemnation for Those Who Follow Him	"...in order that all may be condemned who did not believe the truth but had pleasure in unrighteousness." (2 Thess. 2:12) *For eternal destruction in flaming fire (2 Thess. 1:6-10; cf. Dan. 7:11)*	"If anyone worships the beast and its image and receives a mark . . . he also will drink the wine of God's wrath, poured full strength into the cup of his anger, and he will be tormented with fire and sulfur in the presence of the holy angels and in the presence of the Lamb." (Rev. 14:9-10)

139

The inherent weaknesses of the aforementioned arguments have led many preterists to propose alternative candidates for the Man of Lawlessness. DeMar claims, "There are at least three possible first-century, pre-A.D. 70 candidates: a political figure (Nero or a representative of the Roman government), a religious figure (Phannias or another member of the priesthood), or a zealot (John Levi Gischala)."[48] This list is speculative at best, a mere "grasping at straws". DeMar later suggests Titus as a candidate, an interpretation that is slightly more appealing because he entered the Jerusalem temple in AD 70.[49] DeMar even considers the possibility that the Man of Lawlessness was the office of the high priests who served in the temple during the period between Jesus' atoning death and the destruction of Jerusalem in AD 70. He explains that the high priests are good candidates because they "offered 'strange' sacrifices that violated the provisions of the New Covenant that is now defined by Jesus' blood and no longer by the blood of 'bulls and goats' (Hebrews 10:4). The sin of the high priest was akin to that of Nadab and Abihu. He was the man of lawlessness as defined by the provisions of the New Covenant."[50] The reader is left to wonder if DeMar understands that these sacrifices were already being made when the apostle penned the Thessalonian letters. His suggestion undermines the apostle's entire argument, namely, that the day of the Lord *could not* have arrived because this man had not yet arrived!

Any candidate for the Man of Lawlessness must also take his seat in the Jerusalem temple (2 Thess. 2:4) and remove the daily sacrifice (Dan. 8:11-14; 9:27; 11:31; 12:11; cf. Matt. 24:15). This is the strength of one of DeMar's candidates, as he notes, "John Bray offers another first-century candidate ...John Levi of Gischala ... And he was the cause of the ceasing of the daily sacrifices three and one half years after Vespasian came against the city."[51] The

48 DeMar 1999, p. 290; Similarly Jordan 2014, loc. 341
49 Ibid., p. 291
50 Ibid., p. 299; cf. pp. 301-02
51 Ibid., p. 302

primary weakness with this approach is that John of Gischala was not killed at "the appearance of his [Jesus'] coming" (2 Thess. 2:8; cf. Rev. 19:17-20), an event that preterists believe occurred in AD 70. This weakness plagues many preterist theories about the Man of Lawlessness and the Beast of the Apocalypse. In addition, DeMar, like other preterists who do not identify Nero as the Man of Lawlessness, struggles to identify "the restrainer" (2 Thess. 2:6-7). DeMar wonders if the restrainer could be the Roman government, specifically Herod Agrippa, who served as a civil restrainer of Jewish persecution against Christians.[52] He also suggests that the "strong delusion" (2 Thess. 2:11-12) refers to the enticement of first-century Israel to revolt against Rome.[53] DeMar ultimately admits that the restrainer is a "mystery" and warns that he can "only offer an educated guess" because "we may never know who Paul had in mind."[54]

The Antichrist

A common preterist objection to futurist eschatology is that the solitary figure of the Antichrist is not found in the Olivet Discourse[55] or the book of Revelation.[56] For example, Chilton teaches that "the term *antichrist* is used in a very specific sense, and is essentially unrelated to the figure known as 'the Beast' and '666'. ...The term *antichrist*, therefore, cannot be simply a designation of one individual."[57] Russell also denies that the Antichrist refers to a solitary individual.[58] DeMar makes a similar claim with the added statement that the epistles of John (in 1 John 2:18ff; 4:3-5; 2 John 1:7) were correcting a rumor that the early church had accepted: one man would arise as *the* Antichrist.[59] In contrast

52 Ibid., p. 304, 305-06
53 Ibid., p. 308
54 Ibid., p. 303
55 Ibid., p. 103
56 Chilton 2007, p. 109, 110; DeMar 1999, pp. 267, 269
57 Chilton 2007, p. 109, 110
58 Russell 2003, p. 333
59 DeMar 1999, pp. 267, 269

to DeMar's claim, John does not intimate that he was diminishing the doctrine of a personal Antichrist, but affirming that *additional* antichrists would appear (1 John 2:18, 22; 4:3; 2 John 7; cf. Matt. 24:24-26). Furthermore, the apostle John's individual Beast and the apostle Paul's Man of Lawlessness will display antichrist qualities; this alone establishes the biblical precedent for an individual Antichrist. Finally, the immediate context in 1 John clearly shows that by avoiding the antichrists, when Jesus *"appears*, we may have confidence and not shrink from him in shame at his coming" (1 John 2:28; cf. 3:2; 4:17, emphasis added). This "appearance" is the bodily return of Jesus, a fact suggested by John's use of the word φανερωθῇ (often translated "appear" or "manifested") that occurs elsewhere throughout the epistles with clear reference to the Lord's *bodily* presence (e.g., 1 John 1:2; 3:5, 8; 4:9). This is the glorious appearance of Jesus, when "we shall be like him, because we shall see him as he is" (1 John 3:2).

The historic church has always held a firm conviction about the *future* revelation of a *personal* Antichrist. In addition, the early church fathers equated the Beast, the Man of Lawlessness, and the Antichrist, teaching that he will be destroyed at the return of Jesus Christ. For example, Justin Martyr (circa AD 160) mentioned that Jesus will return from heaven when this "man of apostasy" speaks words "against the Most High" and persecutes the saints.[60] Irenaeus (circa AD 180) believed that the Antichrist is the "lawless one" and "the son of perdition" who will seek to be "worshipped as God." According to Irenaeus, this wicked man will be "endowed with all of the power of the devil" and will arise from a ten-nation confederacy to "reign over the earth for three years and six months" and to "sit in the temple at Jerusalem" until the Lord returns in heavenly clouds.[61]

Hippolytus (circa AD 200) understood the Beast as the future Antichrist who will gather the Jews of the Diaspora so that "he

---

60 Justin Martyr 1.253, 254 in Bercot 1998
61 Irenaeus 1.553, 1.554, 1.560 in Bercot 1998

may be worshipped by them as God."[62] He also taught that the Antichrist will set up the abomination of desolation and remove "sacrifice and oblation" in the middle of the seventieth week of Daniel 9.[63] Hippolytus believed that the Antichrist will reign for "a time, times, and a half," which he says means "three and a half years," to rebuild Jerusalem and to "restore the sanctuary" while "exalting himself above all kings and above every god."[64]

As well, Tertullian (circa AD 210) taught that the resurrection will occur immediately after "the destruction of the Antichrist."[65] Origen (circa AD 248) referenced Daniel 11:31 to teach that the Antichrist will establish the abomination of desolation "on the temple" so that he "'sits in the temple of God, showing himself that he is God.'"[66] Cyprian, Victorinus, and Lactantius each wrote around AD 250-280 and described a future Antichrist who will persecute the saints of God.[67] Victorinus (circa AD 280) believed that the number 666 referred to the name of the Antichrist.[68] Lactantius (circa AD 304-313) taught that Jesus will return to destroy the Antichrist, who will have required worship of himself, called himself God, performed signs and wonders, and "attempt[ed] to destroy the temple of God and persecute the righteous people" during the "forty-two months" of "distress and tribulation, such as there never has been from the beginning of the world."[69]

The testimony of Scripture and the traditions of the early church harmonize and consistently teach a *future* appearance of a *personal* Antichrist. These witnesses demonstrate that the Antichrist is the one identified by 666, the Beast, and the Man of Lawlessness. Applying the term "Antichrist" to this individual appropriately summarizes his character, corroborating the clear

62 Hippolytus 5.214, 5.215 in Bercot 1998
63 Hippolytus 5.182 in Bercot 1998
64 Hippolytus 5.190, 5.184 in Bercot 1998
65 Tertullian 3.565 in Bercot 1998
66 Origen 4.593-94 in Bercot 1998
67 Cyprian 5.346, 349, 556; Victorinus in Bercot 1998
68 Victorinus 7.456 in Bercot 1998
69 Lactantius 4.593-95; 5:204-19; 7.215 in Bercot 1998

teaching of the Bible and the testimony of church history. In addition, the writings of the early church fathers provide evidence of a future restored Jerusalem and Third Temple, which will be made desolate by the Antichrist. This evidence argues against various preterist theories that certain first-century individuals represent the Antichrist or that these prophetic events were fulfilled in the period of the Second Temple.

12

The Prophecy of the Seventy Weeks

The Prophecy of the Seventy Weeks in Daniel 9:24-27 serves a critical purpose in the study of eschatology, largely due to the fact that the Olivet Discourse is widely considered to be an exposition of this prophecy. The angel Gabriel delivered it in response to the prophet's penitential prayer that the Jews be brought back to their homeland after being exiled for seventy years in Babylon (Dan. 9:1-19). Daniel requested that the Lord turn his wrath away from his holy city, Jerusalem, and show favor to the desolate sanctuary of his holy temple (vv. 16-17). The prophecy continues as follows:

> [24] Seventy weeks are decreed about your people and your holy city, to finish the transgression, to put an end to sin, and to atone for iniquity, to bring in everlasting righteousness, to seal both vision and prophet, and to anoint a most holy place. [25] Know therefore and understand that from the going out of the word to restore and build Jerusalem to the coming of an anointed one, a prince, there shall be seven weeks. Then for sixty-two weeks it shall be built again with squares and moat, but in a troubled time. [26] And after the sixty-two weeks, an anointed one shall be cut off and shall have nothing. And the people of the prince who is to come shall destroy the city and the sanctuary. Its end shall come with a flood, and to the end there shall be war. Desolations are decreed. [27] And he shall make a strong covenant with many for one week, and for half of the week he shall put an end to sacrifice and offering. And on the wing of abominations shall come one who makes desolate, until the decreed end is poured out on the desolator. (Dan. 9:24-27)

Preterists and futurists generally agree on several features of the prophecy. First, it is an expansion of Jeremiah's prophecy that predicts the return of the Jews to the land of Israel after seventy

146

years of Babylonian exile (Jer. 25:11-12; 29:10; Dan. 9:2), enumerating the events that would occur during a period of seventy "weeks" שָׁבֻעִים (literally "sevens" or "heptads"). These seventy "weeks" are almost universally understood to mean seventy groupings of seven years (70 x 7 years = 490 years; cf. Gen. 29:27-28). Second, the prophecy pertains to the prophet's people, the Jews, and the Holy City, Jerusalem (Dan. 9:24). Third, the 490-year period consummates the following divine purposes: "to finish the transgression, to put an end to sin, and to atone for iniquity, to bring in everlasting righteousness, to seal both vision and prophet, and to anoint a most holy place" (Dan. 9:24). Some scholars have attempted, with varying degrees of success, to connect all six redemptive actions to the first advent of Jesus Christ. Fourth, most Christian interpreters understand "an anointed one" who would be "cut off" and "have nothing" after the first sixty-nine weeks (483 years) to refer to Christ and his death on the cross (Dan. 9:26; cf. Isa. 53:8).

However, scholars vehemently disagree regarding the timing and events of the seventieth week (the final seven years) of the prophecy. Preterists usually view "the prince who is to come" (Dan. 9:26) as Emperor Vespasian or General Titus,[1] whereas many futurists see this figure to be the future Antichrist. Most interpreters see the destruction of the city (Dan. 9:26) as a reference to the Roman invasion of Jerusalem in AD 70, although some futurists interpret it as referring to the city's future destruction by the Antichrist's forces or as a double entendre.

Many preterists see the one who will "make the strong covenant [alternatively 'strengthen the covenant'] with many for one week, and for half of the week he shall put an end to sacrifice and offering" (Dan. 9:27) as a reference to the ministry and death of Christ (cf. Matt. 26:28).[2] On the other hand, futurists interpret the verse as describing the Antichrist who will deceptively enter into a holy covenant with many nations, but most particularly with

---

1 E.g., Kik 1971, p. 108
2 Ibid., p. 109

147

Israel (Dan. 8:25; 11:21-24, 27-28; cf. Isa. 28:14-16, 18; Ezek. 38:8, 11, 14; 1 Thess. 5:3), before violating it by setting up the abomination of desolation at the mid-point of the final seven years ("...for half of the week he shall put an end to sacrifice and offering. ... on the wing of abominations shall come one who makes desolate" Dan. 9:27). This event will include the forced cessation of the daily sacrifice in the Third Temple (Dan. 9:27; 11:31; 12:11; Matt. 24:12 Thess. 2:4).

Most futurists interpret Daniel's seventieth week as referring to the final seven years prior to the return of Jesus. This requires a gap of nearly 2,000 years between the sixty-ninth and seventieth weeks. DeMar summarizes, "Again, the prophetic scenario is dependent on splitting the seventieth 'week' (seven years) from the previous sixty-nine 'weeks' (483 years) and inserting a 'gap' of nearly two thousand years after the sixty-ninth 'week' and before the seventieth 'week' of Daniel 9:24-27. There is nothing in Daniel 9:24-27 that even hints that there will be a rebuilt temple."[3] While the prophecy does not specify a gap, the grammatical construction of the passage divides the 490 years into *three distinct periods* of seven weeks (49 years), sixty-two weeks (434 years), and one week (7 years). This allows for the possibility of one or two gaps, especially since the angel specified that certain prophetic events would signal the start and completion of each period.

DeMar argues that futurists have "no biblical warrant" for seeing the first sixty-nine weeks and the seventieth week as non-continuous periods of time. He declares, "*The idea of separation and the placement of an indeterminable gap between the two sets of weeks is one of the most unnatural and nonliteral interpretations of Scripture found in any eschatological system.*"[4] He claims that interpreting the prophecy in this manner is a form of "manipulating" Scripture and contriving a novel interpretation so that the passage fits an "already established prophetic system."[5]

---

3 DeMar 1999, p. 95
4 Ibid., emphasis original; Similarly Kik 1971, p. 107
5 DeMar 1999, p. 95; Similarly Hanegraaff 2007, p. 54

Kik states that a gap would indicate that "we would still be in our sins!"[6] DeMar quotes the axiom that "necessity is the mother of invention"[7] and claims that the idea of a future seventieth week originated in the modern period.[8] He quibbles, "Why is there no mention of this 'great parenthesis' either in the Bible or in nearly nineteen hundred years of church history?"[9]

DeMar's complaint about the futurist interpretation of this passage is verifiably false. The testimony of the early church fathers is reason enough to reject his insistence that such teaching is absent from the history of the church. The Fathers taught that Jesus is the Messiah who was "cut off" after the sixty-ninth week, and many of them also held the view that the seventieth week, and more particularly the final 3.5 years, is reserved for fulfillment in our future (see Chapter 11). For example, Irenaeus (circa AD 180) saw the final week as pointing to the final seven years prior to the return of Christ.[10] Hippolytus (circa AD 200) taught that the final week referred to "the last week that is to be at the end of the whole world."[11] He laid out this futurist view of the prophecy: "For when the sixty-two weeks are fulfilled, and Christ has come, and the Gospel is preached in every place, the times will then be accomplished. Then, there will remain only one week (the last) ...And in the middle of it, the abomination of desolation will be manifested. This is the Antichrist, announcing desolation to the world. And when he comes, the sacrifice and oblation will be removed".[12]

DeMar critiques the futurist interpretation of Daniel 9:27, seeing in it the Antichrist (not Jesus, as many preterists argue), who will make or strengthen a covenant with many during the final seven years. He mocks this interpretation by exclaiming, "It's not Jesus who 'will put a stop to sacrifice and grain offering'

6   Kik 1971, p. 108

7   DeMar 1999, p. 325

8   Ibid., p. 328

9   Ibid., p. 95

10 *Irenaeus* 1.553, 1.554, 1.560 in Bercot 1998

11 *Hippolytus* 5.213 in Bercot 1998

12 *Hippolytus* 5.182 in Bercot 1998

through his shed blood (9:27)—*it's the antichrist!*"[13] However, in every reference to the abomination of desolation in the book of Daniel, it is a *self-exalting, evil ruler who removes the daily sacrifice from the sanctuary*:

> And the regular burnt offering was taken away from him [the little horn], and the place of his sanctuary was overthrown. And a host will be given over to it together with the regular burnt offering because of transgression ["that makes desolate" v. 13] (Dan. 8:11b-12a)

> Forces from him [the king] shall appear and profane the temple and fortress, and shall take away the regular burnt offering. And they shall set up the abomination that makes desolate. He shall seduce with flattery those who violate the covenant ... Yet he shall come to his end, with none to help him. (Dan. 11:31-32a, 45)

> And from the time that the regular burnt offering is taken away and the abomination that makes desolate is set up, there shall be 1,290 days. (Dan. 12:11)

Consistent with this motif, the premillennial futurist interpretation of Daniel 9:26-27 applies these actions to the Antichrist (see Table 5).

Table 5: Comparison of the Preterist and Futurist Interpretations of Daniel 9:26-27

Daniel 9:26-27	Preterist Interpretation	Premillennialist Interpretation
And the people of the prince who is to come shall destroy the city and the sanctuary	Vespasian or Titus	The Antichrist
And he shall make a strong covenant with many for one week,	Christ	The Antichrist
and for half of the week he shall put an end to sacrifice and offering.	Christ	The Antichrist

---

13 DeMar 1999, p. 328; Similarly Adams and Fisher 2000, p. 87

Daniel 9:26-27	Preterist Interpretation	Premillennialist Interpretation
And on the wing of abominations shall come one who makes desolate,	Titus	The Antichrist
until the decreed end is poured out on the desolator.	Titus	The Antichrist

All eschatological systems, including preterism, must leave room for a gap before Daniel's final "week" of years. Many preterists, following Clement of Alexandria, allow for a forty-year gap between the Messiah who was "cut off" after the sixty-ninth week and the destruction of Jerusalem during the seventieth week.[14] Nevertheless, DeMar and others reject a gap altogether. He places the "cutting off" of the Messiah in the midpoint of the seventieth week instead of immediately after the sixty-ninth week. He claims that the termination of the seventieth week occurred exactly 3.5 years after the Lord's crucifixion when the evangelistic effort "for Israel" supposedly ended and the apostolic preaching to the gentiles began.[15]

However, this interpretation is incorrect. The prophet Daniel had prayed for the Lord to show mercy to the Jewish nation by turning them from their iniquities and putting an end to the desolations that had come upon Jerusalem (Dan. 9:1-19). DeMar's interpretation strongly implies that the prophetic answer to these prayers was that the Romans would bring ultimate desolation upon Jerusalem. On the other hand, the futurist position is that the prophetic fulfillment of prophecy must include the final salvation of the Jewish nation, the eschatological redemption of Jerusalem, and the glorious return of Jesus Christ to usher in "everlasting righteousness" for the nation. In addition, DeMar's interpretation necessarily separates the abomination of desolation from the removal of the daily sacrifice, requiring the former event to

14 E.g., Adams and Fisher 2000, p. 90; Kik 1971, p. 109
15 DeMar 1999, p. 327

151

have occurred four decades *after* the seventieth week (cf. Dan. 9:26-27).

DeMar charges those who accept the traditional premillennial interpretation with denying the faithfulness of God. He asks, "What would we think of such a deal? Could God ever delay keeping His promise in such a way and still be called a covenant-keeping God? No!"[16] The traditional interpretation teaches that the Lord will fulfill his promise to redeem Daniel's nation, city, and temple, albeit after a mysterious delay. This delay does not mean that God is slack to fulfill his promises but that he is patiently waiting for his people to repent (2 Peter 3:9). Ironically, the preterist position denies God's faithfulness by placing the *terminus ad quem* (endpoint) of Daniel's prophecy in the first century AD without God having answered his prayers and "pleas for mercy" for his desolate nation, city, and sanctuary (Dan. 9:1-19). While the angel predicted specific prophetic events related to the final *redemption* of the nation (Dan. 9:24; cf. Dan. 12:7; Zech. 12:10; Rom. 11:25-27), DeMar's position teaches the exact opposite, that is, that the destruction of the Jewish kingdom in AD 70 was the ultimate and permanent *rejection* of Daniel's people!

Preterists admit that Daniel's prophecy reveals the cyclical nature of divine judgment. Mathison wrote, "Jeremiah provided a specific time text [Jer. 25:11-12; 29:10] that was greatly extended in Daniel [9:24-27]. Leviticus 26, especially verse 18, provides the covenantal basis for such extensions of judgment. Leviticus 26 also indicates that this principle of sevenfold judgment can be repeated many times."[17] DeMar also correctly sees that the seventy years' captivity mentioned in Jeremiah 29:10 provided the pattern for the 490 years of captivity in Daniel 9:24.[18] It is not as apparent to preterists that this pattern of covenantal judgments and blessings will continue until the Antichrist destroys Jerusalem and the

16 Ibid., p. 331
17 Mathison 2004, p. 164
18 DeMar 1999, p. 330

Third Temple, immediately prior to the ultimate restoration and salvation of the Jewish nation.

The mysterious gap in the Prophecy of the Seventy Weeks fits well with "the mystery of the gentiles" taught by the apostle Paul (Rom. 11:25-26; 16:25-26; Eph. 3:3-6; Col 1:26-27). This mystery that believing Jews and believing gentiles were divinely intended to be "fellow heirs" of the promises of Israel was concealed during the ages recorded in the Old Testament, only being revealed in the New Testament era (Rom. 16:25; Eph. 3:5, 9; Col. 1:26). Specifically, this inclusion of the gentiles is taking place between the two advents of the Messiah.

13

The Already and Not Yet

T he "already and not yet" principle is foundational to a proper understanding of New Testament eschatology. The classic example of this principle is called *inaugurated eschatology*, the doctrine that God's kingdom has been *set in motion* by Jesus Christ and his work on the cross *and will be consummated* when he returns. In addition, the future "age to come" has already *penetrated* "this present evil age" (Gal. 1:4) through the dynamic activity of the Holy Spirit in the lives of the Lord's people.

Gerhardus Vos and Oscar Cullman recognized and formally defined inaugurated eschatology in the early-twentieth century, and beginning in the 1950s, George Eldon Ladd further popularized it. Ladd described the kingdom of heaven as "God's rule which men can and must receive in the present" (e.g., Matt. 6:33; 11:11; 12:28; 21:31; 23:13; Mark 10:15; Luke 11:52; 12:31; 16:16; 17:21), but also emphasized the fact that "God's rule will also be eschatologically manifested in the future."[1] He identified different aspects of the kingdom including: (1) God's providential reigning authority (Luke 19:12, 15; 23:42; John 18:36) and (2) the realm of this reign, which is further subdivided into the proleptic present ("already") and future ("not yet") aspects. He demonstrated that Jesus equated his future kingdom reign with the age to come (Matt. 8:11; Mark 9:47; 10:23-25; 14:25; Luke 13:28).

The Gospel of John contains several examples of this "already and not yet" phenomenon. For example, the Lord Jesus employed the phrase "the hour is coming and is now here" to highlight this phenomenon (John 4:23; 5:25; 16:32). He used the phrase "an hour is coming" to predict the eschatological time when the dead will

---

1   Ladd 1974, p. 138, cf. p. 123

hear his voice and be resurrected, and he taught that the resurrection had, in one sense, *already* arrived ("and is now here") (John 5:25, 28). While Jesus maintained the traditional Jewish teaching that the resurrection will occur "on the last day" (John 6:39-44, 54; cf. Dan. 12:1-3), he also taught that those who believe in him have *already* been given eternal life (John 3:36; 5:24; 6:40, 47, 54; cf. 1 John 5:11, 13). He explained that he would soon "go away" to the Father and that his disciples will "see him no longer", but he promised to come to them again "in a little while" (John 14:2-3, 12, 16; 16:5, 7, 10, 16-19, 20-24, 28).

This coming was fulfilled *in one sense* when the Holy Spirit arrived (John 14:16-17, 26-27; 16:7-11, 13-15). However, the versatility of the Master's words can, at times, be understood as referring to the arrival of the Spirit *and* to his personal return on the day of the Lord (John 14:18-20, 23, 28-29; 16:16-19, 20-24). In addition, Jesus saw his crucifixion as the time ("now is") for the casting of Satan from heaven (John 12:31; 16:11; cf. Luke 10:18); however, the apostle John prophesied that Satan will be cast out of heaven at the beginning of the unprecedented tribulation (Rev. 12:4-17). The idea is that the cross of Jesus is the "ground and basis" for Satan's ultimate downfall. Consequently, the Devil will be cast down to the earth *in historical time* at the beginning of the great tribulation when the saints will "have conquered him *by the blood of the Lamb* and by the word of their testimony, for they loved not their lives even unto death" (Rev. 12:11, emphasis added). Similarly, those who crucified Jesus gazed upon his pierced body hanging upon the cross, and John understood this as a fulfillment of Zechariah's prophecy ("They will look on him whom they have pierced" John 19:37; cf. Zech. 12:10). Nevertheless, the exhaustive fulfillment of this prophecy will occur when the surviving inhabitants of Judah and Jerusalem (and all the nations) mourn after looking upon the pierced and risen Savior at his glorious return (Zech. 12:10; cf. Matt. 24:30; Rev. 1:7).

Some preterists are open to the likelihood that the New Testament reveals an "already and not yet" pattern of fulfillment. For example, Mathison freely acknowledges such aspects of New Testament eschatology.[2] He identifies this pattern in the present and future aspects of resurrection in John 5-6, and in the judgment of Satan in John 12:31-32.[3] He also correctly teaches that individual redemption is an "already and not yet" aspect of the new creation (2 Cor. 5:17).[4] He cites the Immanuel prophecy (Isa. 7:14-16) as an example of "a prophecy with multiple fulfillments."[5]

Most Christian commentators posit a double fulfillment of Isaiah's prophecy, primarily due to Matthew's teaching that the virgin birth of Jesus fulfilled it (Matt. 2:20-25), coupled with the prophet Isaiah's explicit prediction that Damascus and Samaria would be plundered before the chosen son, Immanuel ("God is with us"), was old enough to distinguish right from wrong (Isa. 7:15-16). For example, the New Testament scholar, Craig L. Blomberg, commends this interpretation: "Better than both of these approaches, however, is the concept of double fulfillment ... Matthew recognized that Isaiah's son fulfilled the dimension of the prophecy that required a child to be born in the immediate future. But the larger, eschatological context especially of Isa. 9:1-7, depicted a son, never clearly distinguished from Isaiah's, who would be a divine, messianic king."[6]

As demonstrated in previous chapters, Gentry embraces an "already and not yet" fulfillment of many biblical prophecies. He teaches that many of the Savior's teachings contain an "eschatological orientation": proximal events in history prefigure distant, eschatological events.[7] He argues that Jesus' teaching that unbelieving Jews will be cast out "into outer darkness to endure weeping and gnashing of teeth (Matt 8:12) certainly points to God's ultimate judgment. But it also directly pictures the AD 70 judgment

2 Mathison 2004, pp. 169, 203
3 Ibid., pp. 173, 174; p. 171
4 Ibid., p. 174
5 Ibid., p. 167
6 Blomberg, Craig L. in Beale and Carson 2007, p. 5
7 Gentry 2010c, loc. 727-732

when God horribly judges Israel and removes her temple forever. That judgment is a harbinger of the final judgment itself."[8]

Elsewhere, Gentry speaks about the Master's contemporary audience: "Their prideful boasting will be judged on judgment day at the end of history. But in addition, this [Matt. 23:12] seems also to highlight the approaching AD 70 judgment (which also is eschatological, being a pointer to the final judgment)."[9] Gentry provides insights into this perspective: "Theologically, a redemptive-historical link does in fact connect AD 70 with the second advent. This could easily confuse the disciples. That is, the AD 70 episode is an anticipatory foreshadowing of the larger event, the second advent. As Carson expresses it: 'The near event, the destruction of Jerusalem, serves as a symbol for the far event, i.e., the second coming.'"[10] Despite Gentry's admission, many preterists recoil at the notion that the destruction of Jerusalem and its temple in AD 70 functions typologically to point to a much greater eschatological event in the future.

And the Day of Vengeance

Many eschatological passages in the Old Testament Prophets *conceal* the "already and not yet" aspects of God's kingdom by not differentiating between the two. This phenomenon is known as the prophetic perspective. The New Testament *reveals* the mystery of the two advents of the Messiah and assists the reader to identify the portions of the Old Testament prophecies that have been fulfilled and those that will be fulfilled at the end of the age. One classic example of this phenomenon is recorded in the Gospel of Luke (Luke 4:18-19, 21). The passage explains that Jesus of Nazareth opened the scroll of Isaiah the prophet (Isa. 61:1-2a) and read the following passage: "The Spirit of the Lord is upon me, because he has anointed me to proclaim good news to the poor. He has sent me to proclaim liberty to the captives and recovering

---

8 Ibid., loc. 360

9 Ibid., loc. 727-732

10 Ibid., loc. 1004-1009

of sight to the blind, to set at liberty those who are oppressed, to proclaim the year of the Lord's favor ..." Then he claimed, "*Today* this Scripture has been *fulfilled* in your hearing" (Luke 4:18-19, 21, emphasis added). Notably, he quoted the portion of this prophecy that he was presently fulfilling, but at *mid-sentence*, refrained from declaring the following portion:

> ... and the day of vengeance of our God; to comfort all who mourn; to grant to those who mourn in Zion—to give them a beautiful headdress instead of ashes, the oil of gladness instead of mourning, the garment of praise instead of a faint spirit; that they may be called oaks of righteousness, the planting of the LORD, that he may be glorified. They shall build up the ancient ruins; they shall raise up the former devastations; they shall repair the ruined cities, the devastations of many generations. (Isa. 61:2b-4)

Jesus did not recite the remainder of the prophecy because he intended to fulfill those aspects at his second advent. This latter portion of the prophecy is concerned with "the day of vengeance of our God" (Isa. 61:2b), also known as the day of the Lord (cf. Isa. 34:8). Jesus used a variant phrase – "days of vengeance" – in the Olivet Discourse (Luke 21:22). The prophet Isaiah revealed that the day of vengeance is when the Lord will comfort Zion's mourners so that they find everlasting gladness, and rebuild "the ancient *ruins* ... the former *devastations* ... the *ruined* cities" of the land of Israel (Isa. 61:2b-4; cf. 58:12; 60:21; Amos 9:14; Zech. 12:10-14; Matt. 5:4). These prophetic events do not match any first-century events, but represent the "not yet" of prophetic fulfillment.

The King of the North

The final vision in the book of Daniel in chapters 10-12 also reveals the "already" and the "not yet" of biblical prophecy. Most evangelical futurist commentators categorize the various sections of Daniel 11 as follows: the transition from Medio-Persian rule to Macedonian rule under Alexander the Great (vv. 2-3), the Seleucid and Ptolemaic dynasties, with a special emphasis on Antiochus Epiphanes IV (vv. 4-35), and the future Antichrist (vv. 36-45).

Preterist commentators differ widely, with many seeing the proud king described in Daniel 11:36ff as Vespasian, Titus, one of the Herodians, or some other first-century figure. It was demonstrated in other chapters of this book that the future unprecedented tribulation and the resurrection from the dead are thematically and temporally inseparable. This argument sets forth the futurist position that the Antichrist is in view from Daniel 11:36ff, thus prohibiting a preterist paradigm that disallows a future Antichrist. It will now be demonstrated that the Antichrist is in view *beginning as early as verse 21.*

Mathison correctly noted that a change in the subject does not occur beginning in Daniel 11:36:

> Daniel 11:36-12:3 does not provide any indication that the subject has changed, but, unlike the preceding verses, the events described in 11:36-12:3 do not correspond to any known events in the life of Antiochus IV—or anyone else, for that matter. Some suggest that these verses were fulfilled in the first century. Others suggest that they have not yet been fulfilled. In either case, their fulfillment did not occur when the prophecies of Daniel 11:21-35 were fulfilled. The two events were telescoped by Daniel into one continuous prophecy, and no one reading it before any of it was fulfilled would have been able to detect a change of subject at verse 36.[11]

Antiochus IV (Epiphanes) (175-164 BC) fulfilled *many* of the prophetic details of "the king of the north" of Daniel 11:21-35. This interpretation is well established, with much in its defense, and so, will not be reiterated here. However, the futurist position that the final Antichrist will *completely* fulfill these verses is also highly defensible. This interpretation is based on several incontrovertible pieces of evidence.

First, the invasion of the ships of Kittim (Dan. 11:30) is an allusion to Balaam's prophecy, which identifies this event as occurring in "the latter days" (Num. 24:14, 23-24). This period of "the latter days" does not fit with the reign of Antiochus IV in the second century BC.

11 Mathison 2004, p. 167

Second, the events of the unprecedented tribulation in Daniel 12 refer back to events that were detailed previously in the same prophetic vision (Dan. 11:30-36). These events include the king's forcible removal of the daily burnt offering (i.e., the *tamid* offering), the setting up of "the abomination that makes desolate" (Dan. 11:31; 12:11), and the refining, purifying, and whitening of the wise and understanding (Dan. 11:33-35; 12:10). The careful reader should consider that chapters 10-12 comprise a single prophecy, detailed in chapters 10-11 and prophetically elucidated by the "man clothed in linen" in chapter 12.

Third, the antecedent for "the king" (Dan. 11:36) is "the vile/ contemptible person" that was introduced *as early as verse 21.* The subject of the contemptible person is maintained by usage of the third person singular pronouns "he" and "him" throughout verses 21-35, without any indication of a change. Then, verse 36 mentions "the king" without any indication of a subject change. As Mathison points out in his quote above, this use of the noun would be oddly out of place if a subject change had occurred at this point. This lack of subject change is sharply contrasted with the many subject changes prior to verse 21.

Fourth, this king will "exalt himself and magnify himself above every god" and speak blasphemies (Dan. 11:36). The apostle Paul alluded to this passage with reference to the Man of Lawlessness, who will enter the temple (2 Thess. 2:3-4; cf. Rev. 13:5-6) and who is the Antichrist (as argued in Chapter 11).

Table 6: Parallel Passages of Daniel 11

	Daniel 11	Parallel Passages
Ships of Kittim in the Latter Days	"For ships of Kittim shall come against him, and he shall be afraid and withdraw, and shall turn back and be enraged and take action against the holy covenant. He shall turn back and pay attention to those who forsake the holy covenant." (Dan. 11:30)	"Come, I will let you know what this people will do to your people in the latter days. ... Alas, who shall live when God does this? But ships shall come from Kittim and shall afflict Asshur and Eber; and he too shall come to utter destruction." (Num. 24:14, 23-24)
Removal of the Regular Burnt Offering and the Abomination of Desolation is Set Up	"Forces from him shall appear and profane the temple and fortress, and shall take away the regular burnt offering. And they shall set up the abomination that makes desolate." (Dan. 11:31)	"And from the time that the regular burnt offering is taken away and the abomination that makes desolate is set up, there shall be 1,290 days." (Dan. 12:11)
The Wise Will Understand and Some Will Be Refined, Purified, and Made White	"And the wise among the people shall make many understand, though for some days they shall stumble by sword and flame, by captivity and plunder. When they stumble, they shall receive a little help. And many shall join themselves to them with flattery, and some of the wise shall stumble, so that they may be refined, purified, and made white, until the time of the end, for it still awaits the appointed time." (Dan. 11:33-35)	"Many shall purify themselves and make themselves white and be refined, but the wicked shall act wickedly. And none of the wicked shall understand, but those who are wise shall understand." (Dan. 12:10)

	Daniel 11	Parallel Passages
The Lawless One Will Exalt Himself Above Every Deity and Will Speak Blasphemies Against God	"And the king shall do as he wills. He shall exalt himself and magnify himself above every god, and shall speak astonishing things against the God of gods." (Dan. 11:36) "He shall speak words against the Most High . . . and shall think to change the times and the law." (Dan. 7:25)	"…and the man of lawlessness is revealed, the son of destruction, who opposes and exalts himself against every so-called god or object of worship, so that he takes his seat in the temple of God, proclaiming himself to be God." (2 Thess. 2:3b-4; cf. Rev. 13:5-6)

Therefore, in one sense, the historical actions of Antiochus Epiphanes function as *a historical distractor* that divinely conceals the true identity of the king--the Antichrist. This identity will become evident when the prophecy is unsealed and the vision fulfilled. As demonstrated in previous chapters, Jesus alluded to Daniel's abomination of desolation in his Olivet Prophecy (Matt. 24:15-16; Mark 13:14; cf. Dan. 9:27; 11:31, 45; 12:11), and he spoke of it as awaiting a future fulfillment at the end of the age. This means that the abomination did not find exhaustive fulfillment in Antiochus' desecration of the Jerusalem temple in 168 BC.

Some preterists argue that the Olivet Prophecy represents a double fulfillment of this aspect of Daniel's prophecies,[12] but this special pleading is evidenced by the temporal relationship of the abomination with the unprecedented tribulation and the resurrection of the dead (Dan. 12:1-3, 11). Consequently, the ultimate, plenary fulfillment of both prophecies will include the setting up of the Antichrist's abomination in the Third Temple. The partial fulfillment of Daniel's prophecies by Antiochus and the complete fulfillment by the Antichrist illustrate the "already and not yet" pattern characteristic of many biblical prophecies.

These prophecies could be said to demonstrate a *pattern eschatology*, that is, typological cycles of prophetic fulfillment

12 E.g., Mathison 2004, p. 167

that repeat throughout history. These cycles find their basis in the history of covenant enactment and violation, divine retribution, and salvation/redemption as recorded in the books of Leviticus and Deuteronomy. The actions of Antiochus IV Epiphanes in 168 BC and General Titus in AD 70 are similar to previous actions by other individuals, such as Pharaoh, Nebuchadnezzar, Caligula, Domitian, Hitler, and the like, whose actions prophetically foreshadow those of the final Antichrist. The familiar pattern consists of a wicked king who brings covenant discipline by forcing assimilation and idolatry, outlawing the observance of God's commandments, desecrating the holy place(s), demanding cult worship of himself, and attempting to destroy the Jews. However, these historical enemies of Israel only partially fulfilled the prophetic picture of the ultimate enemy. Exhaustive fulfillment awaits the future Antichrist.

Elijah as "Already and Not Yet"

The Old Testament prophet, Elijah, provides an excellent case study depicting the "already and not yet" principle. First of all, Elijah's end-of-life experience was most exceptional; he was taken to heaven in a whirlwind (2 Kings 2:1, 11). At the end of the Old Testament canon, the prophet Malachi prophesied about him, saying, "Behold, I [the LORD] will send you Elijah the prophet before the great and awesome day of the LORD comes. And he will turn the hearts of the fathers to their children and the hearts of children to their fathers, lest I come and strike the land with a decree of utter destruction" (Mal. 4:5-6; cf. Mal. 3:1-2; 4:1-3; Matt. 11:9-10; Mark 1:2; Luke 7:27). Evidently, in the future, Elijah will bring a message of intergenerational repentance so that *God might spare the land of Israel from complete ruin* on the day of the Lord. Malachi also prophesied that the Lord Jesus "will suddenly come to his temple" after Elijah has purified and refined the Levites so that they "bring offerings in righteousness to the LORD" (Mal. 3:1, 3).

In the New Testament, the linkage of John the Baptist with Elijah the prophet is enigmatic. Many preterists argue that the Baptist *exhaustively* fulfilled Malachi's prophecies.[13] On the other hand, futurists teach that John was a typological, partial fulfillment of the prophecies, *and* that Elijah the prophet will return to prepare the Jewish nation for the day of Christ Jesus. Significantly, Jesus never denied the future return of Elijah, but he taught, "Elijah does come first to restore all things. ... I tell you that Elijah has come" (Mark 9:12-13). He also taught that those with spiritual discernment could perceive the truth that John the Baptist was Elijah (Matt. 11:14-15).

On the other hand, the Baptist rejected any self-identification as Elijah (John 1:21). This apparent contradiction is easily reconciled when we understand that John had been given "the spirit and power" of Elijah (Luke 1:17, 76). This is similar to Elisha the prophet receiving the prophetic spirit and prophetic abilities of his master, Elijah, after the latter had been raptured (2 Kings 2:9, 15). Illustrative of this transference of power, Elijah, John the Baptist, and to a lesser degree, Elisha, performed prophetic actions at the Jordan River, wore similar clothing, preached a message of repentance to the nation, and were persecuted by a wicked king.

The preterist view that John the Baptist *exhaustively* fulfilled Malachi's prophecies about Elijah is defective because John did not fulfill the prophetic expectation concerning Elijah - that he would purify the sons of Levi so that they could offer acceptable sacrifices – nor did he usher in a period of national repentance, which could have prevented the utter destruction of the nation of Israel. To the contrary, preterists point out that the land was utterly destroyed in AD 70! N. T. Wright argues that John the Baptist's audience would have understood his prophetic warnings about "a great national disaster, to be interpreted as the judgment of the covenant god."[14] The nation ultimately rejected and murdered both John and Jesus, a rejection that resulted in covenantal curses

---

13 Gentry 2010c, loc. 380; Similarly Russell 2003, p. 4
14 Wright 1996, p. 326

against the land. Chilton admits that the nation refused to repent so that God cursed the land and "placed [it] under the ban, completely devoted to destruction" in AD 70.[15]

Premillennialists teach that many within the Jewish nation will accept Elijah's message of repentance in preparation for the Lord's second coming. The national rejection of John and Jesus contrasts sharply with some of the nation's repentance at the preaching of Elijah and the glorious return of Jesus. Many premillennialists understand the prophet Elijah or another Elijah-like figure to be one of the two witnesses of Revelation 11:3-13. Craig L. Blomberg explains, "Whether one sees John as the complete fulfillment of the prediction depends in large part on one's understanding of the two witnesses in Rev. 11, depicted as mirroring the ministries of Moses and Elijah."[16] The biblical evidence supports the thesis that John the Baptist was a *partial* fulfillment of Malachi's prophecy and that Elijah will return in *complete* fulfillment. The 3.5-year ministry of the two witnesses will usher in nothing short of the day of the Lord Jesus Christ.

There Are Some Standing Here

The Lord Jesus prophesied, "For the Son of Man is going to come with his angels in the glory of his Father, and then he will repay each person according to what he has done. Truly, I say to you, there are some standing here who will not taste death until they see the Son of Man coming in his kingdom" (Matt. 16:27-28; cf. Mark 8:38-9:1; Luke 9:26-27). The other Synoptic Gospels substitute the Matthean phrase "see the Son of Man coming in his kingdom" with "see the kingdom of God after it has come with power" (Mark 9:1) and the more abbreviated "see the kingdom of God" (Luke 9:27). J. Stuart Russell regarded this passage as "the greatest importance in this discussion [about eschatology]," "the key to the right interpretation" of the doctrine of the *Parousia*, and "*the master key* ... which serves to open, not only this, but

15 Chilton 2007, p. 138
16 Blomberg, Craig L. in Beale and Carson 2007, p. 40

many other dark sayings in the prophetic oracles."[17] Most preterists consider this prophecy, as DeMar argues, "a crucial time text" in favor of preterism.[18] However, we will see that this biblical prophecy is a fitting example of the "already and not yet" arrival of God's kingdom.

Gentry summarizes the preterist position that the prophecy "must point to the AD 70 destruction of the temple which occurs forty years later."[19] Preterists reason that the text clearly states that most (but not all) of those who were then with Jesus had to die prior to his glorious coming.[20] They reason that this prophecy cannot be about his second coming because all of his first disciples died almost two millennia ago.[21] Chilton sees no alternative to the preterist interpretation; he wrote, "Was Jesus right or wrong? ... And this was no slight miscalculation: Jesus missed the mark by thousands of years! Can we trust Him as Lord and Savior, and still hold that he was wrong, or that somehow His prophecy got derailed?"[22] Russell explains the preterist rationale for rejecting the futurist interpretations of this passage:

> Or how can we suppose that Christ, speaking of an event which was to take place in about twelve months, would say [this] ... The very form of the expression shows that the event spoken of could not lie within the space of a few months, or even a few years: it is a mode of speech which suggests that not *all* present will live to see the events spoken of; that not *many* will do so; but that *some* will. It is exactly such a way of speaking as would suit an interval of thirty or forty years, when the majority of the persons then present would have passed away, but some would survive and witness the event referred to.[23]

---

17 Russell 2003, pp. 29, 46
18 DeMar 1999, p. viii
19 Gentry 2010c, loc. 428-433, 1550; Similarly Kik 1971, p. 64
20 Gentry 2010c, loc. 1259, 1269
21 Hanegraaff 2007, p.17
22 Chilton 2007, p. 70
23 Russell 2003, pp. 30-31

Preterists emphatically reject the traditional interpretations and believe that this entire passage refers to a supposed judgment "coming" of Jesus in AD 70. J. Marcellus Kik explains, "This [Matt. 16:28] could not possibly refer to the second, personal, visible coming";[24] however, he later argues that Matthew 16:27 confirms that "the final judgment takes place at the second coming of Christ."[25] On the other hand, many futurists argue that the first verse of the prophecy (Matt. 16:27; Mark 8:38; Luke 9:26) refers to the glorious return of Jesus Christ. This interpretation is certain because the Matthean version of the prophecy includes the expression "For the Son of Man is going to come with his angels in the glory of his Father, and *then he will repay each person according to what he has done.*" (Matt. 16:27, emphasis added). The participle "for" (γὰρ) thematically connects this verse with the preceding content, namely, the suffering and deaths of Jesus and his disciples (Matt. 16:21, 24-26).

This shows that the purpose for the Son of Man's coming in verse 27 will be to vindicate Jesus and his disciples by repaying "each person according to what he has done" (Matt. 16:27; cf. Isa. 40:1-5, 9-11; 62:10-11). The biblical writers typically reserved such language of rewards to describe the eschatological, post-mortem judgment (e.g., Rom. 14:10-12; 2 Cor. 5:10; 2 Tim. 4:1).[26] The language is most similar to the Apocalypse's vision of the Lord sitting upon his throne to judge the dead "by what was written in the books, *according to what they had done*" (Rev. 20:12, emphasis added; cf. Rev. 20:13). Those whose names are "not found written in the book of life" will be thrown into hellfire (Rev. 20:15). These punishments and rewards do not fit the historical events of AD 70.

Futurist commentators generally take one of several inter-pretive approaches to the second verse of Jesus' prophecy ("there are some standing here who will not taste death until ..." Matt.

---

24 Kik 1971, p. 38

25 Ibid., p. 167

26 Contra Adams and Fisher 2000, pp. 109, 111

16:28: Mark 9:1; Luke 9:27). One interpretation sees this statement as referring to Peter, James, and John who soon saw the glorified Jesus on the Mount of Transfiguration (Matt. 17:1-13; Mark 9:2-13; Luke 9:28-36). Proponents of this view point out that the account of this event immediately follows the statement of Jesus in all three Synoptic Gospels, and that the time indicators connecting the two events show that the experience on the mountain took place about a week after he made the statement (Matt. 17:1; Mark 9:2; Luke 9:28). One strength of this position is that the apostle Peter identified this event "on the holy mountain" as an "eyewitness" experience of the glorified Jesus (2 Peter 1:16-21). Peter provided this experience as a reason to believe that the apostles "did not follow cleverly devised myths when we made known to you *the power and coming of our Lord Jesus Christ*" (2 Peter 1:16, emphasis added). This statement links the majestic experience on the Mount of Transfiguration with the return of Jesus using language similar to his statement in Matthew 16:28.

An alternative interpretation understands Jesus' statement about the disciples seeing him coming in his kingdom (Matt. 16:28) as referring to his post-resurrection appearances. The strength of this view is that the eleven apostles saw and handled the glorified Jesus (1 John 1:1-2), a powerful and certain foretaste, an "already and not yet" fulfillment, of his second coming. Judas, of course, had died prior to these appearances.

A third interpretation is that the prophecy was fulfilled when some of the disciples saw the glorified Jesus at his Father's right hand (e.g., Stephen in Acts 7:56) or when they received visions in which they saw Jesus returning in glory (e.g., John in Rev. 19:11-16). The remaining disciples died without having yet seen the Lord in his glorious kingdom.

A fourth option is to see the fulfillment as the disciples seeing or recognizing one or more prophetic events in which the kingdom of God had arrived. These events included the Lord's mighty miracles, his post-resurrection appearances and ascension into heaven, the pouring out the Holy Spirit beginning at Pentecost, and the advancement of the gospel throughout the world. The power and certainty of the *whole* was evident in the seeing of the *part*.

DeMar provides the standard preterist critique of the futurist interpretations:

> Some claim that the 'coming' Jesus had in mind was the transfiguration. But the transfiguration cannot be its fulfillment since Jesus indicated that *some* who were standing with Him would still be alive when He came but *most* would be dead. If we adopt this view that the transfiguration is the fulfillment, we must conclude that most of the people with whom Jesus spoke were dead within a week of Jesus' prediction (Matt. 17:1)! ... Others see Pentecost, with the coming of the Holy Spirit, as the fulfillment. But the same problem arises—nearly all the disciples would have had to die within a period of a few months after the events described by Jesus in Matthew 16:27-28.[27]

Contrary to DeMar's claims, the Lord's statement (Matt. 16:28) does not indicate that *most* of the original hearers would die prior to the Lord's coming; it simply states that *some* would remain alive. The difference is subtle, yet of great importance, because it provides explanatory power for the various futurist interpretations. The preterist interpretation is flawed for another reason. The apostle John's explicit *denial* that Jesus had predicted that John would remain alive until the Lord's coming (John 21:20-23) would have been unnecessary if this "coming" did not refer to the future return of Christ, but to an event in AD 70 that the Holy Spirit knew would occur during the apostle's lifetime (cf. Matt. 16:28).

During the Lord's trial before the Jewish Sanhedrin, the high priest, Caiaphas, put Jesus under a legal obligation to answer a question about his identity. The passage reads, "But Jesus remained silent. And the high priest said to him, 'I adjure you by the living God, tell us if you are the Christ, the Son of God.'

---

27 DeMar 1999, p.44; Similarly Gentry 2010c, loc. 1550 and Sproul 1998, pp. 61, 62

Jesus said to him, 'You have said so. But I tell you, from now on you will see the Son of Man seated at the right hand of Power and coming on the clouds of heaven'" (Matt. 26:63-64; cf. Mark 14:62; Luke 22:69).

R. T. France explains that preterist interpreters have recently challenged the traditional interpretation of this passage. He states, "The 'coming on the clouds of heaven' cannot be read as a reference to the parousia, as has been the traditional exegesis until relatively recently."[28] He teaches that the elders of the Sanhedrin soon saw, in the destruction of Jerusalem in AD 70, the vindication of the Messiah after they had failed to suppress the movement of Christianity.[29] Many preterists correctly note that the phrase ἀπ' ἄρτι in Matthew 26:64 is often translated "hereafter" but can be translated "from now on," meaning from that point in time until the indefinite future.[30] However, this contradicts the preterist interpretation that members of the Sanhedrin did not recognize ("see") his coming until AD 70. R. C. Sproul admits, "Jesus' words . . . may refer to an indefinite future. ...'seeing' the coming of Christ in the 'hereafter' does not demand a first-century fulfillment."[31]

The traditional approach to this passage is to understand Jesus' response (Matt. 26:68), which is a combined allusion to Psalm 110:1 and Daniel 7:13, as a description of *the entire period of his heavenly reign at God's right hand* that will be completed when he returns on clouds of glory (e.g., Luke 19:12ff). Blomberg explains, "Christ is *first* in God's presence and then coming on the clouds, presumably therefore coming from heaven to earth."[32] Jesus' statement encapsulates the mystery of his twofold advent, the two-stage process of redemption that began with his crucifixion, resurrection, and ascension and will be completed at his

28 France 2007, pp. 1027-28
29 Ibid. Similarly DeMar 1999, pp. 162-163; Gentry 2010b, pp. 36, 45; Hanegraaff 2007, p. 27
30 France 2007, pp. 1027-28; Gentry 2010c, loc. 598; Mathison 2004, p. 183
31 Sproul 1998, p. 100
32 Blomberg, Craig L. in Beale and Carson 1996, p. 87-88

glorious return. Christ was not claiming that Caiaphas and the Sanhedrin would conclude that he is the glorified Son of Man soon after his death and resurrection, or as preterists claim, when Jerusalem was destroyed in AD 70. The correct interpretation is that the larger nation, of which the Sanhedrin were primary representatives, began the historical process ("from now on") of recognizing and understanding that Jesus is the glorified Messiah. This process will be completed when Jesus returns from heaven and the entire nation sees the pierced and resurrected Lord and is saved (see Chapter Seven). This interpretation of Matthew 26:63-64 favors the fourth interpretation of Jesus' statement in Matthew 16:28, as discussed above.

The examples of inaugurated eschatology discussed in this chapter provide a snapshot of how the biblical writers portrayed the *eschaton*. Preterism, with its forced, two-dimensional hermeneutic, fails to leave room for this multifaceted diamond of biblical prophecy. As we have seen throughout the chapters of this book, many of the faulty claims of preterism arise from a deficient understanding of the "already and not yet" principle. Such a deficiency, coupled with a noble desire to maintain a consistent hermeneutic, leads many preterists to cast prophecies about the future in a first-century mold.

On the other hand, the common Christian experience of the resurrected glory of Jesus *in the present age* corroborates the futurist interpretation of the biblical texts. Furthermore, Christians, in a very real sense, "already" experience the inaugurated realities of the end of the age. These include such realities of tribulation, resurrection and eternal life, the presence of the resurrected Jesus in the person of the Holy Spirit, dimensions of the kingdom of God, and other glories of the age to come. Although these events will take place in their proper time ("not yet"), we *no less see them* in the present ("already").

14

The Millennium

Premillennialism (otherwise known as millennialism or chiliasm) is the doctrine that Jesus will return to establish his kingdom on Earth for 1,000 years. Although the Old Testament prophets often depicted millennial conditions, the primary biblical text describing the *length* of the millennium is Revelation 20:1-10. Premillennial eschatology was arguably the predominant view in the earliest centuries of Christianity, and the testimony of the early church fathers reveals an abundance of evidence in support of premillennialism. For example, Papias, a disciple of the apostle John, believed that Jesus will personally reign on the earth during the millennium.[1] Justin Martyr taught that "right-minded Christians" are convinced that Christ will reign from the rebuilt Jerusalem during this time.[2] Theophilus, Irenaeus, and Tertullian described the pristine conditions that will exist on Earth.[3] Irenaeus argued that the land promises given to Abraham will be fulfilled after the resurrection of the righteous, and he taught that the earthly Jerusalem "will be rebuilt after the pattern of the Jerusalem above."[4] Hippolytus, likely influenced by Jewish millennial teachings, quoted Psalm 90:4 in his defense of the millennium.[5] Tertullian taught that the glorified Jerusalem will be established on the earth after the resurrection and during the millennium.[6] Commodianus, Methodius, and Lactantius also taught a literal millennial reign of Christ.[7]

---

1 Papias cited by *Irenaeus* 1.153, 154 in Bercot 1998
2 Justin Martyr 1.239, 240 in Bercot 1998
3 Theophilus 2.101; Irenaeus 1.561, 562, 563; Tertullian 3.483 in Bercot 1998
4 Irenaeus 1.562, 562, 565 in Bercot 1998
5 Hippolytus 5.179 in Bercot 1998; cf. The Epistle of Barnabas 15:4
6 Tertullian 3.342 in Bercot 1998
7 Commodianus 4.211, 212; Methodius 6.347; Lactantius 7.212, 218 in

On the other hand, most preterists deny that the Bible predicts a literal millennium.[8] For example, Gentry claims, "I will show that the 1000 years began in the first century, has already consumed 2000 years of time, and is not yet over."[9] Preterists usually follow the Augustinian amillennialist construct where the phrase "a thousand years" means nearly 2,000 years and represents the *totality* of the Christian era.[10] They argue that the phrase must refer to "a long period of time" because the qualifier "thousand", when used elsewhere in Scripture, confers the sense of *totality* upon the noun it modifies. For example, God stated that he owns "the cattle on a thousand hills" (Ps. 50:10), which is a poetic manner of saying that he lays claim to *every* hill. However, this line of reasoning does not support the conclusion of preterists about the millennium because a *totality* of years would be much longer than the New Testament period, indicating that the millennium cannot refer to a period of nearly 2,000 years, as these preterists argue. In addition, preterists reject the plain sense of John's millennium passage, that is, that "a thousand years" means an actual 1,000 years, in order to maintain their presupposition that the millennium began in the first century AD.

In the Scriptures, the prophetic vision of Revelation 20 begins with the binding of Satan:

> Then I saw an angel coming down from heaven, holding in his hand the key to the bottomless pit and a great chain. And he seized the dragon, that ancient serpent, who is the devil and Satan, and bound him for a thousand years, and threw him into the pit, and shut it and sealed it over him, so that he might not deceive the nations any longer, until the thousand years were ended. After that he must be released for a little while. (Rev. 20:1-3)

However, preterists commonly maintain that the binding of Satan is a symbol for the curtailing of his power during the first

Bercot 1998

8   E.g., Gentry 2010c, loc. 1565

9   Gentry 2010b, p. 105

10 E.g., Kik 1971, p. 41

century so that the gospel could "progress into all the world".[11] Gentry references the Master's casting out of demons and his analogy of the binding of "the strong man" (Matt. 12:29) to argue that Jesus bound Satan during his earthly ministry. However, Gentry admits that Satan "continued (and still continues!) to work among men."[12] Also, he teaches that the death and resurrection of Jesus legally bound Satan so that he now has all authority to "disciple the nations."[13] Similarly, Russell sees the exorcisms performed by Christ as the binding event depicted in Revelation 20:1-4, resulting in "a marked and decisive check to the power of Satan" that decreased "the presence of moral evil" throughout the world.[14] Kik also argues, "Nations were not to be deceived entirely. This does not mean that individuals within nations or even a portion of them would not be entirely deceived.... He [Satan] cannot deceive the nations as he did".[15]

Such arguments reveal a glaring anachronism. The binding of Satan described by the apostle John (Rev. 20:1-4) *cannot* be equated with the miracles and passion of Jesus. The prophetic sequence of events in the book of Revelation is that the binding of Satan immediately follows the glorious appearance of Jesus and his slaying of the Beast (the Antichrist) and the False Prophet (Rev. 19:11-21). This indicates that the binding of Satan takes place *because of* the return of Jesus and is not a mere theological assertion that is disconnected from its immediate context.

Other preterists, such as James Jordan, teach that the binding of Satan and the millennium began in AD 70.[16] He describes this process of binding: "This does not mean that Satan can do nothing, but that he can no longer deceive the nations and keep the Kingdom from them."[17] This interpretation is less than satis-

---

11 Gentry 2010b, p. 105; Similarly Kik 1971, p. 41
12 Gentry 2010b, p. 108; cf. p. 106
13 Ibid., pp. 107, 110
14 Russell 2003, p. 516; cf. p. 515; Similarly Kik 1971, pp. 193, 203, 204
15 Kik 1971, p. 194
16 Jordan 2014, loc. 577
17 Ibid.

fying for a variety of reasons. First of all, the apostolic gospel had been successfully preached *and accepted* throughout the conquered nations of the Roman Empire for many years prior to AD 70. Furthermore, subsequent history revealed that Satan has continued to deceive the nations even into our present era, resulting in significant rejection of the gospel, just as in the apostolic period. Jordan cannot credibly maintain his position that Satan no longer deceives the nations in the face of historical realities.

But even without reference to the distant past, only present, ongoing deception by Satan can explain the worldwide and continuous destruction among the nations: the continued expansion of radical Islam into former Christian nations, two World Wars, the Holocaust, Stalin's Gulag, the spread of Communism, and more recent genocides (Cambodia, Bosnia-Herzegovina, Rwanda) and atrocities (South Sudan and Myanmar). Understatedly, Kik admits that "all appearances seem to be against the view that we are in the millennium now."[18]

Gentry claims that premillennialism depends on the millennium passage in Revelation 20, whereas other eschatological positions do not.[19] While the exact length of the millennium is not *explicitly* revealed elsewhere in Scripture, the concepts depicted in John's millennium passage originate in the Old Testament. For example, the prophet Isaiah explained that demons and earthly kings will receive a lengthy imprisonment and eschatological punishment. He prophesied, "On that day the Lord will punish the host of heaven, in heaven, and the kings of the earth, on the earth. They will be gathered together as prisoners in a pit; they will be shut up in a prison, and after many days they will be punished" (Isa. 24:21-22; cf. "kings of the earth" in Rev. 19:18-21).

Furthermore, an earthly age that will extend beyond the day of the Lord is *a necessary inference* based on a plethora of Old Testament prophecies. Kik explains, "Isaiah gives us many beau-

18 Kik 1971, p. 205
19 Gentry 2010b, p. 118

tiful pictures of the millennium."[20] Other prophets also foresaw a blissful kingdom era that will exist on the earth (e.g., Ps. 2:8; 22:27-31; Hab. 2:14; Zeph. 2:11; Zech. 8:20-23; 9:10; 14:9, 16-19).

The First Resurrection

The apostle John continued his millennium passage with a description of the resurrection of the dead and the kingdom reign of Christ and the saints:

> Then I saw thrones, and seated on them were those to whom the authority to judge was committed. Also I saw the souls of those who had been beheaded for the testimony of Jesus and for the word of God, and those who had not worshiped the beast or its image and had not received its mark on their foreheads or their hands. They came to life and reigned with Christ for a thousand years. The rest of the dead did not come to life until the thousand years were ended. This is the first resurrection. Blessed and holy is the one who shares in the first resurrection! Over such the second death has no power, but they will be priests of God and of Christ, and they will reign with him for a thousand years. (Rev. 20:4-6)

The preterist framework necessarily rejects the traditional interpretation of "the first resurrection" as the actual resurrection of the saints at the return of Jesus (1 Thess. 4:13-18; 1 Cor. 15:20-28, 50-58). Many preterists argue that John's first resurrection is a symbol for the spiritual aspect (the "already") of resurrection that occurs when an individual first believes in Jesus (John 5:24-26; Rom. 6:4; Eph. 2:6; Col. 2:12; 3:1).[21] Chilton advocated this view, saying that Christians are *now* partakers in the First Resurrection" and that the first resurrection is "Spiritual and ethical, our regeneration in Christ and ethical union with God, our re-creation in His image."[22] Gentry also originally held to this position; he once argued, "Therefore, what John teaches through symbolic imagery is that the first resurrection refers to salvation

---

20 Kik 1971, p. 207
21 E.g., Jordan 2014, loc. 586; Kik 1971, pp. 43, 185, 188
22 Chilton 2007, p. 197

and the second resurrection to a literal, bodily arising again from physical death. The first resurrection, then, occurs throughout Christian history (the 1000 years of Christ's reign); the second resurrection only at the end of history, on the 'last day.'"[23]

Nevertheless, Gentry changed his view after interacting with other scholarly arguments. He humbly admits, "John could be symbolically presenting the new birth as the first resurrection and the bodily resurrection from death as the second resurrection. This is the Augustinian view—a view I myself held when I wrote the first edition of this book. But since then, I have engaged in a deeper and more focused analysis of Revelation 20 and how it fits in John's larger narrative."[24]

Gentry explains that he changed his position about the first resurrection (Rev. 20:4-6) after considering two pieces of biblical evidence. First, verse four depicts this resurrection as occurring *after* the martyrs are slain for refusing to take the mark of the Beast, a mark that would be received during the unprecedented tribulation (Rev. 13:5-18). This consideration exposes Gentry's former interpretation as anachronistic because it would require that the martyrs of the Neronian persecution died *before* they converted to Christ. Second, the Greek syntax of the passage shows that the first resurrection is the answer to the martyrs' prayers for vindication (Rev. 6:9-11).[25] Gentry explains that the apostle John concluded that the martyrs' "coming to life" after being beheaded was "a fulfillment of the promise given to them after they are already in heaven (Rev. 6:11)".[26] Consequently, Gentry admits that the first resurrection must be something experienced in a post-mortem setting.[27]

Gentry's current interpretation is that the first resurrection is a symbol for the vindication of the martyrs, which he believes took

---

23 Gentry 2008, pp. 112-13

24 Gentry 2010b, p. 117

25 Ibid., p. 119

26 Ibid., pp. 119, 121

27 Also Jordan 2014, loc. 307

place in AD 70. He also teaches that God rewarded the martyrs at that time so that they could "arise to new life",[28] although it is uncertain what he means by this phrase. He also maintains that the general resurrection of the dead will occur at the return of Jesus.

> John appears to be stating that by AD 70, the martyrs will be vindicated ... Thus, their "coming to life," a fulfillment of the promise given to them *after they are already in heaven* (Rev. 6:11), appears to be an image of their vindication in the death of their opponents in AD 70, rather than at the very moment when the martyrs enter heaven ... They are *deceased* Christians in *heaven,* who were *martyred* in the *first century.*[29]

Gentry's humility and willingness to change his view in light of the Scriptures is highly commendable. However, his novel approach presents many formidable difficulties. One difficulty is that the Bible never presents vindication by itself as a resurrection. Kik explains, "The fact that it [Rev. 20:4-6] is a resurrection knocks out the thought that it is descriptive of the life of the soul in the intermediate state....But when the Christian soul leaves the body to dwell in heaven, it is not a *resurrection.*"[30] In addition, preterists generally recognize that the New Testament "very seldom uses the Greek term 'psuche' to describe the disembodied spirit."[31] Consequently, Gentry is forced by his preterist hermeneutic to invent a new type of "resurrection" that is foreign to Judaism and Christianity.

Another problem with Gentry's view is that the apostle John explained that *"the rest of the dead"*, those *not* resurrected at the first resurrection, will be resurrected after the millennium (Rev. 20:5, emphasis added). This statement *excludes* the martyrs from the postmillennial resurrection because they had *already* been "resurrected" at the first resurrection.[32] Therefore, Gentry's inter-

---

28 Gentry 2010b, p. 123

29 Ibid., pp. 120-21

30 Kik 1971, p. 42; cf. p. 180

31 Ibid., p. 226; cf. p. 228

32 Cf. Gentry 2008, pp. 111-12

pretation implies that these martyrs will be denied bodily resurrection! He does attempt to avoid this difficulty by arguing that the expression "the rest of the dead" should be equated with "the rest" (Rev. 19:21), that is, the people that Jesus will kill at his coming.[33] However, the expression "the rest of the dead" is a parenthetical statement that appears between two other statements concerning the first resurrection ("came to life ... for a thousand years" in Rev. 20:4 and "the first resurrection" in Rev. 20:5b). This grammatical structure demonstrates that the "the rest of the dead" are those who will *remain* dead after the righteous dead have received the first resurrection.

Gentry objects to the premillennial view that Revelation 20 reveals two resurrections from the dead, namely, the premillennial resurrection of the righteous and the postmillennial general resurrection. He claims, "If Revelation teaches two physical resurrections, it is the *only* place in Scripture that does so."[34] Ironically, Gentry's view requires at least three resurrections! He must allow for (1) the spiritual resurrection accorded to Christians by the Spirit upon conversion, (2) a "resurrection" of a vindicated martyr class in AD 70, and (3) the bodily resurrection of all the dead at the return of Jesus. Furthermore, Gentry fails to understand that the mystery of these two resurrections is similar to the mystery that the Messiah would be raised as the Firstfruits of those who would be resurrected thousands of years later (1 Cor. 15:12-26). Neither of these resurrection mysteries were *fully* revealed until the resurrection of Jesus Christ. In addition, Isaiah prophesied that the wicked dead will *not* be resurrected when the Lord arrives to raise the dead:

> They [the wicked] are dead, *they will not live*; they are shades, *they will not arise* ... Your [Israel's] dead shall live; their bodies shall rise. You who dwell in the dust, awake and sing for joy! For your dew is a dew of light, and the earth will give birth to the dead.... For behold, the LORD is coming

33 Gentry 2010b pp. 121-23.
34 Ibid., p. 113

out from his place to punish the inhabitants of the earth for their iniquity, and the earth will disclose the blood shed on it, and will no more cover its slain. (Isa. 26:14, 19, 21; emphasis added)

Daniel 12 and the Resurrection

The angel gave the prophet Daniel a vision that includes an important statement regarding the resurrection of the dead:

> [1] **At that time** shall arise Michael, the great prince who has charge of your people. *And there shall be a time of trouble, such as never has been since there was a nation till that time.* But **at that time** *your people shall be delivered, everyone whose name shall be found written in the book.* [2] And many of those who sleep in the dust of the earth shall awake, some to everlasting life, and some to shame and everlasting contempt. [3] And those who are wise shall shine like the brightness of the sky above; and those who turn many to righteousness, like the stars forever and ever. [4] But you, Daniel, shut up the words and seal the book, until the time of the end. (Dan. 12:1-4)

This portion of Daniel's prophecy must be understood as a specific prediction about the resurrection of the dead, a point argued by futurist commentators.[35] The phrase "**at that time**," used twice in verse one, clearly connects the timing of the deliverance of Daniel's people and the resurrection of the dead (Dan. 12:1b-3) with the unprecedented tribulation (Dan. 12:1) that starts with the abomination of desolation as shown in the preceding verses (Dan. 11:30ff; cf. Dan. 12:11; Matt. 24:15). Most commentators agree that the statement by "the man clothed in linen" that Daniel "shall rest and shall stand in your allotted place at the end of the days" (Dan. 12:12) continues this resurrection theme. The idea is that the prophet would "rest" in sleep, a euphemism for physical death (e.g., Mark 5:39; John 11:11; 1 Thess. 5:6-10), and later "stand" in resurrection "at the end of the days" to receive his eternal inheritance ("allotted place") in God's kingdom (cf. Job 19:23-27). This Danielic prophecy undoubtedly gave rise to the

---

35 E.g. Miller 1994; Calvin 2012, pp. 402-03

first-century Jewish belief that the resurrection will occur "on the last day" (John 6:44; 11:24; cf. John 6:39-40, 54).

Those who interpret Daniel 12:1-3 as predicting anything other than a literal resurrection unwittingly compromise the central claim of Christianity—the resurrection of Jesus Christ—for this prophecy formed the basis of the teaching of Jesus and his apostles regarding the resurrection of the dead (Matt. 25:46; John 5:28-29; Acts 24:15; Rev. 20:4-6, 12-15). I. Howard Marshall noted that the apostle Paul's defense of the resurrection (Acts 24:14-15) uses essentially the same vocabulary as Daniel 12:1-3.[36] In addition, although many Old Testament prophecies predicted the resurrection (e.g., Isa. 25:9; 26:17-19, 21; Ezek. 37:4-14; Job 19:23-29), many scholars recognize that Daniel's prophecy is perhaps *the most unambiguous prophecy* of the resurrection in the Old Testament. Those who deny that this prophecy predicted the resurrection implicitly concede to the arguments of the critics of Christianity in their assessment that Jesus and his apostles invented a doctrine not found in "the law or the prophets," a notion rejected by the apostles (e.g., Acts 26:21-23). Consequently, the statement about the resurrection in Daniel 12:2 should not be interpreted as figurative, referring to conversion or the vindication of the martyrs, as partial preterists maintain.

Gentry once argued correctly that Daniel 12:1-3 is about the resurrection of the dead that will take place at the end of the age.[37] He has since abandoned this position and now teaches that the passage was fulfilled in AD 70,[38] but his interpretive shift illustrates another preterist dilemma. Preterists who believe that all the events of Daniel 12 were fulfilled in the first century must either (1) abandon preterism, (2) deny that Daniel 12:1-3 predicts a literal, bodily resurrection, or (3) embrace the heresy of consistent preterism. This dilemma is evident in how partial preterists inter-

---

36 Marshall, I. Howard in Beale and Carson 2007, p. 598

37 Gentry 1990, p. 142; Similarly Adams and Fisher 2000, p. 105

38 Gentry 2009 p. 538; cf. Gentry, Kenneth L. as quoted in Sullivan 2012 website

pret the statement that the righteous "shall shine like the brightness of the sky ... and like the stars" at the time of the end (Dan. 12:3). The Lord Jesus echoed this in his teaching that "at the end of the age ... the righteous will shine like the sun in the kingdom of their Father" (Matt. 13:39, 43). DeMar, Jordan, Leithart, McDurmon, and others consistently interpret both prophecies as having an AD 70 fulfillment. On the other hand, Gentry *inconsistently* sees the Danielic passage as having an AD 70 fulfillment, while Jesus' statement in Matthew 13 points to the end of the age in our future.

Sam Frost describes another preterist method for interpreting Daniel 12:1-3.

> Then we read, "And many of those who sleep in the dust of the earth shall awake, some to everlasting life, and some to shame and everlasting contempt." There is no "time" indicator here. If it read, "at that time many of those who sleep shall awake" we would have a different issue. But it doesn't. "And" (waw) can be seen as a simple connector. Those who suffered will be delivered, *and, by the way, they are also promised to awake unto eternal life*. A good number of scholars take this approach.[39]

A few observations demonstrate the fallacy of Frost's argument. The man clothed in linen swore to the prophet that at the terminus of the "time, times, and half a time ... when the shattering of the power of the holy people comes to an end *all these things would be finished*" (Dan. 12:7, emphasis added). The "all these things" that will be accomplished during this period includes all the events in the preceding verses (Dan. 12:1-4) including the resurrection of the dead (Dan. 12:2). Preterists cannot argue that "all these things" in Matthew 24:34 must include the coming of the Son of Man in its preceding verses (Matt. 24:27, 30) while denying the same logic as it pertains to this passage! Frost then argues that "the end" (Dan. 12:13) should not be equated with "the end of the days" that occurs in the same verse:

---

39 Frost 2012

Daniel was told to "go your way till **the end**. And you shall rest and shall stand in your allotted place at **the end of the days**." The last phrase is an equivalent to "the last day" and resurrection is to occur on that day. *Bodily* resurrection. The first phrase, however, is the end of Daniel's life. Obviously, for the angel is not telling Daniel to "go your way" until "the time of the end"! (note the Septuagint *in loc*). Neither is the "end of the days" referring to the 1,290 or 1,335 days. The "end of the days" is in reference to *Dan* 12.2, the resurrection of the dead. Daniel, who will eventually die (reach his end) is promised participation in the resurrection. No notation of time is given for that time other than "the last day" or "end of the days" of history (which was thoroughly common in Second Temple Judaism)[40].

Frost's "piecemeal approach" to dividing the chapter is forced and unconvincing. He wants to convince the reader that the unprecedented tribulation (Dan. 12:1) occurred in AD 70, but that the resurrection of the dead (Dan. 12:2) will be fulfilled in our future. He also wants to divorce the 1,290 days (Dan. 12:11) from "the end of the days" (Dan. 12:13). He then separates "the end" (Dan. 12:13), which he interprets as instruction for the prophet to wait for his death, from "the end of the days" within the same verse. However, the language of "the end" is found elsewhere in the prophecy, where it clearly means the end of the age (Dan. 11:27, 35, 40; 12:4).

The correct meaning of the passage is that the prophet would experience death ("you shall rest") and wait until "the end of the days" (Dan 12:13), the antecedent of which includes the 1,290 days (Dan. 12:11-12), the vast majority of which will comprise the unprecedented tribulation of 3.5 years. This fits appropriately with the argument in previous chapters of this book that the return of Jesus and the resurrection of the dead will *immediately* follow the unprecedented tribulation.

---

40 Ibid.

Millennial Temple and Sacrifice

Most premillennial interpretations of Ezekiel 40-48 allow for a millennial temple with sacrifices. DeMar admits that Ezekiel's temple prophecy describes sacrifices that result in atonement. However, he objects to the premillennial interpretation on the following grounds:

> This supposed millennial temple is of special interest since it depicts animal sacrifices 'to make atonement' (Ezek. 45:15, 17, 20). The word 'atonement' is used in the Pentateuch to describe Old Testament propitiatory sacrifices, the very thing Jesus came to abolish through His own shed blood ... Such a millennial temple would require Jesus to officiate over the very animal sacrifices that He shed His blood to replace. ... This vision should not be projected nearly twenty-five hundred years into the future into some earthly millennial kingdom where sacrifices will be offered *for atonement* in the presence of the crucified Christ.[41]

Most premillennial schemas for Ezekiel's temple prophecy interpret the sacrifices here as having a *memorial* function comparable to how the Eucharist or Lord's Supper memorializes the Lord's sacrificial death (Luke 24:35; 1 Cor. 11:24-26). Yet Hanegraaff asks, "Does the Bible indeed prophesy a rebuilt temple with reinstituted temple sacrifices that are 'for atonement rather than a memorial'"?[42] Hanegraaff sees the prophecy as providing the reader with an "either-or" interpretive decision. The writer of the book of Hebrews wrote, "For it is impossible for the blood of bulls and goats to take away sins" (Heb. 10:4), yet we know that the offerings atoned for sins during the Old Testament period. We can reconcile this apparent discrepancy by recognizing that the blood of animals could not atone for sins except *as the offerings looked beyond to the eternal blood of the new covenant in Jesus Christ.* Animal sacrifices by themselves did not take away sins offered prospectively in the Old Testament, nor will they *retrospectively* in the millennium.

41 DeMar 1999, pp. 97, 98
42 Hanegraaff 2007, p. xxvii

The prophet Ezekiel depicted a future, literal temple that will exist during the millennium (Ezek. 40-48 cf. Isa. 60:3, 13; 62:9; 66:18-23; Jer. 33:17-22; Mic. 4:1-3; Joel 3:18; Zech. 14:20-21; Mal. 3:2-4). This temple cannot be the Second Temple, even after Herod's renovation, because this structure was infinitesimally smaller than the edifice depicted by the prophet Ezekiel. Similarly, the city and temple complex in the prophecy cannot be equated with the new Jerusalem in the book of Revelation because the latter structure will be exponentially larger (Rev. 21:16-17). Many preterists posit that Ezekiel's prophecy is an *allegory*, describing only the New Testament church. As expected, DeMar insists that the premillennial interpretation of Ezekiel's temple is incompatible with the new covenant church as the greater temple. He remarks, "But this passage [Ezek. 40-48] is simply a visionary expression of the faithful remnant that returned after the exile and the glorious future they would have. ... By extension, Ezekiel's temple is a picture of the New Covenant, under which the church, made up of believing Jews and Gentiles, is the new temple."[43]

However, the prophet spilled much ink describing the temple and its city, providing the reader with nine lengthy chapters that detail minute architectural dimensions, sacrificial procedures, marriage and grooming laws, festival laws, and geographical boundaries that were never fulfilled. This is hardly a proof text for an allegory! The details of this blueprint prohibit any consistent allegorical interpretation.

A New Creation

Premillennialism maintains the traditional interpretation that Jesus Christ will personally usher in a thousand years of peace, tranquility, justice, and abundance upon Earth. This will begin when God's original creation, "the heavens and the earth" (Gen. 1:1-2:1), is transformed into a state of "paradise restored" (Isa. 65:17-25; 66:22ff; 2 Peter 3:12-13; Rev. 21:1-22:5).

---

43 DeMar 1999, pp. 95-96

By contrast, many preterists argue that the appearance of this new creation, "a new heaven and a new earth" (Rev. 21:1), symbolizes the arrival of the new covenant in the first century AD, most often seen as having occurred during the so-called "transition period" between the crucifixion of Jesus and the destruction of the earthly Jerusalem in AD 70,[44] or less often, during one of these two events. The dissolution of the old cosmos is believed to symbolize the "passing away" of the Mosaic covenant during this period. Many preterists interpret the harlot city of Babylon as a symbol for the earthly Jerusalem, which they believe was destroyed in AD 70 to make way for the heavenly descent of the virgin bride--"the holy city, new Jerusalem" (Rev. 21:2). They also see the new Jerusalem as a symbol for the new covenant or the new covenant church.

The preterist interpretation of the new creation reveals a glaring anachronism. The apostle John saw that the old cosmos must completely "pass away" *before* the new cosmos can arrive. He wrote, "Then I saw a new heaven and a new earth, for the first heaven and the first earth had passed away. And I saw the holy city, new Jerusalem, coming down out of heaven from God" (Rev. 21:1-2; cf. 20:11-12). The participle γὰρ ("for") is causative and demonstrates that the new cosmos will appear *because* the old cosmos will have been removed. The implication for the preterist position is that the new covenant could not have arrived before the old covenant passed away or before the harlot city is destroyed. This logically means that the new covenant could *not* have begun at the cross, but had to wait for Jerusalem's destruction in AD 70, an implication that contradicts the Lord's teaching (e.g., Luke 22:20).

Many preterists teach that the new Jerusalem descended from heaven in AD 70, despite adhering to the postmillennial doctrine of Dominion Theology, which teaches that the new cosmos symbolizes a fully-Christianized planet in our future. These preterists want to "have their cake and eat it too" by interpreting the new

44 Jordan 2014, loc. 51, 75-84

creation *figuratively*, as a symbol for the new covenant, *and literally*, as a transformed Earth under Christ's dominion. Gentry summarizes this position in the following statements:

> John's picture of the new creation, however, *represents a present reality* which *the consummate order eventually fulfills, perfects, and replaces.* John's image is a picture of new covenant salvation *coming into the world in the first century* ... it seems *exegetically unlikely that we could surmise that the preceding actually applies to a reality thousands of years in the future* ...In other words, we expect the New Jerusalem order to immediately replace the Old Jerusalem, just as the new covenant immediately superseded the old covenant (Heb 8:13). *A gap seems unreasonable*—especially in light of the stated time frame [Rev 22:6][45].

> The new creation begins flowing into and impacting history in the first century long before the consummate order ... Like the mustard seed which grows to a great plant, so the first century church will work its message of peace into all the world ... In the *consummate* New Creation, this will, of course, come to full and perfect fruition as we enter into eternal bliss in our resurrected bodies (Matt. 25:34). But in the present gospel-based new creation redemptive order, we experience this *in principle*.[46]

The partial preterist view that the new creation is continually and *progressively* arriving during an extended millennium of the present church age creates significant difficulties. Most preterists teach that the new Jerusalem *fully* descended from heaven by AD 70, meaning that the new covenant descended to a new earth that at that time, only existed, to borrow Gentry's expression, "*in principle*". This interpretation is also hermeneutically inconsistent. It teaches that the passing away of the old creation is a *metaphor* for the dissolution of the Jewish kingdom and old covenant in AD 70, while maintaining that the appearance of the new creation describes a *literal* recreated universe in our future! In addition, Gentry backs himself into a corner by demanding that the arrival

---

45 Gentry 2008, pp. 114-15
46 Gentry 2010b, pp. 126, 129, 130

of the new creation (Rev. 21:1-22:5) be included in the events that "must soon take place" (Rev. 22:6). He wrote, "It seems exegetically unlikely that we could surmise that the preceding description actually applies to a reality thousands of years in the future."[47] This is an odd contention because he agrees with the futurist claims that the new creation has *not yet* fully arrived and that it did not "soon take place."

Most preterists do not see the millennium as having been fulfilled in AD 70 because this would mean that the general resurrection also took place in the first century, as full preterists argue. The general resurrection and judgment of the dead will occur after the millennium (Rev. 20:5, 11-15), most likely when the old cosmos disappears (Rev. 20:11; 21:1). The apostle John wrote, "Then I saw a great white throne and him who was seated on it. From his presence *earth and sky fled away*, and no place was found for them. And I saw the dead, great and small, standing before the throne ... And the dead were judged" (Rev. 20:11-12). Despite their attempts to escape this conclusion, partial preterists *must* accept that the old cosmos (i.e., the Mosaic covenant according to their interpretation) had passed away by AD 70; nevertheless, they cannot accept this without accepting the heretical notion that the resurrection and judgment also took place at that time.

An alternative preterist interpretation sees a fully consummated new creation as having arrived in AD 70. This tragic implication, associated with the full preterist position, compromises the fundamental Christian doctrine that sin and death will be forever vanquished in the new creation. The apostle John described these conditions in the new Jerusalem: "[the Lord] will wipe away every tear from their eyes, and death shall be no more, neither shall there be mourning, nor crying, nor pain anymore, for the former things have passed away" (Rev. 21:4). If this prophecy was fulfilled in AD 70, it must be dismissed as mere allegory by preterists who hold to this interpretation of the new creation. Furthermore, this interpretation leaves these preterists without any exegetical

47 Ibid., p. 126

grounds to suggest that sin and death will be terminated at any point in the future.

15

The Cost of Consistency

Many preterists recognize the artificiality of dividing the Olivet Discourse and other eschatological prophecies into preterist and futurist components. Some preterists, such as R. T. France and Kenneth Gentry, argue that dividing these prophecies is not hermeneutically inconsistent (see Chapter Nine). Other preterists, such as Gary DeMar and N. T. Wright, argue that most eschatological prophecies were *entirely* fulfilled in the first century AD. This viewpoint presents an entirely different set of difficulties. For example, this position does not leave these preterists *with a single reference* in the Synoptic Gospels that mentions the bodily return of Jesus Christ! Suffice to say, it is highly unlikely that Matthew, Mark, and Luke omitted an event of such theological magnitude. This chapter will explore many other implications that arise from preterist hermeneutics.

The Representative You

The Lord Jesus taught, "When they persecute *you* in one town, flee to the next, for truly, I say to *you*, *you* will not have gone through all the towns of Israel before the Son of Man comes" (Matt. 10:23, emphasis added). The historic church has understood this verse as referring to the Lord's second advent. The second person plural ("you") in this passage and in the Olivet Discourse has a *representative* function and refers to the Lord's disciples in general (i.e., the church) and not to the Twelve in a restricted sense. Sproul explained that Reformers such as John Calvin interpreted the Olivet Discourse in this manner. He wrote, "Though Calvin acknowledged that the problem of false christs plagued the early church after the resurrection of Christ, he applied the warning to the church of all ages, not limiting it to the church of the first century. This application is quite legitimate, as the appearance of imposters is a perennial problem."[1]

Preterists vehemently disagree with this approach, arguing that "you" in these passages must be understood as referring *only* to the original disciples.[2] They see the coming of the Son of Man (Matt. 10:23) as a metaphor for the ascension of Jesus and the destruction of Jerusalem in AD 70.[3] Gentry suggests this verse means that the apostles would preach the gospel of Christ so as to seal their nation's judgment: "As Israel sinfully continues to reject him, they [i.e., the apostles] will effectively secure and oversee Israel's judgment in AD 70."[4] Regarding Jesus' statement, Gentry quips, "Surely he is not referring to an event hundreds upon hundreds of years away."[5] DeMar explains that this argument also applies to the Olivet Discourse:

> ... notice how many times Jesus used the plural *you* in Matthew 24 and in the parallel passages ...Now if *you* heard Jesus say that all these things would happen to 'this genera-tion' while you were standing there listening to Him, and in every other instance of its use 'this generation' meant the present generation, and you also heard Him say that when 'you' would see these things, what would you conclude? The most natural (literal) interpretation is that it would happen to *your generation*, and maybe even to you personally.[6]

The full preterist, Ed Stevens, explains that such arguments are based on the premise of audience relevance. He wrote, "The New Testament was not written to us originally. We are reading someone else's mail."[7] Likewise, Hanegraaff claims that in these passages Jesus was "directly and obviously addressing a first-cen-

1 Sproul 1998, p. 41
2 DeMar 1999, pp. 30, 573; Hanegraaff 2007, pp. 5-7, 72, 81, 87, 89, 94; Mathison 2004, p. 175; Russell 2003, p. 115; Sproul 1998, pp. 41, 55
3 Gentry 2010c, loc. 373; Hanegraaff 2007, p.18; Mathison 2004, p. 175
4 Ibid., loc. 470
5 Ibid., loc. 1252, 1259
6 DeMar 1999, p. 59
7 Stevens, Edward as quoted in Russell 2003, p. ix

tury audience. When someone attempts to convince them otherwise, their baloney detectors should immediately register full."[8]

Preterists are unable to bear the burden of proving that Jesus restricted his intended audience to those *first* disciples who heard the sound of his voice. The textual evidence demonstrates that Christ often employed the second person plural ("you") to address his disciples *through all time*. Consider the following teachings in Matthew's Gospel where the specified subject is "you": the moral imperatives in the Sermon on the Mount (Matt. 5:11-7:20), the requirement of absolute righteousness (Matt. 5:20), the knowledge of the secrets of the kingdom (Matt. 13:11-17), the imperative to become like little children (Matt. 18:3), instructions on church discipline (Matt. 18:15-19), the command to be servants (Matt. 20:25-27; 23:11), the promise of answered prayer (Matt. 21:21-22), the command to observe the Lord's Supper (Matt. 26:27-29), and the command to fulfill the Great Commission (Matt. 28:16-20). A consistent application of the preterist argument regarding the second person plural would mean that these teachings were *only* intended for the original hearers and not for the historic church! In essence, the preterist's failure to recognize the fluidity of language unwittingly compromises any modern application of the message of Jesus.

The preterist argument about the second person plural also requires Jesus' original audience to have personally witnessed the events described in the Olivet Discourse. The Lord prophesied, "So when *you* see the abomination of desolation ... standing in the holy place" (Matt. 24:15, emphasis added). Preterists contend that the "you" here refers only to the small band of original disciples or to the Twelve (cf. Matt. 24:3; Mark 13:3). This interpretation requires the original hearers to have seen the abomination of desolation. Nevertheless, nearly all the original hearers of the discourse died before the First-Jewish Roman War of AD 67-70. This consideration is based on the ages of the hearers when the discourse was given and the historical records regarding the deaths

8   Hanegraaff 2007, p. 86

of the apostles. The few who were still alive, such as the apostle John, likely lived outside the vicinity of Jerusalem at this time so that they did not see any such event at the temple.

The second person plural ("you") argument is a double-edged sword for preterists because consistency demands that the argument would equally apply to the third person plural ("we"). In other words, if Jesus and the apostles used "you" to refer *in the restricted sense* to their immediate audiences, they must *necessarily* have included themselves with their immediate audience when they used "we". The apostle Paul *did* address his readers as "we who are alive, who are left until the coming of the Lord" (1 Thess. 4:15), "we who are alive, who are left, will be caught up together with them in the clouds to meet the Lord in the air" (1 Thess. 4:17), and "we shall not all sleep" (1 Cor. 15:51). J. Stuart Russell pointed this out, saying, "But the question for us is, To whom does the apostle refer when he says, '*We* shall not all sleep,' etc.? Is it to some hypothetical persons living in some distant age of time, or is it of the Corinthians and himself that he is thinking?"[9] Thus preterists extract the implication that Paul's original audience lived to see the return of Jesus and was included in the rapture! Russell argued that this preterist argument, when consistently applied, leads the preterist into *full* preterism.

Consistent Preterism

Many preterists adopt consistent, or full, preterism in order to maintain a consistent hermeneutic. Full preterism is the view that every prophecy of the Bible was fulfilled no later than the destruction of Jerusalem in AD 70. The most notable examples of such prophecies include the glorious return of Jesus, the general resurrection of the dead, the day of the Lord, and the arrival of the new heaven and new earth. The strength of this position lies in its agreement with the biblical testimony that the unprecedented tribulation would be *immediately* followed by the Lord's return from heaven and the resurrection of the dead. Partial preterists have

9   Russell 2003, p. 208

given this eschatological position the label "hyper-preterism" and have joined futurists in rejecting full preterism as blatant heresy. This book aims to critique the foundations of preterism and does not undertake the task of dismantling full preterism per se. However, the negative *implications* of consistent preterism will be briefly examined in this chapter.

Most seriously, consistent preterism steals away the blessed hope of the resurrection from the dead. R. C. Sproul correctly notes, "The great weakness of full preterism—and what I regard to be its fatal flaw—is its treatment of the final resurrection."[10] Full preterists reject the ancient Jewish and Christian teachings regarding the nature of resurrection: according to traditional instruction, corpses are reconstituted, resuscitated, and given immortal glory.[11]

Ed Stevens' Individual Body at Death position (IBD) represents one example of this rejection. His position is based on the premise that modern Christians will never be resurrected because the resurrection was a singular event that took place in AD 70. Stevens and his colleagues argue that essentially, resurrection consisted only of *disembodied souls being raised out of Sheol or Hades.*[12] This view reduces resurrection to a mere transmigration of the soul reminiscent of Gnosticism, Manichaeism, and Neo-Platonism. Other full preterists have embraced Max King's Collective Body View (CBV).[13] King contended that the resurrection is *not concerned with individual corpses or the afterlife*! He defined resurrection as the corporate or collective experience of Israel that transformed "the dead carcass of Judaism" into the new covenant church during the years leading up to AD 70. The IBD and CBV views deny that the resurrection is about the rising of individual bodies from the tombs and graves.

10 Sproul 1998, p. 217
11 For a full evaluation of the Jewish and Christian views, see Wright, N. T. 1996
12 Stevens 2003; Harding 2005
13 See Preston 2012; Similarly King 1987

Contrary to the claims of full preterism, the Bible affirms that resurrection is *the miraculous raising of corpses from the tombs and graves into a glorified state of existence.* The prophet Isaiah foretold, "Your [Israel's] dead shall live; their bodies shall rise. You who dwell in the dust, awake and sing for joy! ... The earth will give birth to the dead ... the Lord is coming out from his place . ... The earth will disclose the blood shed on it, and will no more cover its slain" (Isa. 26:19, 21). The book of Daniel, alluding to Isaiah's prophecy, reads as follows: "And many of those who sleep in the dust of the earth shall awake, some to everlasting life, and some to shame and everlasting contempt" (Dan. 12:2). In addition, the resurrected body of our Lord Jesus Christ consisted of "flesh and bones" (Luke 24:39), and the *bodies* of the saints that emerged from the tombs were recognizable to the inhabitants of Jerusalem (Matt. 27:51-53). Finally, the apostle Paul taught that God "who raised Christ Jesus from the dead will also give life *to your mortal bodies* through his Spirit who dwells in you" (Rom. 8:11, emphasis added; cf. Rom. 8:17-25, 30; 1 Cor. 6:13-15), and "will *transform our lowly body* to be like his glorious body" (Phil. 3:21, emphasis added; cf. 1 Cor. 15:43-44).

Consistent preterism is the modern expression of the ancient Hymenaean heresy. This heresy appeared during the apostolic period, as evidenced by the apostle Paul's warnings to Timothy about certain men who were teaching *that the resurrection had already happened.* Paul warned, "But avoid irreverent babble, for it will lead people into more and more ungodliness, and their talk will spread like gangrene. Among them are Hymenaeus and Philetus, who have swerved from the truth, saying that the resurrection has already happened. They are upsetting the faith of some" (2 Tim. 2:17-18). The apostle considered the Hymenaean doctrine a form of blasphemy that was causing believers to reject "faith and a good conscience" and to make "shipwreck of their faith" (1 Tim. 1:18-20). The results of such teaching was (and is!) ungodliness (2 Tim. 2:17). Similarly, Paul warned the saints in Thessalonica to avoid the notion that the day of the Lord had already taken place. He admonished, "Now concerning the coming of our Lord Jesus Christ and our being gathered together to him, we ask you, brothers, not to be quickly shaken in mind or alarmed, either by a spirit or a spoken word, or a letter seeming to be from us, to the effect that the day of the Lord has come. Let no one deceive you in any way" (2 Thess. 2:1-3).

Full preterists deny that the Bible *explicitly* addresses the issue of the afterlife for Christians who live beyond AD 70. Consequently, the implication for this view is that any Christian hope of a glorious afterlife, eternal reward, or eternal inheritance is *based entirely on conjecture, inference, and deductive speculation, having no clear prophetic precedent in the Scriptures.* Chilton explained, "According to this interpretation (which might be called *post-everythingism*), we are now living in a never-ending limbo era, with literally no prophecies left to be fulfilled. The world will just go on and on and on and on, until ... ?"[14] The result is that full preterists often find themselves engaged in theological speculations, bizarre conundrums, and unnecessary doubts. According to full preterism, the answers to life's ultimate questions are based on a "theology of inference" instead of clear Scriptural reasoning. What follows are examples of the awkward questions that necessarily arise from the full preterist system:

- Did Jesus retain his physical body upon his ascension if resurrection is not about glorified, physical bodies?

- Do modern Christians have a mandate to "make disciples of all nations" if the Great Commission was fulfilled at the end of the Jewish age?

- Can Satan tempt people today if he was thrown into the eternal lake of fire in AD 70?

- Can modern Christians *actually* sin if we live in the new heaven and new earth where sin, death, and hell do not exist?

---

14 Chilton 2007, p. 138

- Can we live godly lives now if the day of the Lord is the raison d'etre for godly living (Matt. 25:31-46; Col. 1:22-23; 1 Thess. 5:23-24; 2 Thess. 1:6-10, 12; 2 Peter 3:11) and it occurred in AD 70?

- Do we need spiritual gifts, such as pastors and teachers, if the church has attained to "the knowledge of the Son of God, to mature manhood, to the measure of the stature of the fullness of Christ" (Eph. 4:13)?

- Should we observe the Lord's Supper if we were commanded to do it to proclaim the Lord's death "until he comes" (1 Cor. 11:26)?

- Does the church, "the pillar and buttress of the truth" (1 Tim 3:15), need to exist in a post-AD 70 setting?

Full preterism rejects the consistent testimony of the historic church that Jesus Christ will return in the future, and it dismisses the ecumenical creeds, the theological guardrails accepted by historic Christianity to protect the church from heresy. The creeds clearly communicate that Jesus "will come to judge the living and the dead." Not surprisingly, full preterists stumble over many other doctrines that are fundamental to Christianity. For example, Don Preston undermines the doctrine of the hypostatic union of Christ by teaching that Jesus of Nazareth no longer has a physical body and is no longer human. Other full preterists, such as Max King, have embraced universalism, the teaching that all people will be saved regardless of whether they believed in Jesus during their lifetimes. Others have abandoned Christianity altogether. Even some partial preterists have rejected orthodoxy by claiming that the day of the Lord took place in the historical past (2 Thess. 2:1-3).[15]

---

15 E.g., Sproul 1998, pp. 108, 110-11, 115

The Meaning of "Mello": Soon or Certain?

Full preterists often contend that the Greek verb μέλλω always (or nearly always) conveys a sense of imminence or immediacy, and that it should be translated "be on the point of, be about to."[16] They argue that the translational biases of futurist translators have led to this verb being translated in a manner that conveys *certainty* (i.e., that an event certainly will occur) instead of *immediacy* (i.e., that an event will occur soon or immediately). They argue that the glorious return of Jesus, the resurrection of the dead, judgment day, and the arrival of the new Jerusalem must have occurred in the first century AD because of the presence of this verb (μέλλω) with respect to these events. Derivatives of this verb appear in the following eschatological passages:

> [God] "has fixed a day on which he will [μέλλει present active indicative] judge the world in righteousness by a man whom he has appointed; and of this he has given assurance to all by raising him from the dead." (Acts 17:31)

> "...having a hope in God, which these men themselves accept, that there will be [μέλλειν present active infinitive] a resurrection of both the just and the unjust." (Acts 24:15)

> "For I consider that the sufferings of this present time are not worth comparing with the glory that is to be [μέλλουσαν present active participle] revealed to us." (Rom. 8:18)

> "I charge you in the presence of God and of Christ Jesus, who is to [μέλλοντος present active participle] judge the living and the dead, and by his appearing and his kingdom,..." (2 Tim. 4:1)

> "For here we have no lasting city, but we seek the city that is to [μέλλουσαν present active participle] come." (Heb. 13:14)

The consistent preterist argument regarding μέλλω has caused some difficulties for partial preterists. For example, Gentry once argued, "When used with the aorist infinitive – as in Revelation 1:19 – the word's preponderate usage and preferred meaning is: 'be on the point of, be about to.' The same is true when the

16 Russell 2003, pp. 223, 262, 291, 304, 369, 386; cf. DeMar 1999, p. 430

word is used with the present infinitive, as in Rev. 3:10. The basic meaning in both Thayer and Abbott-Smith is 'to be about to.' Indeed 'mello' with the infinitive expresses imminence (like the future)."[17] Apparently Gentry was unaware of the implications of his statement. He limited the meaning of imminence for μέλλω to its present and aorist infinitive uses, yet he failed to consider that Acts 24:15 (above) uses the present infinitive. The implication of his position is that this verse would support the full preterist teaching that the general resurrection occurred in the first century. He later revised his view and presented it in a subsequent statement. At first glance, it appears that Gentry merely qualified his original statement, but a closer examination reveals that he failed once again to mention that Acts 24:15 uses the present infinitive. He presented his revised view in the following:

> The supposed evidence for hyperpreterism lies in the phrase "there shall certainly be a resurrection." Here the Greek words behind "there shall certainly be" is *mellein esesthai*. Since the base word *mello* can mean "about to," this statement is thought to demonstrate that Paul stated that the resurrection is "about to" happen. This is a misreading of Paul . . . In the Arndt-Gingrich-Danker *Lexicon* (p. 500) we read that when *mello* is used with a future infinitive it "denotes certainty that an event will occur in the future." That, and nothing more. This is why *all* the standard translations of the Acts 24:15 do not translate *mello* as expressing nearness, but simply as a future fact.[18]

The correct translation of a Greek word should ultimately be based upon its common usage in first-century Greek literature which is reliably conveyed in virtually all lexicons; nevertheless, preterists will likely continue to debate the correct translation of the verb μέλλω. The translation of this verb is a relative non-issue for futurist interpreters, who understand that the biblical authors portrayed the day of the Lord as *always* pressing into the present (see Chapter Two). Futurists understand that the imminence

17 Gentry 2010a, pp. 141-42
18 Gentry, Kenneth L. as quoted in Sullivan 2012 website

expressed in prophecy represents the prophetic perspective, and as such, this verb does not indicate an immediate, first-century fulfillment. The glorified Jesus is always about to judge the living and the dead.

Square Peg in A Round Hole

Those who adopt preterism must face the difficult challenge of preserving their eschatological model when it does not fit the biblical data. The temptation for the preterist is to see everything through the various lenses, or presuppositions, of preterism. Abraham Maslow once said, "I suppose it is tempting, if the only tool you have is a hammer, to treat everything as if it were a nail."[19] The interpretive framework of preterism pushes preterists to search for first-century fulfillments of prophecy, often with ridiculous outcomes. For example, Gentry interprets the great earthquake that removes every mountain (Rev. 16:18-21; cf. 6:14) as a symbol for the successful demolition crews of the Roman legions who "labored to overcome the mountainous defenses facing them."[20] He also claims that the talent-sized hailstones (Rev. 16:21) represent the stones (not comprised of ice!) that the Romans hurled at Jerusalem in AD 70.[21] He even claims that the scarlet-colored Beast speaks of Nero's *red* beard![22]

Some preterists argue that the parables of Jesus suggest that he promised to vindicate and reward his first-century saints within their lifetimes, which supposedly took place when God judged Jerusalem in AD 70. DeMar reasons that Christ promised to bring speedy justice to his elect during their lifetime because the widow in the parable of the unrighteous judge received justice *during her lifetime* (Luke 18:7-8).[23] Other preterists make the same argument with the parables found in the Olivet Discourse, including the Parable of the Faithful Servant (Matt. 24:42-51), the Parable

19 Maslow 1966 p. 15
20 Gentry 2010b, p. 94
21 Ibid., p. 99
22 Gentry 1998, p. 217
23 E.g., DeMar 1999, p. 382

of the Ten Virgins (Matt. 25:1-13), and the Parable of the Talents (Matt. 25:14-30). No futurist commentator considers this kind of interpretation as valid because the parables were never intended to be forced into this theological straitjacket. Hanegraaff admits, "Some say that a parable is not designed to walk on all fours. In other words, every detail in the story doesn't have to have an analogy. That is probably true."[24]

Preterists often force the historical evidence to fit biblical prophecies. One example is James Jordan and Gary DeMar's thesis that the attempted genocide of the Jews by Haman in the fifth century BC fulfilled Ezekiel's prophecy regarding Gog and Magog (Ezek. 38:1-39:24).[25] The fatal flaw in their arguments is that the prophetic events described by the prophet Ezekiel contradict the historical events recorded in the book of Esther. For example, Ezekiel's prophecy predicts that Gog's vast army will be utterly defeated *in the land of Israel* by a great earthquake, sword, pestilence, and "torrential rains and hailstones, and fire and sulfur" (Ezek. 38:19-22; 39:2-6). However, Haman never took a vast army into the land of Israel, and the Jews slaughtered their enemies *with swords* throughout the provinces of Persia without a single mention of an earthquake, rain, hail, or descending fire (Est. 9:2-10). Ezekiel also prophesied that the Jews living in the land of Israel will take spoils from Gog's defeated army (Ezek. 39:10), whereas the book of Esther mentions that the Jews *refused* to take plunder from their enemies (Est. 8:10, 15-16). In addition, Ezekiel's prophecy predicts that the wars of Gog and Magog will occur in "the latter years" and "the latter days" (Ezek. 38:8, 16), but the events in the book of Esther predate the first century AD, "the latter days" according to preterism, by nearly 540 years![26] Furthermore, two of the stated purposes of the war of Gog and Magog will be to ensure that the nations *never again* profane the Lord's name (Ezek. 39:7; cf. 38:16, 23; 39:6), and that "Israel shall

---

24 Keathley 2017
25 DeMar 1999, p. 368; DeMar 2012 website
26 DeMar 1999, p. 366

know that I am the LORD their God, *from that day forward*" (Ezek. 39:22, emphasis added). The complete fulfillment of Ezekiel's prophecies will mean nothing less than the nation of Israel finally and forever inheriting the blessings of the new covenant (cf. Ezek. 39:25-29). Obviously, these events await a future fulfillment, evidenced by the fact that the particular conclusions - the ultimate result specified by the prophets has, to this point, never been fully manifested in Israel or the nations.

On the other hand, preterists generally interpret the Old Testament prophets in a highly allegorical manner, resulting in, as DeMar admits, an interpretation which asserts that many prophecies had been fulfilled when the Jews returned from the Babylonian exile, or when the first-century Jewish church was established.[27] The preterist interpretation of Zechariah 14 illustrates this allegorical method of interpretation. The prophecy reads as follows:

> [1]Behold, a day is coming for the LORD, when the spoil taken from you will be divided in your midst. [2]For I will gather all the nations against Jerusalem to battle, and the city shall be taken and the houses plundered and the women raped. Half of the city shall go out into exile, but the rest of the people shall not be cut off from the city. [3]Then the LORD will go out and fight against those nations as when he fights on a day of battle. [4]On that day his feet shall stand on the Mount of Olives that lies before Jerusalem on the east, and the Mount of Olives shall be split in two from east to west by a very wide valley, so that one half of the Mount shall move northward, and the other half southward. [5]And you shall flee to the valley of my mountains, for the valley of the mountains shall reach to Azal. And you shall flee as you fled from the earthquake in the days of Uzziah king of Judah. Then the LORD my God will come, and all the holy ones with him. [6]On that day there shall be no light, cold, or frost. [7]And there shall be a unique day, which is known to the LORD, neither day nor night, but at evening time there shall be light. [8]On that day living waters shall flow out from Jerusalem, half of them to the eastern sea and half of them to the western sea. It shall continue in summer as

27 DeMar 1999, p. 408

in winter. [9] And the LORD will be king over all the earth. On that day the LORD will be one and his name one. [10] The whole land shall be turned into a plain from Geba to Rimmon south of Jerusalem. But Jerusalem shall remain aloft on its site from the Gate of Benjamin to the place of the former gate, to the Corner Gate, and from the Tower of Hananel to the king's winepresses. [11] And it shall be inhabited, for there shall never again be a decree of utter destruction. Jerusalem shall dwell in security. (Zech. 14:1-11)

This prophecy predicts the return of Christ Jesus and the deliverance of the Jewish remnant from the forces of the invading nations at the end of the age (Zech. 14:1-5; cf. Ezek. 38-39; Zech. 12:9-10; 14:12-21). The prophet Zechariah predicted that the Lord will go forth to "fight against those nations [that had gathered against Jerusalem = v. 2] as when he fights on a day of battle" (Zech. 14:3) and "his feet shall stand on the Mount of Olives" (v. 4), resulting in a massive earthquake. Zechariah prophesied that the earthquake will create a new valley through which those in the vicinity of Jerusalem can flee (Zech. 14:5). He explains that at that time, "the LORD my God will come, and all the holy ones with him" (Zech. 14:5; cf. 12:9-10; Matt. 25:31), but only God knows the exact day on which this will take place (Zech. 14:6; cf. Matt. 24:36; Mark 13:32). The prophet details the topographical changes that will alter the land of Israel (Zech. 14:8, 10). He explains that "the LORD will be king over all the earth" and "Jerusalem shall dwell in security" (Zech. 14:9, 11). Nothing in this passage indicates that it should be interpreted metaphorically.

N. T. Wright admits that Jesus delivered his Olivet Prophecy on the Mount of Olives because it served as a reminder of the eschatological prophecy of Zechariah 14. He explains, "The context is the coming of the divine kingdom (Zechariah 14.9) and the coming great battle of the nations against Jerusalem (14.1-3). Zechariah 14.4-5 speaks of Israel's god standing on the Mount of Olives, and of a great earthquake, after which 'YHWH your god will come, and all the holy ones with him'."[28] The Mount of

28 Wright 1996, p. 344

Olives described in Zechariah's prophecy is also reminiscent of the angel's promise, given in that very location, predicting that the glorified Jesus "will come in the same way as you saw him go into heaven" (Acts 1:11). This promise, coupled with Zechariah's prophecy, strongly suggests that Christ will descend from heaven to stand upon the Mount of Olives and to make war with his enemies.

Many preterists equate the eschatological battle of Zechariah 14 with the Roman destruction of Jerusalem in AD 70. The greatest difficulty with this interpretation is that the prophecy predicts that the Lord will arrive with his angels to *deliver* the Jewish people and to fight against those who had destroyed Jerusalem (Zech. 14:3-5; cf. 12:7-9). Aware of this difficulty, DeMar argues that this prophecy was fulfilled when God turned his wrath against Rome after using the empire to judge Jerusalem.[29] However, the Roman Empire prospered for several centuries beyond Jerusalem's fall in AD 70. DeMar continues his allegorical interpretation of the prophecy by arguing that the mountains (Zech. 14:4-5) are not actual mountains, but symbols that represent kingdoms![30] He also claims that the earthquake at the Mount of Olives (Zech. 14:4) is a metaphor for the "breaking down of the Jewish/Gentile division" (cf. Eph. 2:14).[31] DeMar simply cannot allow for a literal fulfillment of the prophecy because it supports the traditional, futurist interpretation.

One hallmark of preterism is its insistence upon the early date (circa AD 67-68) for the writing of the book of Revelation.[32] This position rests upon several considerations, which were discussed in previous chapters. Certain scholars of the late-date persuasion have adequately addressed these considerations, and therefore, they will not be detailed in this book. However, one consideration worth mentioning is the preterist contention that the fiery destruc-

29 DeMar 1999, p. 439
30 Ibid., p. 437
31 DeMar 2017 website
32 See Gentry 1998, p. 115

tion of the great harlot city of Babylon (Rev. 14:8; 16:19; 17-18) was fulfilled in the destruction of Jerusalem in AD 70. Some futurist interpreters accept many of the arguments in favor of this identification, but see the harlot city as referring, at least in part, to the *future* Jerusalem that will be subjugated by the Antichrist (Dan. 11:41, 45; 2 Thess. 2:4).

Preterist conclusions drive many of its proponents to innovate novel interpretations, but which are based on sloppy exegesis. Worse yet, many of these innovations are examples of the extreme "newspaper exegesis" of which they accuse dispensationalists; in fact, they make Hal Lindsey's "Cobra helicopters" seem comparatively mild. Proper exegesis would lead preterists to the literal interpretations found in respected conservative commentaries. But as we have demonstrated, they would rather completely rework the eschatological passages than embrace the futurist position. Those who stop short of embracing consistent preterism are still compelled, by the magnetism of their presuppositions, to conform the data accordingly, thus running roughshod over many exegetical considerations. Consequently, they are driven by constraint to maintain extreme interpretations that strain credulity.

16

Preterism as Replacement Theology

The heart of preterism is supersessionism, otherwise known as replacement theology or fulfillment theology. This is the teaching that the new covenant church has *completely* replaced the Jews as the covenant people of God. According to preterism, the destruction of the Jewish kingdom and temple in AD 70 demonstrates that God has divorced the Jews for disobeying him and rejecting his Son. According to preterism, God no longer considers the Jews his covenant nation. Consequently, any remnants of Judaism beyond AD 70 represent a mere façade of the covenant that had previously existed between the Lord and his elect nation. For example, Hanegraaff teaches that the genealogical relationship of the Jews to Abraham is no longer meaningful since "The true church is true Israel, and true Israel is truly the church."[1] Gentry explains that "Israel has been rejected as the favored people of God" so that Christianity now is the "new approach to God."[2] He surmises that Jesus rebuked Israel for its "corporate failure as the people of God" and that now "God is turning from the Jews to the world".[3] According to Gentry, the fall of Jerusalem in AD 70 concluded the old covenant and freed the church from "its bondage to Judaism."[4] He also claims that the theme of the book of Revelation is the divorce of old covenant Israel "as God's people" so that he may "take a new wife", the new covenant church.[5] Chilton emphasized the apparent irreversibility of this action by adding that Jerusalem has been "divorced

---

1 Hanegraaff 2007, p. 49
2 Gentry 2010b, p. 143
3 Gentry 2010c, loc. 620, 700-05
4 Ibid., loc. 2411, 2369
5 Gentry 2010b, pp. 141, 140

and executed".[6] J. Stuart Russell agrees that the Jews "ceased to be the covenant nation" when the theocratic nation of Jews was dissolved in AD 70.[7] He explained that the removal and repudiation of the Jewish economy demonstrated this reality:

> Although, therefore, the great barriers to the introduction of all men, without distinction, into the privileges of the children of God were virtually removed by the death of Christ upon the cross, yet the formal and final demonstration that 'the way into the holiest of all' was now thrown open to all mankind, was not made until the whole framework of the Mosaic economy, with its ritual, and temple, and city, and people, was publicly and solemnly repudiated; and Judaism, with all that pertained to it, was for ever swept away.[8]

> We are given to understand also that the close of the Jewish dispensation, the abrogation of the legal economy, and the destruction of the city and temple of Jerusalem, indicated the dissolution of the peculiar relation between Jehovah and the nation of Israel. The nation had rejected its King, and the King had judged the nation; and the Messianic mission, both for mercy and for judgment, was then fulfilled. ... and the whole frame and fabric of Judaism were shattered and destroyed for ever. ... His [Jesus'] mission as the *King of Israel* is fulfilled; the covenant-nation no longer exists ...[9]

Preterist James Jordan details how many preterists understand the implications of AD 70 for the identity of God's chosen people. He writes the following:

> The Church is the new chosen people, the new priestly nation. With the elimination of the old chosen people in AD 70, the designation of everyone else as 'Gentiles' ceased to have any meaning. While people who are racially and culturally Jewish and Greek and Roman continued to exist after AD 70, these people no longer had the particular callings they had in the Old Creation. The Roman Empire was no longer a special Guardian Beast, and the Jews were no longer a special

---

6   Chilton 2007, p. 191
7   Russell 2003, pp. 204, 546
8   Ibid., p. 230
9   Ibid., p. 537

priestly nation. After AD 70, all that remain are believers and unbelievers.[10]

To a Nation Producing Its Fruit

Preterists tout many of the Bible passages that other supersessionists use to promote replacement theology. One such passage is Jesus' Parable of the Wicked Husbandmen (Matt. 21:33-46; Mark 12:1-12; Luke 20:9-19). The parable is a retelling of Isaiah's song about God's vineyard where the symbolic vineyard is identified as "the house of Israel" (Isa. 5:1-7). Jesus' parable describes a master who plants a vineyard, leaves for another country, and sends his servants to gather his fruit from the master's tenants. In a shocking act of defiance, the tenants beat and murder the servants and the master's son-heir. The parable describes the consequences for such insolence: "'When therefore the owner of the vineyard comes, what will he do to those tenants?' They [the chief priests and elders] said to him, 'He will put those wretches to a miserable death and let out the vineyard to other tenants who will give him the fruits in their seasons.' ... 'Therefore I [Jesus] tell you, the kingdom of God will be taken away from you and given to a people producing its fruits'" (Matt. 21:40-41, 43).

Preterists subtly advance a supersessionist interpretation by neglecting the fact that the New Testament church is comprised of believing gentiles *and Jews*. Gentry correctly observes that the kingdom of God was effectively taken away from national Israel and given to Christianity, a new "holy nation" (cf. 1 Peter 2:9), in the first century AD.[11] Chilton took this a step further by claiming that this parable refers to *a gentile nation* replacing the nation of Israel.[12] Similarly, Kik declares that "the Gentiles would take their [the Jews'] place."[13]

10 Jordan 2014, loc. 482
11 Gentry 2010c, loc. 527, 557, 1902; Gentry 2010b, pp. 37, 55
12 Chilton 2007, p. 78
13 Kik 1971, p. 78

Contrary to these claims, the statement that "the kingdom of God will be taken away from you and given to a people producing its fruits" (Matt. 21:43; cf. Deut. 32:21) refers to God stripping the kingdom from the largely unrepentant nation (Matt. 21:45) and giving it to his disciples, specifically, to the *Jewish* apostles and the *Jewish* and gentile converts who received their gospel. This interpretation is further supported by the Master's statement in the preceding context that the Jewish tax collectors and prostitutes would enter God's kingdom (Matt. 21:31), the very ones that people normally presume would be the last to enter, thereby confirming the essence of God's election, which is always independent of merit or demerit, and always confounds the proud. Furthermore, this stripping of the kingdom from the Jewish nation began shortly after Pentecost and did not wait for the destruction of Jerusalem in AD 70. Finally, it may be preferable to interpret the arrival of the vineyard owner as the return of Christ at the end of the age to destroy the ungodly and to reward his saints (cf. 2 Thess. 1:7-10; 2 Peter 3:4-7).

Preterists also advance their supersessionism by appealing to the narrative of Jesus' cursing of the barren fig tree (Matt. 21:18-22; Mark 11:12-14, 20-25; cf. Luke 13:6-9). Matthew recounted this event: "In the morning, as he [Jesus] was returning to the city, he became hungry. And seeing a fig tree by the wayside, he went to it and found nothing on it but only leaves. And he said to it, 'May no fruit ever come from you again!' And the fig tree withered at once" (Matt. 21:18-19). Many preterists teach that the barren fig tree in this prophetic drama is a metaphor for the kingdom of Israel.[14] Gentry suggests that the cursing of the tree signifies the destruction of Jerusalem in AD 70.[15] In his view, the curse functioned as a warning that the Jewish nation had "reached a point of no return."[16]

---

14 Chilton 2007, p. 80; DeMar 1999, p. 400; Gentry 2010b, p. 142
15 Gentry 2010c, loc. 303, 519
16 Ibid., loc. 519

A few observations about the passage are helpful at this point. First, the purpose of the narrative is to demonstrate that the prayer of faith is effective (Matt. 21:21-22; Mark 11:21-25), not to depict the cursing of the Jewish nation in perpetuity. Second, although the barren fig tree likely functions as a metaphor (cf. Mic. 7:1; Hos. 9:10), the larger context limits the symbol to the *contemporary* kingdom and its leaders--the chief priests, scribes, and Pharisees (Matt. 21:15, 23, 45). Furthermore, the Jewish disciples of Jesus produced *good* fruit (Matt. 3:10; 7:17-19; 13:23; John 15:2-8, 16), and the Lord made his Jewish apostles the leaders of his new nation (Matt. 19:28; Eph. 2:20; Rev. 21:10-14). The prophetic message of the cursed fig tree includes the idea that the contemporary, wicked shepherds of Israel and those who followed them would never again belong to God's kingdom. They were rejected and eventually destroyed for not recognizing the time of the Lord's visitation (Luke 19:41-44; Matt. 23:37-39), yet Jesus held out hope that the nation would eventually receive him as King (Matt. 23:39; cf. Luke 21:24; see Chapter 17).

A New Temple

Preterists have developed several theological principles related to the destruction of the Jerusalem temple in AD 70. Gentry sees this event as "the final cessation" of the sacrificial system, which he believes began with Abraham.[17] He believes that the "permanent removal" of the temple "made with hands" along with its sacrifices was essential to the establishment of the new covenant.[18] He concludes, "Now I understood the catastrophic consequences of the transition from the old covenant, temple-based economy to the New Testament, spiritual economy. God removed his temple from the earth so that men might seek him in spiritual, non-bloody worship."[19] Gentry provides several implications of the removal of the old covenant temple system:

---

17 Ibid., loc. 166, 360, 1884
18 Gentry 2010b, p. 130
19 Gentry 2010c, loc. 123

[This was] the removing of the old covenant temple system so that the new covenant kingdom may remain in its place (Heb 12:27-28). In fact, the New Testament looks with holy anticipation to the final change from the old order to the new order, as the Temple system approaches its dramatic disestablishment in AD 70. This transition leads to "the restoration of all things" (Matt 17:11), "the regeneration" (Matt 19:28), the "times of refreshing" (Acts 3:19), the "times of the restitution of all things" (Acts 3:21), the "time of reformation" (Heb 9:10), a "new heavens and a new earth" (Rev 21:1; cp. 2 Cor 5:17; Gal 6:17), "all things new" (Rev 21:5 [cf. 22:6, 10]; cp. 2 Cor 5:17; Gal 6:15).[20]

Gentry incorrectly suggests that all of the above events occurred when the Second Temple was destroyed in AD 70. As argued in Chapter Six, the language of Hebrews 12:27-28 is about the eschatological day of the Lord and is not concerned with "the old covenant temple system." Ironically, Gentry's previous quote alludes to several "times" that are restricted as referring to the millennial reign of Christ, with the likely exception of "the time of reformation" (Heb. 9:10). Although many events associated with these times have "already and not yet" aspects with regard to the new covenant, none of Gentry's references point to events of AD 70. The most revealing of these biblical references is the "times of refreshing ... for restoring all the things", which the apostle Peter stated will occur when God will "send the Christ appointed for you, Jesus, whom heaven must receive until" this time arrives (Acts 3:20-21). In other words, the New Testament teaches that these times of refreshing and restoration will begin when the Lord returns from heaven! Presumably, Gentry does not realize that his quote supports the full preterist argument that the second coming of Jesus took place in AD 70.

DeMar also believes that the new covenant church is the new temple that effectively replaced the Second Temple.[21] He teaches that the Lord "rejected His once-covenanted people and their

---

20 Ibid., loc. 1555
21 DeMar 1999, pp. 62, 70; Similarly Kik 1971, p. 87

temple of stone because of the nation's rejection of the promised Son of Man" and that the new covenant nation "arose from the ashes of the temple".[22] He argues that a rebuilt temple with sacrifices would be tantamount to a wholesale rejection of the atoning blood of Jesus:

> Does the Bible, especially the New Testament, predict that the temple will be rebuilt? It does not. Why are Jews wanting to rebuild the temple? For the same reason that the temple was maintained prior to its destruction in A.D. 70—apostate Jews do not believe that Jesus is the promised Messiah. If the Jews once again build a temple and begin to offer sacrifices, this will only confirm their rejection of the atoning blood of Jesus.[23]

DeMar, alluding to Isaiah 66, proclaims that those who continued to offer animal sacrifices after the crucifixion of Jesus offered them as "the equivalent of 'swine's blood'".[24] This statement expresses the sentiment of many preterists that the sacrificial system is incompatible with the new covenant. One difficulty with this view is that the biblical prophets spoke of a future temple and sacrificial system in complete compatibility with the new covenant (as argued in Chapter 14). An additional difficulty with this statement is that it undermines the fact that the apostle Paul and the thousands of Christian Jews who lived in Judea meticulously kept the law of Moses, at the center of which is the priestly system of sacrifices and offerings, *after the death of Jesus.*

> And they [the Jerusalem elders] said to him [Paul], "You see, brother how many thousands there are among the Jews of those who have believed. They are all zealous for the law, and they have been told about you that you teach all the Jews who are among the Gentiles to forsake Moses, telling them not to circumcise their children or walk according to our customs … Take these men and purify yourself along with them and pay their expenses, so that they may shave their heads. Thus all will know that there is nothing in what they have been told

22 DeMar 1999, p. 277
23 Ibid., p. 94
24 Ibid., p. 98

about you, but that *you yourself also live in observance of the law.*" (Acts 21:20-21, 24, emphasis added)

The apostle Paul's detractors *falsely* accused him of breaking the law of Moses, refusing circumcision, and violating Jewish customs. However, Paul received ritual purification and kept a vow specifically to demonstrate that he had not willing to violate the commandments of the Torah or command the Diaspora Jews to transgress them. In his trial before the Roman governor, Festus, Paul argued, "Neither against the law of the Jews, nor against the temple, nor against Caesar have I committed any offense" (Acts 25:8). Whereas the Jerusalem Council had strongly dissuaded *gentile* Christians from observing the law of Moses (Acts 15), the Scriptures above prove beyond dispute that the *Jewish* believers continued to zealously observe the laws and ordinances *after* the counsel made its ruling. Torah observance among Jewish believers presumably continued until the destruction of the temple in AD 70 rendered it impossible.

The biblical evidence presented here reveals DeMar's dilemma. He must either (1) admit the compatibility of the gospel and Jewish observance of the law of Moses, as many futurists maintain, (2) argue that Spirit-filled Jews of the apostolic period committed abominations on the level of "offering swine's blood," or (3) deny that the sacrifices, offerings, vows, festivals, and purification requirements are integral to the observance of the law of Moses (cf. Acts 21:20-24; 25:8). Other preterists contend that the Torah was mandatory for the earliest Christians but only until the Romans destroyed the temple in AD 70. However, this argument implies that the destruction of the temple was in some manner necessary to fulfill the legal requirements of the Torah. This option betrays a fundamental misunderstanding about the nature of fulfillment and misses the significance of the cross of Jesus Christ in redemptive-covenantal history.

Most preterist schemas, unlike futurism, portray a simplistic view of the new covenant church replacing the Jerusalem temple. However, the Bible presents multiple *holy* temples during the new covenant administration. For example, the Scriptures describe the physical temple in Jerusalem (Matt. 24:15; Rev. 11:1-3), the actual body of Jesus as the temple (John 2:19-22; 4:10-14), individual Christians as temples (John 7:38; cf. Ezek. 47:1ff), the corporate church as the temple (1 Cor. 3:16; 6:19; Eph. 2:19-22; 1 Peter 2:4-5), the temple in heaven (Heb. 9:11-12, 23-24; Rev. 11:19; 15:5; cf. Rev. 8:3-5), and the millennial temple (Ezek. 40-47).[25] Unlike preterists, the biblical authors were comfortable with the *concurrent* existence of these new covenant temples. In addition, preterists often neglect the fact that the Jerusalem temple finds its basis in the Davidic covenant (2 Sam. 7:1-29) and not in the Mosaic covenant, forgetting that the Mosaic constructions were fashioned after heavenly designs that God showed Moses (Exod. 25:40; Heb. 8:5). Although the desert tabernacle served as a template for Solomon's temple, the Pentateuch does not formally mention a temple. Therefore, the preterist insistence that the Jerusalem temple must forever remain in ruins, because the Mosaic covenant has been transcended by the new covenant, is misguided.

The End of What?

As mentioned in previous chapters, the Old Testament describes a future period known as "the latter days" or "the last days." This period will be characterized by the unprecedented tribulation, which will result in Israel's national repentance and acceptance of the Messiah (Deut. 4:30-31; Dan. 10:14; 12:1-2; Hos. 3:5; cf. Jer. 23:20; 30:24). During this period, Israel's Messiah will destroy its enemies (Num. 24:14, 17-19), the war of Gog and Magog will occur (Ezek. 38:8, 16), the eschatological Spirit of the Lord will be poured out on everyone, and the day of the Lord will arrive (Joel 2:28-32; cf. Acts 2:16-17). The resurrection of the dead will also take place at this time (Dan. 12:1-2; cf. 10:14), more specifically on "the last day" (John 6:39-54; 11:24; 12:48). The

---

25 Similarly, Gentry recognizes the use of the term "body of Christ" to refer to the actual body of Jesus and to his corporate church in Gentry 2010b, p. 58.

holy temple in Jerusalem will be exalted above the mountains, and the nations will make pilgrimage to seek Israel's God there (Mic. 4:1-4; Isa. 2:1-5; cf. Zech. 14:9-11, 16-19).

The New Testament authors clearly taught that "the last days" and "the last hour" had arrived during the apostolic period (Acts 2:16-17; Heb. 1:1-2; 1 Peter 1:20; 1 John 2:18). Scholars have interpreted this phraseology in various ways. Many futurist scholars define the last days as the interval between the first and second advents of Christ, namely, the Christian era. Interestingly, Gentry agrees with this approach. He wrote, "The last days begin in earnest in the transitional era between Christ's death and the temple's destruction; they stretch from the first coming to his second coming, ending with the 'last day' at the resurrection (John 6:39-44; 11:24)."[26] One strength of this position is that the prophets and apostles sometimes juxtaposed "the latter days" and "the former days" (Ezek. 38:16-17; Zech. 8:11; Mal. 3:4; Rom. 15:4; Heb. 10:32).

Perhaps, it is preferable to view the eschatological "last days" and "end of all things" as having "already" arrived, in one sense, with the *inauguration* of the new covenant. This interpretation can be understood as compatible with the first. Futurists who take this approach understand "the last days" as including the final years of eschatological events (the "not yet") that will include the glorious return of Jesus to *consummate* his kingdom. Those who hold this view contend that the last days arrived in an "already and not yet" sense with the first coming of Jesus Christ (1 Peter 1:20; Heb. 1:1-2), the arrival of the eschatological Spirit (Acts 2:16-17), the conversion of the gentiles (Acts 15:16), the appearance of false prophets and antichrists (1 John 2:18-19), the manifestation of increasing lawlessness (2 Tim. 3:1-9; 2 Peter 3:3), the outbreak of tribulation (Rev. 1:9), the arrival of the new creation (2 Cor. 5:17), and the like.

Another opinion is the preterist view that "the last days" refers to the final period of the old covenant that supposedly

26 Gentry 2010c, loc. 1565

ended with Jerusalem's destruction in AD 70.[27] Many of these preterists consider the end of the age to refer to the end of Jewish polity in AD 70. J. Stuart Russell considered the end of the age the "extinction" and "termination of the Jewish age or dispensation" and the time for the "passing away" of the Mosaic economy.[28] He summarized, "It was the winding up of the Mosaic dispensation; the end of the long probation of the Theocratic nation; when the whole frame and fabric of the Jewish polity were to be swept away, and 'the kingdom of God to come with power.'"[29] R. T. France describes it as the transferring of the national kingdom of Israel to the "international people of God."[30] Gentry concurs with this assessment and adds his opinion that the destruction of Jerusalem in AD 70 terminated the old covenant age and economy.[31] He states, "This horrible judgment of God punctuates the end of the old covenant era and the beginning of Christ's kingdom on earth."[32] DeMar considers the fall of Jerusalem to be the end of "the Old Covenant order," the "consummation" of the new covenant, and the time when the new covenant was "realized in all its fullness."[33] He explains, "This fullness [of the gospel] was accomplished with the obliteration of the symbols of the Old Covenant: the temple, priesthood, and sacrificial system."[34] The age to come, in DeMar's view, designates the Christian era.[35] David Chilton states, "We must remember that 'the end' ... is *not* the end of the world, but rather *the end of the age*, the end of the temple, the sacrificial system, the covenant nation of Israel, and the last remnants of the pre-Christian era".[36] Hank Hanegraaff considers

---

27 Chilton 2007, p. 119; DeMar 1999, pp. 36, 38, 292; Mathison 2004, p. 189; Sproul 1998, p. 97
28 Russell 2003, pp. 242, 59, 25, 37, 204
29 Ibid., p. 121
30 France 1985, p. 337; Similarly DeMar 1999, p. 189
31 Gentry 2010b, pp. 91, 166
32 Gentry 2010c, loc. 1839
33 DeMar 1999, pp. 37, 55, 173
34 Ibid., p. 226
35 Ibid., p. 191
36 Chilton 2007, pp. 89, 97

AD 70 as "the end of the old covenant age" that was based on temple and sacrifices.[37] R. C. Sproul calls this the end of "the 'age of the Jews' or the Jewish dispensation."[38]

Preterists often point out that the "ends of the ages" (I Cor. 10:11), "consummation of the ages" (Heb. 9:26), "these last times" (1 Peter 1:20), "the end of all things" (1 Peter 4:7), and "the last hour" (1 John 2:18) had *arrived* during the apostolic period.[39] Sproul asked the question "What does Jesus [in the Olivet Discourse] mean by the end? The end of what? Is Jesus speaking of the end of the temple? The end of the world? The end of the age?"[40] Sproul answered, "Fundamental to preterism is the contention that the phrase 'end of the age' refers specifically to the end of the Jewish age and the beginning of the age of the Gentiles, or the church age."[41] As expected, DeMar interprets these expressions as meaning that Jerusalem and the temple would soon be destroyed in AD 70.[42] He declares, "The end of what? Jesus [in the Olivet Discourse] is answering questions about the destruction of the temple and the 'end of the age,' the end of the Jewish dispensation, the Old Covenant order."[43] DeMar reasons that the destruction of Jerusalem in AD 70 must have been "the end" because it was "the only proximate eschatological event" on the horizon.[44] DeMar's statement betrays the *faulty premise* that the destruction of Jerusalem was the only proximate event. As demonstrated in Chapters Two and Six, the day of Christ Jesus is ever near, soon, and at hand.

However, Gentry breaks rank with other preterists and agrees with futurists that the end of the age will be completed when Jesus returns in glory. He explains, "As noted, sunteleia ["end"] appears

37 Hanegraaff 2007, pp. 84-85

38 Sproul 1998, p. 56

39 Russell 2003, p. 197; Sproul 1998, pp. 96-97

40 Sproul 1998, p. 43; Similarly Sproul 1998, p. 96

41 Ibid., pp., 79-80, cf. Sproul 1998 pp. 100, 115

42 DeMar 1999, pp. 70, 87; cf. Russell 2003, p. 272

43 Ibid., p. 86

44 Ibid., p. 190

first in Matthew 24:3 and points to the end of history."[45] One difficulty with Gentry's position, not shared by the futurist view, is that it requires a distinction between "the end" of the so-called Jewish age in AD 70 and the end of the age at Christ's return. Gentry also agrees with futurism that the angelic separation of the righteous from the wicked and the subsequent fiery destruction of the wicked will occur in our future at the end of the age (Matt. 13:39-40, 49).[46] This contrasts sharply with other preterists, such as DeMar and Sproul, who consistently see the end of the age as referring to the fiery destruction of the kingdom of Israel in AD 70.[47]

Russell erroneously accused futurists of teaching that the end of the age refers to "the close of human history, the end of time, and the destruction of the earth".[48] Preterists commonly present this straw man argument against futurism. Contrary to this argument, premillennialists do *not* teach that the end of the age is the end *of the planet*. Premillennialism says that the Earth will be "destroyed" only in a limited sense, and that human history will continue well beyond the return of the Lord Jesus (see Chapter 14). By definition, premillennialism understands that the *consummated* kingdom of God will arrive "on earth as it is in heaven" and will endure for 1,000 years, climaxing in the perfect state.

Keith Mathison makes the excellent point that the reader should not "automatically assume that a reference to 'the end' means 'the end of the *Jewish* age.'"[49] Sproul admitted, "There are four references in Matthew's Gospel to 'the end of the age.' None explicitly specifies the *Jewish* age. This must be supplied on the assumption that the phrase is elliptical and the term Jewish is tacitly understood."[50] The careful reader who examines the pertinent biblical passages recognizes that the end of the age is *not*

45 Gentry 2010c, loc. 1037
46 Ibid., loc. 1032-1037
47 E.g., Sproul 1998, p. 108
48 Russell 2003, p. 121
49 Mathison 2004, p. 166
50 Sproul 1998, pp. 94-95

the termination of the Mosaic covenant or the destruction of the Jewish kingdom in AD 70. As argued in Chapter Seven, the end of the age will be concurrent with the glorious return of Christ (Matt. 24:3, 6, 14, 30). Jesus taught that God will separate the wicked from the righteous and will subsequently burn the wicked with fire at this time (Matt. 13:39-40, 49). In the age to come, the Lord will resurrect the righteous dead (Luke 20:34-35) and reward the faithful with eternal life (Mark 10:30; Luke 18:30). These descriptions of the end of the age demonstrate that it means the completion of "the present evil age" (Gal. 1:4) that is characterized by sin and death (cf. 1 Cor. 15:24). Nevertheless, once preterists decide that these end-time prophecies are *only* concerned with the events of AD 70, they necessarily redefine what "end" the apostles had in mind.

The writer of the book of Hebrews explained that Christians "have tasted the heavenly gift, have shared in the Holy Spirit, and have tasted the goodness of the word of God and the powers of the age to come" (Heb. 6:4-5). In one sense, these believers had approached the *heavenly* Jerusalem; he continues, "But you have come to Mount Zion and to the city of the living God, the heavenly Jerusalem, and to innumerable angels in festal gathering, and to the assembly of the firstborn who are enrolled in heaven, and to God, the judge of all, and to the spirits of the righteous made perfect, and to Jesus, the mediator of the new covenant" (Heb. 12:22-24). These saints had approached the heavenly Jerusalem *just as they had approached the other heavenly persons.* The writer enumerated these persons as (1) a myriads of angels, (2) the assembled saints "who are enrolled in heaven," (3) God the Father, (4) the perfected spirits of the righteous, and (5) the resurrected Jesus. He also emphasized that Christ is *in heaven* (Heb. 1:3-4, 13; 4:14; 9). Therefore, we can surmise that these enumerated *heavenly* persons belong to the *heavenly* Jerusalem. These Hebrew Christians had "already" approached the heavenly city *in the same manner* that they had approached these heavenly persons. They had "not yet" approached these beings in a literal sense *but in a certain spiritual and proleptic manner.* This passage represents another example of how believers have received the promises in an "already and not yet" manner. The present accessibility of the heavenly Jerusalem does not militate against a restored, millennial Jerusalem any more than it does against a perfected, post-millennial Jerusalem in the new heavens and new earth.

It is preferable to understand the biblical passages regarding the arrival of the last days, the last hour, and the end of the age(s) as representing the "already and not yet" principle of prophecy. Solid exegesis does not lend credence to the preterist teaching that these phrases refer to the supposed end of the Mosaic age or to the destruction of the Second Temple. In addition, the historic church has always understood that the age to come awaits a future fulfillment at the return of Jesus. This is evidenced by the statement in the Nicene Creed that "We look for the resurrection of the dead and the life of the world [literally 'age'] to come."[51] The preterist interpretation is a *derived necessity* to support preterist claims. It also supports their faulty premise that the cross of Jesus and the outpouring of the Holy Spirit did not sufficiently inaugurate the new covenant but that it would be fully inaugurated only after the Jewish kingdom had been decimated. One tragic result of this interpretation is that the prophetic future for the nation of Israel is rejected as theologically "out of bounds."

A New Creation

Russell summarizes the common preterist sentiments regarding the dissolution of the Mosaic covenant and its relationship to the dissolution of the old cosmos:

> What, then, is the great catastrophe symbolically represented as the shaking of the earth and heavens? No doubt it is the overthrow and abolition of the Mosaic dispensation, or old covenant; the destruction of the Jewish church and state, together with all the institutions and ordinances connected

---

51 "Nicene Creed," *Wikipedia*, on August 18, 2017. https://en.wikipedia.org/wiki/Nicene_Creed; The Greek phrase translated here "and life in the age to come" is ζωὴν τοῦ μέλλοντος αἰῶνος.

therewith. There were 'heavenly things' belonging to that dispensation: the laws, and statutes, and ordinances, which were divine in their origin, and might be properly called the '*spiritualia*' of Judaism—these were the *heavens*, which were to be shaken and removed. There were also 'earthly things:' the literal Jerusalem, the material temple, the land of Canaan—these were the earth, which was in like manner to be shaken and removed. The symbols are, in fact equivalent to those employed by our Lord when predicting the doom of Israel... . that is to say, the reference can only be the judgment of the Jewish nation and the abrogation of the Mosaic economy at the Parousia.[52]

As explained in Chapter Six, many preterists interpret the new heaven and earth replacing the old heavens and earth as a metaphor for the destruction of Jerusalem in AD 70 and the transition from the old to the new covenant, which they believe was completed at that time.[53]

Preterists often quote Hebrews 8:13 to support their contention that the old covenant passed away in AD 70.[54] The writer of Hebrews wrote, "In speaking of a new covenant, he [God] makes the first one obsolete. And what is becoming obsolete and growing old is ready to vanish away" (Heb. 8:13). DeMar summarizes the preterist interpretation: "With the destruction of Jerusalem in A.D. 70 the Old Covenant that had faded in glory was obliterated."[55] DeMar correctly interprets the first sentence of this passage as referring to the new covenant rendering the Mosaic covenant fulfilled in Christ. However, he reads his foregone conclusion that the "vanishing away" or supposed "obliteration" of the Mosaic covenant refers to the destruction of Jerusalem in AD 70.

The Babylonian armies under Nebuchadnezzar destroyed the kingdom of Judah and its capital, Jerusalem, razed the First

---

52 Russell 2003, pp. 289-90

53 DeMar 1999, p. 192; Gentry 2010c, loc. 1555; Kik 1971, p. 32; Russell 2003, p. 121

54 DeMar 1999, pp.37, 38; Gentry 2010c, loc. 132, 1550-55; 2192; Gentry 2010b, p. 47; Hanegraaff 2007, p.19

55 DeMar 1999, p. 225

Temple, and exiled most of the remaining Jews to Babylon in the sixth century BC. These catastrophic events effectively ended Jewish polity, yet *this did not signify the end of a future hope for the Jewish nation.* After seventy years of captivity, the small remnant of Jews returned to the Holy Land and rebuilt the holy city and temple under the direction of Nehemiah and Ezra. The reconstituted nation continued to thrive for more than six centuries, despite the fact that preterists interpret the same cosmos-ending, day of the Lord language as having been fulfilled in the Babylonian destruction of Jerusalem (Joel 2:1-11, 30-31; 3:15-16). This has substantial implications for the continuance of the Jewish nation *after* the destruction of Jerusalem in AD 70, because these events did not represent the *permanent* dissolution of the Jewish nation. Consequently, Christians should not be surprised that the Jews returned to the Holy Land to establish the State of Israel in 1948, and have plans to construct the Third Temple.

It is very disturbing that preterists believe that the crowning event of the new covenant was the *permanent* rejection of God's elect nation. At very least, the preterist theology of the permanent destruction of everything Jewish in AD 70 creates a wide berth for the anti-Semitic attitudes that have prospered under this presupposition. The discerning reader can further inquire as to whether preterists get satisfaction with the AD 70 solution to the Jewish question. Suffice it to say that the above evidence shows that preterism supports the theology of supersessionism.

17

Restoring the Kingdom to Israel

The Lord made an *everlasting* covenant with Abraham and his posterity that included giving them "all the land of Canaan for an everlasting possession" (Gen. 17:1-14). This covenant would continue as long as the nation existed ("throughout their generations," Gen. 17:7, 9), and the land of the Canaanites would henceforth belong to Abraham and his offspring (Gen. 13:15). The Bible uses the strongest Hebrew words available to communicate *the eternal perpetuity* of the land promises of the Abrahamic covenant. This is the same language that was used for God's "everlasting covenant" with Noah and every living creature on the earth: that he would never again ("for all future generations") destroy the earth with a flood (Gen. 9:12-16). The Lord promised to remember the land promises of the Abrahamic covenant "for a thousand generations." The psalmist wrote, "He [the LORD] remembers his covenant forever, the word that he commanded, *for a thousand generations*, the covenant that he made with Abraham, his sworn promise to Isaac, which he confirmed to Jacob as a statute, to Israel as an *everlasting* covenant, saying, 'To you *I will give the land of Canaan* as your portion for an inheritance'" (Ps. 105:8-11, emphasis added; cf. 1 Chron. 16:15-22).

Preterists typically deny that the land of Israel has any future prophetic significance. Hank Hanegraaff asserts, "For Palestine was but a preliminary phase in the patriarchal promise ... The climax of the promise would not be Palestine regained but Paradise restored."[1] He then rehearses a common misperception about typology, claiming that the land and the city of Jerusalem are types

---

1   Hanegraaff 2007, p. 53

of Jesus himself.[2] Preterists are unable to offer solid exegesis in support of this interpretation.

DeMar scoffs at the traditional futurist position that "the land promises were never completely fulfilled."[3] This contention betrays a fundamental misunderstanding of the nature of the land promises because *complete fulfillment* of the promises requires the conjunction of a *permanent* holding on the entire land by a *completely righteous* people. During a few brief periods of Israelite history, the nation possessed almost all the land that had been sworn to the Patriarchs. The promised boundaries of the land of Israel were to extend from the River of Egypt to the Euphrates River (Gen. 15:18-21; cf. 13:14-18). The Israelites never completely drove out the foreign nations from the land of Israel (Josh. 23:4-13; 1 Kings 4:21), despite the fact that the nation's territory extended throughout most of these boundaries after the conquest under the prophet Joshua (Josh. 21:43) and during the reign of King Solomon (1 Kings 4:21). In addition, the nation was unable to retain the land due to national disobedience. To reiterate, a temporary acquisition of the majority of the Holy Land could never fulfill the eternal land promises because only a permanent possession of the whole land by the entire nation, having obtained everlasting righteousness, will suffice.

The first return of Jacob's descendants to the Holy Land occurred after God raised up the prophet Moses to deliver them after nearly four centuries of servitude in Egypt. The Assyrians eventually destroyed the Northern Kingdom of Israel and exiled its population in 722-21 BC. The Babylonians exiled the Southern Kingdom of Judah during the years 597-581 BC and destroyed Jerusalem and the First Temple in 587-586 BC. Many Jewish exiles returned after the decree of the Persian King Cyrus in 539 BC and began construction of the Second Temple around 537 BC. The Romans under General Titus enslaved and exiled most of the Jews who survived the First Jewish-Roman War in

2 Ibid., p. 170
3 DeMar 1999, p. 398

AD 70. More recently, the Jews have suffered pogroms, the Inquisition, blood libels, the Holocaust, and Islamic jihad. Against all odds, the Jews have miraculously survived to return to the land once again, largely after the creation of the State of Israel in 1948. Despite being vastly outnumbered by Arab forces, the Jewish nation miraculously won several decisive battles in the War of Independence (1947-49), the Sinai War (1956), the Six-Day War (1967), and the Yom Kippur War (1973). The modern world is faced with the question of the secret to Jewish survival and the reason for their most recent return to the land of Israel. R. C. Sproul wondered, "What is the significance of modern Israel and Jerusalem to biblical prophecy?"[4]

The New Covenant

The Lord promised to remember his everlasting covenant by bringing the nation back to the land of Israel once they had repented of their iniquities (Lev. 26:40-45). The prophet Moses explained that this national repentance will occur in the latter days, the period when the Lord promised to reveal himself to them:

> But from there [the Diaspora] you [Israel] will seek the LORD your God and you will find him, if you search after him with all your heart and with all your soul. *When you are in tribulation, and all these things come upon you in the latter days, you will return to the Lord your God and obey his voice.* For the Lord your God is a merciful God. He will not leave you or destroy you or forget the covenant with your fathers that he swore to them. (Deut. 4:29-31, emphasis added)

There are roughly 21.7 million living Jews, with 6.3 million Jews in the State of Israel. However, this regathering to the land must be understood as preliminary and provisional because it does *not* attain to the final and permanent regeneration of the entire nation, as the prophets had promised. The modern State of Israel is largely secular and vastly different from the glorious-

---

4   Sproul 1998, p. 30

ly-transformed Jewish remnant that will have looked upon the returning Christ. This gathering will not occur until the nation repents of idolatry, humbles its uncircumcised heart, and prayerfully repents from its iniquities (Lev. 26:40-42; 1 Kings 8:33-53, 59-60; 2 Chron. 6:24-39), having been transformed by the LORD at his return (Zech. 12:10-14; cf. Isa. 66:8; Ezek. 37:11-14).

These redemptive elements form the basis for *the new covenant promises* that Moses enumerated in Deuteronomy 30:

> And when all these things come upon you [Israel], the blessing and the curse, which I have set before you, and you call them to mind among all the nations where the Lord your God has driven you, and return to the Lord your God, you and your children, and obey his voice in all that I command you today, with all your heart and with all your soul, then the Lord your God will restore your fortunes and have mercy on you, and he will gather you again from all the peoples where the Lord your God has scattered you. If your outcasts are in the uttermost parts of heaven, from there the Lord your God will gather you, and from there he will take you. And the Lord your God will bring you into the land that your fathers possessed, that you may possess it. And he will make you more prosperous and numerous than your fathers. And the Lord your God will circumcise your heart and the heart of your offspring, so that you will love the Lord your God with all your heart and with all your soul, that you may live. (Deut. 30:1-6)

This prophecy emphasizes the *certainty* of the future redemption and the Lord's intention to fulfill his salvific promises. Moses promised the nation that the Lord God *will* (1) restore their fortunes, (2) have mercy on them, (3) gather them again from all the peoples where he had scattered them (repeated phrase), (4) bring them into the land to possess the land that their fathers had previously possessed, (5) make them more prosperous and numerous than their fathers, and (6) circumcise their heart and their offspring's heart so that they love the Lord with all their heart and soul and have life. The stated promise that the God of Israel will regather the nation even if they are scattered to "the uttermost parts of heaven" (Deut. 30:4) shows that no obstacle, even 2,000 years of exile, will prevent him from bringing his people back to the promised land. The Holy One who scattered them will faithfully bring them back again, to bless them and to circumcise their hearts so that they can properly love him (Deut. 30:5-6). This will occur "in the latter days", after the nation experiences tribulation (Deut. 4:29-31; Jer. 30:6-7).

The Old Testament prophets enumerated the many blessings that the nation of Israel will receive under *the new and everlasting covenant.*

The Eternal Promises of the New Covenant

1. **The Holy Spirit and Eternal Righteousness:** The Lord will *no longer* hide his face from the nation, but will pour out his Spirit upon them (Ezek. 39:29). He will remove their stony hearts and replace them with "one heart and a new spirit" (Ezek. 11:19-20; 36:26), and he will write his law upon their heart so that they will no longer break it (Jer. 31:32-33; 32:39), but will carefully obey *all* his rules and statutes (Ezek. 11:20; 36:27; 37:24). The Spirit and fear of the Lord will prevent them from ever again turning away from him, and they *all* will be righteous (Isa. 60:21; Jer. 32:39-40; 50:20; Ezek. 36:29). He will forgive all their iniquities and never again remember their sins (Jer. 31:34; Ezek. 16:63; 36:25).

2. **The Jewish Messiah:** The Davidic Messiah will *eternally* rule over them as their king, shepherd, and prince (Ezek. 37:24-25; cf. 34:31).

3. **The Land of Israel:** The Lord will gather the entire nation to live *eternally* and peacefully in the land where the Patriarchs once lived only as aliens (Jer. 32:37, 41; Ezek. 11:17; 34:25-29; 36:24, 28; 37:25-26; 39:26-28). They will remove all abominations (Ezek. 11:18) and rebuild the waste places

once they arrive (Ezek. 36:33-34). God will multiply their population (Ezek. 37:26).

4. **God's Presence:** He will place his dwelling place and sanctuary "in their midst forevermore" (Ezek. 37:26-27). He will be their God, and they shall be his people (Jer. 31:33; 32:38; Ezek. 11:20; 34:30-31; 36:28; 37:27), and they will all know him so that no longer need to be evangelized (Jer. 31:34).

5. **National Identity:** The nation is as permanent as "the fixed order" of the solar system, as promised, "If this fixed order departs from before me, declares the Lord, then shall the offspring of Israel cease *from being a nation* before me *forever*" (Jer. 31:36; cf. 31:35; 33:23-26, emphasis added). The descendants of Israel will *never again* be "cast off" for their iniquities (Jer. 31:37).

These passages show that the consummation of the new covenant will include the final return of the *entirety* of Jacob's descendants to a *permanent* state of holiness and security in the promised land. Nothing short of a *permanent* and *complete* salvation of Israel's surviving children in Jesus Christ will suffice. The same new covenant that was inaugurated by the bloody death of Jesus (Luke 22:20; 1 Cor. 11:25) and sealed by the writing of the Holy Spirit upon believers' hearts (2 Cor. 3:1-6) will be consummated when the righteous nation entirely dwells in permanent security in Christ.

The Old Testament prophets expected a *literal fulfillment* of the land promises that had been given to the Patriarchs. First, the prophet Ezekiel precisely identified the topographical boundaries of the land of Israel at the time of the final return from exile and consummation of the new covenant (Ezek. 47:13-48:29). Furthermore, the Lord Jesus and his apostles did not speak in depth about the land promises, presumably because they took the traditional interpretation of these expectations as a given. Not to mention that, as any father knows, for the children to wait for him to call more than once to them about a matter is a great presumption. Neither did they teach that the new covenant promises would be fulfilled *allegorically*. The reader should find abundant evidence of radical modifications or reinterpretations of these expectations if Christ or his new covenant church had fulfilled the land promises; however, we find *nothing* about any supposed fulfillment in the New Testament. Astonishingly, many preterists continue to teach that the land promises were fulfilled by AD 70.

The Everlasting City

The final rebuilding and glorification of Jerusalem is a common theme throughout the Prophets. The Holy City is divinely ordained to serve as the *eternal* capital of God's kingdom, the throne for Christ's eternal reign, and the quintessential glory of Israel and of the world. The Lord promised to make Jerusalem his eternal resting place (Ps. 132:13-14) and the place for his name to remain forever (1 Kings 9:3; 2 Kings 21:7; 2 Chron. 7:16; 33:7). He promised, "And Jerusalem shall be holy, and strangers shall never again pass through it" (Joel 3:17); the fact that strangers once passed through demonstrates that the city will be on earth. The prophet Isaiah received a message concerning the future blessedness of Jerusalem:

> I [the LORD] will rejoice in Jerusalem and be glad in my people; no more shall be heard in it the sound of weeping and the cry of distress. No more shall there be in it an infant who lives but a few days, or an old man who does not fill out his days, for the young man shall die a hundred years old, and the sinner a hundred years old shall be accursed. They shall build houses and inhabit them; they shall plant vineyards and eat their fruit. They shall not build and another inhabit; they shall not plant and another eat; for like the days of a tree shall the days of my people be, and my chosen shall long enjoy the work of their hands. They shall not labor in vain or bear children for calamity, for they shall be the offspring of the blessed of the Lord, and their descendants with them. Before they call I will answer; while they are yet speaking I will hear. The

wolf and the lamb shall graze together; the lion shall eat straw like the ox, and dust shall be the serpent's food. They shall not hurt or destroy in all my holy mountain. (Isa. 65:19-25)

This prophecy demonstrates that Jerusalem will be gloriously transformed in the age to come, *yet will continue to exist on the earth.* The passage reveals that the inhabitants of the city will toil with their hands, engage in agricultural endeavors, eat, construct houses, give birth to children, and die (vv. 20-22). However, the people will no longer experience sorrow but will experience long lives filled with joy and peace (vv. 18-25).

These blessed conditions of the future millennial kingdom have not yet been fulfilled. They also describe *conditions on earth,* which can either be understood literally within the framework of futurism, or be "explained away" by the allegorizing hermeneutic of preterism.

The Old Testament prophets taught that the Lord will have compassion on Jerusalem and that *its ancient ruins will be rebuilt* (Isa. 58:12; Jer. 30:17-20; 31:38-40; cf. Jer. 33:6-13). In his prophecy about the new covenant, the prophet Jeremiah taught that the same rebuilt city will never again be "plucked up or overthrown forever," and he provided the *specific geographical details* of the city.

Behold, the days are coming, declares the Lord, *when the city shall be rebuilt* for the Lord from the Tower of Hananel to the Corner Gate. And the measuring line shall go out farther, straight to the hill Gareb, and shall then turn to Goah. The whole valley of the dead bodies and the ashes, and all the fields as far as the brook Kidron, to the corner of the Horse Gate toward the east, shall be sacred to the Lord. *It shall not be plucked up or overthrown anymore forever.* (Jer. 31:38-40, emphasis added)

These prophecies demonstrate that the new Jerusalem will be *a renewal and glorification of the old city,* yet with qualities of the new covenant. The city will not be in heaven, but it will be endowed with *heavenly* qualities. The prophet Ezekiel also detailed the precise dimensions of the new Jerusalem:

> These shall be the exits of the city: On the north side, which is to be 4,500 cubits by measure, three gates, the gate of Reuben, the gate of Judah, and the gate of Levi, the gates of the city being named after the tribes of Israel. On the east side, which is to be 4,500 cubits, three gates, the gate of Joseph, the gate of Benjamin, and the gate of Dan. On the south side, which is to be 4,500 cubits by measure, three gates, the gate of Simeon, the gate of Issachar, and the gate of Zebulun. On the west side, which is to be 4,500 cubits, three gates, the gate of Gad, the gate of Asher, and the gate of Naphtali. The circumference of the city shall be 18,000 cubits. And the name of the city from that time on shall be, The Lord Is There. (Ezek. 48:30-35)

The prophet Zechariah foretold that the Lord will cause Israel's cities to flourish and "will *again* comfort Zion and *again* choose Jerusalem" (Zech. 1:17, emphasis added; cf. Zech. 2:12). The inhabitants of the Holy City will live in complete safety, without man-made walls, because God "will be to her a wall of fire all around ... the glory in her midst" (Zech. 2:4-5; cf. Isa. 4:5). Zechariah explained that the topography of Jerusalem and its surrounding region will be transformed at the Lord's return (Zech. 14:3-9) so that the city is given an exalted position of *everlasting* peace and security. He prophesied: "The whole land shall be turned into a plain from Geba to Rimmon south of Jerusalem. But Jerusalem shall remain aloft on its site from the Gate of Benjamin to the place of the former gate, to the Corner Gate, and from the Tower of Hananel to the king's winepresses. And it shall be inhabited, for there shall never again be a decree of utter destruction. Jerusalem shall dwell in security." (Zech. 14:10-11; cf. Isa. 2:1-5). The prophet also revealed that the world's inhabitants will make pilgrimage to Jerusalem to seek the Lord's favor:

> Thus says the Lord of hosts: Peoples shall yet come, even the inhabitants of many cities. The inhabitants of one city shall go to another, saying, "Let us go at once to entreat the favor of the Lord and to seek the Lord of hosts; I myself am going."

Many peoples and strong nations shall come to seek the Lord of hosts in Jerusalem and to entreat the favor of the Lord. Thus says the Lord of hosts: In those days ten men from the nations of every tongue shall take hold of the robe of a Jew, saying, "Let us go with you, for we have heard that God is with you." (Zech. 8:20-23)

This prophecy shows that Jerusalem will be the spiritual heart of the whole earth, the lodestar for the world's pilgrims in the age to come (cf. Zech. 14:16-21; Rev. 21:24). The God of Abraham, Isaac, and Jacob will be recognized as preeminent throughout the world. The compelling attraction of Zion in the example above induces a *minyan* or delegation of ten men from the nations to grasp the robe "of a Jew" in earnest desire to make pilgrimage with him to Jerusalem because God is with the Jewish nation (Zech. 8:23).

Restoring the Kingdom to Israel

If the Olivet Prophecy is about the *permanent desolation* of the Jewish kingdom in AD 70, the reader must wonder why Jesus' disciples later asked him if he was going to immediately "restore the kingdom to Israel" (Acts 1:6). Preterists would have us believe that the disciples misunderstood the very foundation of the Lord's teaching about "the kingdom of God" after they had spent more than three years learning about it from his own lips, proclaiming its message, and hearing him teaching about it for an additional forty days after his resurrection (Acts 1:3)! Hanegraaff teaches, "Jesus reoriented their thinking [in Acts 1:6] from a restored Jewish state to a kingdom that knows no borders or boundaries,"[5] but this conclusion is misguided. The apostles were not confused about the Master's teaching regarding the *nature* of God's kingdom, and they correctly understood the Old Testament prophecies concerning the final restoration of Israel's kingdom. Their question in Acts 1:6 ("Lord, will you at this time restore the kingdom to Israel?") indicates that they were ignorant of the *timing* of the kingdom being restored to Israel (cf. Luke 19:11).

5 Hanegraaff 2007, p. 182

In addition, the Lord's answer did not deny the future restoration of the nation, but it showed the disciples that they had not yet been given the knowledge of the divinely-ordained "times or seasons" (Acts 1:7). He commanded them to bring the testimony of the gospel to "the end of the earth" once they had received power from the Holy Spirit (Acts 1:8). At this point, they were still ignorant of "the mystery of the Gentiles," namely, that the nations would first be grafted into Israel's promises through faith in Christ (e.g., Rom. 11:25-26; Eph. 3:6; Col. 1:27).

Preterist David Chilton summarized the "serious problem" that preterists face regarding the divine election of the Jews:

> Old Israel has been excommunicated, cut off from the covenant by the righteous judgment of God. On the surface, this presents a serious problem: What about God's promises to Abraham, Isaac, and Jacob? God had sworn that He would be the God of Abraham's seed, that the covenant would be established with Abraham's seed "throughout their generations, for an everlasting covenant" (Gen. 17:7). If salvation has gone from the Jews to the Gentiles, what does that say about God's faithfulness to His word? Is there a place for ethnic Israel in prophecy? These questions are answered most directly in Scripture by the Apostle Paul in Romans 11. God never *totally* rejected ethnic Israel.[6]

Some preterists teach, based largely on Romans 11, that the Jewish nation will receive the gospel.[7] Chilton continues, "The people of Israel, as a whole, will turn back to the faith of their fathers and will acknowledge Jesus Christ as Lord and Savior. Their fall into apostasy is not permanent, says Paul."[8] Even DeMar admits, "Israel may yet have a role to play in prophecy"[9].

However, preterists often stipulate certain caveats to this promise. For example, Gentry claims, "[Israel's] special place of prominence in God's plan has been removed, however. Her geopolitical distinctiveness has ended; she will not be exalted above

6 Chilton 2007, p. 125
7 Ibid., p. 126; Gentry 2010c, loc. 826; Gentry 2010b, p. 89; Kik 1971, p. 81
8 Chilton 2007, p. 126
9 DeMar 1999, p. 344

or distinguished from the other nations."[10] In the same vein, J. Marcellus Kik provides this explanation:

> Even in the present time there are some within the Church who simply cannot believe that the old dispensation has been terminated. They still look for a temporal Jewish kingdom whose capital, Jerusalem, will hold sway over all the earth. This was the carnal conception of his kingdom which Christ fought and the apostles opposed, and against which his Church must still fight. It is true that we look forward to the conversion of the Jewish nation, and that the whole world will be blessed by this conversion. But this is something entirely different from the idea of a temporal Jewish kingdom holding sway over all the nations of the world.[11]

The apostle Paul taught the future certainty of the national redemption of Israel in his Letter to the Romans. Throughout the letter, he employed the term "Israel" to describe *the ethnic descendants of Jacob* in the context of their largely obstinate, disobedient, and reprobate condition (Rom. 9:6, 27, 31; 10:19, 21; 11:2, 7, 11, 25, 26). He variously called them "my kinsmen, according to the flesh" and "my fellow Jews" (Rom. 9:3; 11:14). On the other hand, Paul also taught that God's covenants and promises continued to belong to these ethnic Israelites (Rom. 9:4), and he called them "his [God's] people" (Rom. 11:1). He earnestly prayed for their salvation (Rom. 10:1), and expressing the intercessory heart of Jesus, Paul would have, if possible, suffered curse and separation from Christ "*for the sake of* my brothers, my kinsmen according to the flesh" (Rom. 9:3). In Romans 11, the apostle contrasted these unbelieving Israelites with the gentiles and remnant of Jews who had trusted in Jesus Christ. He employed the pronouns "they," "them," "their," and "those," highlighted here in **bold** for emphasis, to describe this *unbelieving Jewish nation*:

> [1] I ask, then, has God rejected his people? By no means! For I myself am an Israelite, a descendant of Abraham, a member of the tribe of Benjamin. [2] God has not rejected his people

10 Gentry 2010b, p. 89
11 Kik 1971, pp. 75-76

whom he foreknew. Do you not know what the Scripture says of Elijah, how he appeals to God against Israel? ³"Lord, **they** have killed your prophets, **they** have demolished your altars, and I alone am left, and **they** seek my life." ⁴But what is God's reply to him? "I have kept for myself seven thousand men who have not bowed the knee to Baal." ⁵So too at the present time there is a remnant, chosen by grace. ⁶But if it is by grace, it is no longer on the basis of works; otherwise grace would no longer be grace. ⁷What then? **Israel** failed to obtain what it was seeking. The elect obtained it, but the rest were hardened, ⁸as it is written, "God gave **them** a spirit of stupor, eyes that would not see and ears that would not hear, down to this very day." ⁹And David says, "Let **their** table become a snare and a trap, a stumbling block and a retribution for **them**; ¹⁰let **their** eyes be darkened so that they cannot see, and bend their backs forever." ¹¹So I ask, did **they** stumble in order that **they** might fall? By no means! Rather, through **their** trespass salvation has come to the Gentiles, so as to make <u>Israel</u> jealous. ¹²Now if **their** trespass means riches for the world, and if **their** failure means riches for the Gentiles, how much more will **their** full inclusion mean! ¹³Now I am speaking to you Gentiles. Inasmuch then as I am an apostle to the Gentiles, I magnify my ministry ¹⁴in order somehow to make <u>my fellow Jews</u> jealous, and thus save some of **them**. ¹⁵For if their rejection means the reconciliation of the world, what will **their** acceptance mean but life from the dead? (Rom. 11:1-15)

Paul described the nation of Israel as those who had rejected the Lord and his prophets, failed to obtain salvation because of pursuing it on the basis of works, and not received the gospel due to their hardened hearts (Rom. 11:3-10). The gentiles had received salvation because Israel had rejected it *and* so that they might make Israel jealous unto salvation (Rom. 11:11-12, 14, 31; cf. Deut. 32:21). The apostle contrasted Israel's failure to obtain the promises, a rejection that resulted in reconciliation for the nations, with their future acceptance and full inclusion into the promises. This acceptance will result in greater riches for the nations, including the resurrection of the dead (Rom. 11:2, 15)! Paul continued to contrast unbelieving Israel with the largely gentile assembly of believers with the analogy of the olive tree:

¹⁶ If the dough offered as firstfruits is holy, so is the whole lump, and if the root is holy, so are the branches. ¹⁷ But if some of the branches were broken off, and you, although a wild olive shoot, were grafted in among the others and now share in the nourishing root of the olive tree, ¹⁸ do not be arrogant toward the branches. If you are, remember it is not you who support the root, but the root that supports you. ¹⁹ Then you will say, "Branches were broken off so that I might be grafted in." ²⁰That is true. **They** were broken off because of **their** unbelief, but you stand fast through faith. So do not become proud, but fear. ²¹ For if God did not spare the natural branches, neither will he spare you. ²² Note then the kindness and the severity of God: severity toward **those** who have fallen, but God's kindness to you, provided you continue in his kindness. Otherwise you too will be cut off. ²³ And even **they**, if **they** do not continue in **their** unbelief, will be grafted in, for God has the power to graft **them** in again. ²⁴ For if you were cut from what is by nature a wild olive tree, and grafted, contrary to nature, into a cultivated olive tree, how much more will **these**, the natural branches, be grafted back into **their** own olive tree. (Rom. 11:16-24)

The gentile believers were being grafted into the olive tree, a symbol for the nation of Israel, whereas many of "the natural branches" (i.e., ethnic Jews) had been broken off because of their unbelief (Rom. 11:16-24). The apostle warned these gentile believers not to be arrogant towards ethnic Israel because the nations were being grafted into these promises because the unbelieving Jews had been broken off (vv. 18-20) and the gentiles could also be broken off (v. 22). Paul then introduced the concept of the Lord grafting ethnic Jews back into the promises through faith in Jesus Christ (vv. 23-24). He concluded with the following synopsis of Israel's future, national redemption:

²⁵ Lest you be wise in your own sight, I do not want you to be unaware of this mystery, brothers: a partial hardening has come upon Israel, until the fullness of the Gentiles has come in. ²⁶ And in this way all Israel will be saved, as it is written, "The Deliverer will come from Zion, he will banish ungodliness from Jacob"; ²⁷ "and this will be my covenant with them when I take away **their** sins."²⁸ As regards the gospel, **they**

are enemies for your sake. But as regards election, **they** are beloved for the sake of their forefathers. [29] For the gifts and the calling of God are irrevocable. [30] For just as you were at one time disobedient to God but now have received mercy because of **their** disobedience, [31] so **they** too have now been disobedient in order that by the mercy shown to you **they** also may now receive mercy. [32] For God has consigned all to disobedience, that he may have mercy on all. (Rom. 11:1-32)

The apostle taught the *mystery* of the national restoration of Israel. He explained that this "partial hardening" of the Jewish nation will continue "until the fullness of the Gentiles has come in" (Rom. 11:25). The larger context indicates that this "fullness" includes the provocation of Israel by the believing gentiles so that the *entire nation* finds salvation in Jesus Christ ("all Israel will be saved" in v. 26).

This reaches a climax when Jesus returns in glory from heaven (i.e., "The Deliverer will come from Zion" v. 6; cf. Isa. 59:20-21) and completely eradicates sin and ungodliness from the descendants of Jacob (Rom. 11:26-27; cf. Isa. 27:9). This restoration of Israel is intrinsically bound up with the consummation of the new covenant ("my covenant with them when I take away their sins" Rom. 11:27) and the irrevocable gifts and election of the nation that God promised the Patriarchs (Rom. 11:28). Chilton correctly saw the sequence of Israel's restoration in the prophecy of Romans 11. He sequenced it as follows: "1. The Jewish apostasy resulted in the salvation of the Gentiles; 2. The salvation of the Gentiles will someday bring about the restoration of ethnic Israel; and, finally, 3. The restoration of Israel will cause an even greater revival among the Gentiles, which (compared to everything earlier) will be much greater 'riches' (v. 12), like 'life from the dead' (v. 15)."[12]

Most preterists reject the notions that the Lord will return in glory to restore the kingdom to Israel and that he will bring the light of his glory to all the nations through their priestly stewardship. Nevertheless, the Lord recognized that the children of Jeru-

---

12 Chilton 2007, p. 126

salem were not yet able to be gathered "under her wings" (Matt. 23:37; Luke 13:34), but he explained that they would yet praise him with the words "Blessed is he who comes in the name of the Lord" (Matt. 23:39).

National lamentation and repentance will accompany the salvation of the entire surviving remnant of Jews (Deut. 4:30-31; 32:36; Isa 4:2-3; 6:9-13; Matt. 23:39; cf. Isa. 10:20-23). The Lord promised, "And I will pour out on the house of David and the inhabitants of Jerusalem a Spirit of grace and pleas for mercy, so that, when they look on me, on him whom they have pierced, they shall mourn for him, as one mourns for an only child, and weep bitterly over him, as one weeps over a firstborn" (Zech. 12:10; cf. Isa. 35:10; 51:11). The prophet Jeremiah also described the weeping of the descendants of Jacob, who will go up to Jerusalem to join themselves to the Lord with an *everlasting* covenant. He prophesied, "In those days and in that time, declares the Lord, the people of Israel and the people of Judah shall come together, weeping as they come, and they shall seek the Lord their God. They shall ask the way to Zion, with faces turned toward it, saying, 'Come, let us join ourselves to the Lord in an everlasting covenant that will never be forgotten'" (Jer. 50:4-5).

Stumbling Over a Mystery

Preterists cannot adequately account for the modern State of Israel. This is especially true for preterists who entirely disconnect the nation from the new and everlasting covenant and see its existence as historical happenstance. Furthermore, the supersessionist claim that the nation is the result of a self-fulfilling prophecy of Christian Zionism betrays an ignorance of God's *preservation* of a unique Jewish identity throughout history. No other people has endured as much longstanding persecution as the Jews, and no other nation has been exiled three separate times over three millennia, only to later return to its homeland. These historical circumstances defy human logic and demonstrate the Lord's providence regarding his ancient nation.

Preterism, as a form of supersessionism, regards modern Jews as vestigial organs of the Lord's ancient covenant nation. Also, it views the Christian church, comprised of righteous gentiles and a mere remnant of believing Jews, as having *entirely replaced* the Israelite nation as the holy people of God. According to preterism, the Jewish nation will *never* obtain the full measure of salvation in Jesus Christ. This is tantamount to God having brought the Jewish nation to the point of labor pains without deliverance—a "giving birth to wind" (Isa. 26:18). As we have seen, preterism allegorizes and minimizes the importance of many detailed prophecies regarding the final return of the Jews to the promised land, and treats the prophecies about the conditions and detailed geographical boundaries of the rebuilt Jerusalem and the ultimate restoration of the Jewish nation in the same way. David Baron, a nineteenth-century Christian Jew, wrote in detail about this interpretive blunder:

> There is, first of all, the old-fashioned way of so-called spiritualizing the prophecies—making Israel and Zion to mean the Church, and The Land to signify heaven; but I confess this system of interpretation has no consistency about it, and makes the Word of God the most meaningless and unintelligible book in the world. For instance, we read here "I will bring again the captivity of My people Israel and Judah ... and I will cause them to return to the land that I gave to their fathers." (`KJV) If Israel be the Church, who is Judah? If Judah be the Church, who is Israel? What is the "captivity" the Church has endured? And where is "the land" from which the Church has been driven out, and to which it will return? ... In what particular locality in heaven are the tower of Hananel and the corner gate? And what will our allegorical interpretations make of the hill Gareb, and Goah, and the brook Kidron? All these are known to me in the environs of the literal Jerusalem in Canaan; but I confess some difficulty in locating them in heavenly places. If Israel does not mean Israel, and "the land God gave to the fathers" does not mean Palestine, then I do not know what is meant. The announcement is: "He that scatters Israel will gather him." (Jer. 31:10) Now, when it comes to scattering—of course, this is allowed to refer to literal Israel,

to the Jews, "scattered and peeled"; but when, in the same sentence, a gathering of the same people is mentioned—oh, this is the gathering of the spiritual Israel. What consistency or honesty, I pray, is there in such interpretations![13]

The biblical evidence and the testimony of the historic Christian church is that the Lord Jesus has faithfully preserved the nation of Israel as "the apple of his eye" (Deut. 32:10; cf. Ex. 4:22). This author's distant uncle, Mark Twain, outlined the miracle of Israel's preservation:

If the statistics are right, the Jews constitute but one quarter of one percent of the human race. It suggests a nebulous puff of star dust lost in the blaze of the Milky Way. Properly, the Jew ought hardly to be heard of, but he is heard of, has always been heard of. He is as prominent on the planet as any other people, and his importance is extravagantly out of proportion to the smallness of his bulk. His contributions to the world's list of great names in literature, science, art, music, finance, medicine and abstruse learning are also very out of proportion to the weakness of his numbers. He has made a marvelous fight in this world in all ages; and has done it with his hands tied behind him. He could be vain of himself and be excused for it. The Egyptians, the Babylonians and the Persians rose, filled the planet with sound and splendor, then faded to dream-stuff and passed away; the Greeks and Romans followed and made a vast noise, and they were gone; other people have sprung up and held their torch high for a time but it burned out, and they sit in twilight now, and have vanished. The Jew saw them all, survived them all, and is now what he always was, exhibiting no decadence, no infirmities, of age, no weakening of his parts, no slowing of his energies, no dulling of his alert but aggressive mind. All things are mortal but the Jews; all other forces pass, but he remains. What is the secret of his immortality?[14]

---

13 Baron 1894, pp. 12-14
14 Twain, Mark. Quote from September 1897 as published in *The National Jewish Post & Observer* for June 6, 1984.

18

Repenting of Preterism

My journey into preterism began in earnest during my seminary training at Midwestern Baptist Theological Seminary in 2000. Like many of my colleagues, I struggled to find biblical support for the ubiquitous pre-tribulational dispensationalist perspective, which proliferates on the Christian theological landscape. Although many of my Hebrew and Greek professors held to the historic premillennial position, they provided me with little solid exegesis of eschatological scriptures during my academic training. At this time, I became increasingly confused by the time statements in the New Testament that indicate a "near," "soon," and "at hand" coming of the Son of Man (see Chapter Two).

However, I became persuaded that the preterist perspective interpreted these statements more coherently. My position was reinforced after becoming familiar with preterist works, especially the writings of R. C. Sproul, Hank Hanegraaff, N. T. Wright, Gary DeMar, Kenneth Gentry, David Chilton, and R. T. France. My conviction was further strengthened after Hank Hanegraaff announced his conversion to preterism and began promulgating these views on his radio program.

Initially, I spent several years as a partial preterist, but then began seriously considering full preterism. Along with most futurists and partial preterists, I had considered full preterism to be a blatant heresy, largely due to its rejection of the historic creeds and its denial of an individual, bodily resurrection of the saints. Full preterism differs from biblical Christianity in every area of theology, including soteriology, ecclesiology, pneumatology, angelology, and of course, eschatology (see Chapter 15). I was introduced to full preterist books, beginning with the works of J.

Stuart Russell, Don K. Preston, and Edward Stevens. Eventually, I began the arduous process of embracing the full preterist position, in order to maintain a consistent hermeneutic (see Chapter 15), which ultimately proved to be a noble but misguided gambit.

Later, I became a teacher at a preterist church and defended preterist eschatology as the host of a weekly radio program, *Fulfilled Life*, on Covenant Key FM. By 2013, I had finished writing a book defending preterism, *Let No Man Separate: How Partial Preterists Divide Scripture*, and was scheduled to be a conference speaker at Don Preston's prophecy conference, Preterist Pilgrim Weekend, in Ardmore, Oklahoma. During this time, I found myself engaged in sharp disagreements over trivialities, and embroiled in arrogant controversies about foundational doctrines of Christianity. As well, my striving against biblical and ecclesiastical authority that the Lord has placed in his church robbed me of much joy and peace.

In his own due time, the Lord showed great mercy to me by revealing that I had been deceived by preterism. On the very night that I received the first box of 100 books from my publisher, the Lord spoke to my heart to freshly examine the biblical doctrine of the resurrection of the dead, which led me to repent of my involvement with full preterism. The process of fully abandoning partial preterism took several additional months, but the rewards have been immeasurable. I have gained a new appreciation and devotion to the traditional eschatology of the historic church, namely, post-tribulational historic premillennialism.

In 2017, God placed a fresh burden on my heart to write a book that introduces a proper biblical eschatology, while providing a roadmap for refuting preterism. I completed this book in only three months, impelled by a prophetic urgency in the writing. I have attempted to advance a solid biblical exegesis in order to provide the reader with a pre-Augustinian eschatology, and in accordance with this exegesis, I subsequently seek to dismantle the faulty foundations of preterist theology.

The Implications of Preterism

As demonstrated throughout this book, preterism reinterprets many passages that are concerned with the future unprecedented tribulation, the glorious return of Jesus, and the millennial kingdom of God. Consequently, those who have embraced preterism will not be prepared for the unprecedented tribulation that is coming upon all the world (Rev. 3:10; 13:8). They will likely experience theological confusion during the construction of the Third Temple in Jerusalem, being caught off guard, which will leave many subject to the prophesied "strong delusion", when the Antichrist appears to set up the abomination of desolation and begin his worldwide assault on the saints (2 Thess. 2:8-12).

In addition, preterists have created unnecessary divisions, hindering theological unity within the body of Christ, because preterism undermines a proper understanding of many biblical prophecies that describe our blessed hope at the appearance of Jesus Christ. Many preterists have descended into theological confusion. To reiterate, some have unwittingly accepted the ancient heresy that the day of the Lord has already arrived (2 Thess. 2:1-3). Others have stopped short of embracing full preterism, not because of a proper understanding of biblical eschatology, but because of their purported commitment to orthodoxy as defined in the ecumenical creeds.

That many people will repent of the false doctrines of preterism is my prayer and purpose for writing this book. As demonstrated herein, the subtle allure of preterism lies in its claim that its interpretation of the time statements of Scripture is based on clear, logical argumentation. However, the entire preterist hermeneutic is built upon an inadequate understanding of these statements, of the prophetic perspective, and of the "already and not yet" principle of eschatology. My desire is that Christians who read this book will become more informed about preterism and better equipped to challenge its arguments, in order to warn others of its dangers.

Acknowledgments

I would like to thank Reggie Kelly, Tom Quinlan, and Robert Weiss for their assistance with editing my manuscript in its entirety. A special thanks also belongs to Jayne Lampley, Travis Bennett, Jamie Lundy, and Sam Frost for their contributions to the editing of this book and Tom Quinlan for preparing the manuscript for publication. I want to thank Travis Bennett for creating the figures found throughout the book. I am also grateful for Jeremy Thompson's consultations regarding the preparation, publishing, and promoting of the book. A special thank you belongs to Phil Norcom for his cover art of the demolished stones of the Second Temple. Finally, I want to thank my wife Staci and our four daughters for sacrificing time with me as I prepared this book.

Appendixes

Appendix A: A Comparison of the Courtroom Scenes of Daniel 7 and Revelation 4-5

	Daniel 7	Revelation 4-5
"I Looked" God Seated On His Throne Other Thrones	As I looked, thrones were placed, and the Ancient of Days took his seat; his clothing was white as now, and the hair of his head like pure wool (Dan. 7:9)	After this I looked (Rev. 4:1)... a throne stood in heaven, with one seated on the throne. (Rev. 4:2) ... Around the throne were seated twenty-four thrones (Rev. 4:4)
Fire Before the Throne of God	his throne was fiery flames; its wheels were burning fire. (Dan. 7:9) A stream of fire issued and came out from before him;	From the throne came flashes of lightning, and rumblings and peals of thunder, and before the throne were burning seven torches of fire, which are the seven spirits of God, (Rev. 4:5)
Multiple Thousands Ministering to God	a thousand thousands served him, and ten thousand times ten thousand stood before him;	I heard around the throne and the living creatures and the elders the voice of many angels, numbering myriads of myriads and thousands of thousands (Rev. 5:11)

	Daniel 7	Revelation 4-5
Scrolls/Books Opened for Judgment	the court sat in judgment, and the books were opened. (Dan. 7:10)	Then I saw in the right hand of him who was seated on the throne a scroll written within and on the back, sealed with seven seals. ... he [the Lion of Judah] can open the scroll and its seven seals. (Rev. 5:1, 5)
The Beast Speaks Great Blasphemies **He is Killed and Thrown Into the Fire**	I looked then because of the sound of the great words that the horn was speaking. And as I looked, the beast was killed, and its body destroyed and given over to be burned with fire. (Dan. 7:11)	*Parallel account in Rev. 13:5; 19:20*
The Son of Man Arrives with Heavenly Clouds	I saw in the night visions, and behold, with the clouds of heaven there came one like a son of man,	*Parallel account in Rev. 14:14; 19:11-16*
He Appears Before the Throne of God the Father	and he came to the Ancient of Days and was presented before him. (Dan. 7:13)	And between the throne and the four living creatures and among the elders I saw a Lamb standing, as though it had been slain ... And he went and took the scroll from the right hand of him who was seated on the throne (Rev. 5:6, 7)

	Daniel 7	Revelation 4-5
The Son of Man Receives a Kingdom that Includes Every People, Tribe, Nation, and Language	And to him was given dominion and glory and a kingdom, that all peoples, nations, and languages should serve him; his dominion is an everlasting dominion, which shall not pass away, and his kingdom one that shall not be destroyed. (Dan. 7:14)	and by your blood you ransomed people for God from every tribe and language and people and nation, and you made them a kingdom and priests to our God, and they shall reign on the earth. (Rev. 5:9)
The Prophet Alarmed	As for me, Daniel, my spirit within me was anxious, and the visions of my head alarmed me. (Dan. 7:15)	And I began to weep loudly because no one was found worthy to pen the scroll or to look into it. (Rev. 5:4)
One Interprets the Vision	I approached one of those who stood there and asked him the truth concerning all this. So he told me and made known to me the interpretation of the things. (Dan. 7:16)	And one of the elders said to me, "Weep no more; behold the Lion of the tribe of Judah, the Root of David, has conquered, so that he can open the scroll and its seven seals." (Rev. 5:5)
The Saints Receive the Everlasting Kingdom	But the saints of the Most High shall receive the kingdom and possess the kingdom forever, forever and ever. (Dan. 7:18)	And you have made them a kingdom and priests to our God, and they shall reign on the earth." (Rev. 5:9)

Appendix B: Comparison of the Judgment Scenes in Daniel, Revelation, and Matthew

	Daniel 7	Revelation 19-20	Matthew 25
The Son of Man Coming With the Clouds of Heaven	With the clouds of heaven there came one like a son of man (Dan. 7:13)	behold, a white cloud, and seated on the cloud one like a son of man (Rev. 14:15)	When the Son of Man comes in his glory (Matt. 25:31; cf. Matt. 24:30: "on the clouds")
Myriads of Angels	ten thousand times ten thousand stood before him (Dan. 7:10)	many angels, numbering... thousands of thousands (Rev. 5:11)	and all the angels with him (Matt. 25:31)
God Seated On His Throne	the Ancient of Days took his seat; his clothing was white as snow ... his throne (Dan. 7:9)	I saw a great white throne and him who was seated on it (Rev. 20:11)	then he will sit on his glorious throne (Matt. 25:31)
All Peoples Included	all dominions (Dan. 7:27)	I saw the dead, great and small, standing before the throne (Rev. 20:12)	Before him will be gathered all the nations (Matt. 25:32)
Thrones Placed For Judgment	As I looked, thrones were placed ... the court sat in judgment (Dan. 7:9-10)	I saw thrones and seated on them were those to whom the authority to judge was committed (Rev. 20:4)	when the Son of Man will sit on his glorious throne, you who have followed me will also sit on twelve thrones, judging (Matt. 19:28)
Scrolls/Books Opened	and the books were opened (Dan. 7:10; cf. 12:1)	and books were opened (Rev. 20:12)	----

	Daniel 7	Revelation 19-20	Matthew 25
The Wicked Ones Throne Into Fire	the beast was killed, and its body destroyed and given over to be burned with fire (Dan. 7:11)	[the beast and false prophet] were thrown alive into the lake of fire that burns (Rev. 19:20) . . . and the devil who had deceived them was thrown into the lake of fire . . . and they will be tormented day and night forever and ever (Rev. 20:10)	Depart from me, you cursed, into the eternal fire prepared for the devil and his angels (Matt. 25:41)
and Tormented With Everlasting Punishment	some to shame and everlasting contempt. (Dan. 12:2)		these will go away into eternal punishment (Matt. 25:46)
The Righteous Receive God's Everlasting Kingdom	And the kingdom ... shall be given to the people of the saints of the Most High; his kingdom shall be an everlasting kingdom (Dan. 7:27; cf. 7:22; 12:2)	*Cf. Rev. 21:1-22:5*	Come, you who are blessed by my Father, inherit the kingdom prepared for you (Matt. 25:34) the righteous into eternal life (Matt. 25:46)

Sources

Adams, Jay E., and Milton C. Fisher. *The Time of the End*. Hackettstown, NJ: Timeless Texts, 2000.

Baron, David. *The Jewish Problem, Its Solution; or, Israel's Present and Future ... Introduction by Rev. A. T. Pierson*. London: Morgan & Scott, 1894.

Beale, G. K. *The New International Greek Testament Commentary*. Carlisle: Paternoster Press, 1999.

----------. *1-2 Thessalonians*. The IVP New Testament Commentary Series. Downers Grove, IL: InterVarsity Press, 2003.

Beale, G. K., and D. A. Carson. *Commentary on the New Testament Use of the Old Testament*. Grand Rapids: Baker Academic, 2007.

Bell, William E., Jr. *"A Critical Evaluation of the Pretribulational Rapture Doctrine in Christian Eschatology,"* (Th.D. dissertation, New York University, April 1967): 249-50.

Bercot, David W. *A Dictionary of Early Christian Beliefs: A Reference Guide to More Than 700 Topics Discussed by the Early Church Fathers*. Peabody, MA: Hendrickson Publishers, Inc, 1998.

Bruce, F. F. *The Epistles to the Colossians, Philemon and to the Ephesians*. Grand Rapids: Eerdmans, 1984.

Caird, G. B. *Jesus and the Jewish Nation*. London: University of London, the Athlone Press, 1965.

Caird, G. B., and L. D. Hurst. *New Testament Theology*. Oxford: Clarendon Press, 1994.

Calvin, John. *Commentary on a Harmony of the Evangelists, Matthew, Mark, and Luke*. Trans. William Pringle, vol. 3. Grand Rapids: Baker, 1984.

----------. *Reformation Commentary on Scripture: Ezekiel, Daniel.* Edited by Carl L. Beckwith. Downer's Grove, IL: InterVarsity PressAcademic, 2012

Carson, D. A., "Matthew," in Frank E. Gaebelein, ed., *The Expositor's Bible Commentary*, vol. 8. Grand Rapids: Zondervan, 1984.

Chilton, David. *The Days of Vengeance: An Exposition of the Book of Revelation.* Horn Lake, MS: Dominion Press, 2006.

Chilton, David. *Paradise Restored: A Biblical Theology of Dominion.* Horn Lake, MS: Dominion Press, 2007.

Danker, Frederick W., Walter Bauer, and William F. Arndt. *A Greek-English Lexicon of the New Testament and Other Early Christian literature.* 3rd ed. Chicago: University of Chicago Press, 2000.

DeMar, Gary. *Last Days Madness: Obsession of the Modern Church.* Atlanta: American Vision, 1999.

----------. "But Is It In The Bible?" As of October 24, 2012. *Grace Online Library.* http://www.graceonlinelibrary.org/eschatology/dispensationalism/but-is-it-in-the-bible-by-gary-demar

----------. "Zechariah 14 and the Coming of Christ." As of August 8, 2017. *Preterist Archive.* http://www.preteristarchive.com/Modern/2001_demar_zechariah-14.html

Fee, Gordon D. *The First and Second Letters to the Thessalonians.* Grand Rapids: William B. Eerdmans Publishing, 2009.

France, R. T. *The Gospel According to Matthew: An Introduction and Commentary.* Tyndale New Testament Commentaries. Leicester, UK: InterVarsityPress, 1985.

----------. *The Gospel of Mark: a Commentary on the Greek Text.* Grand Rapids: W.B. Eerdmans, 2002.

----------. *The Gospel of Matthew. The New International Commentary on the New Testament.* Grand Rapids: William B. Eerdman's Publishing, 2007.

Frost, Sam. [Article title unknown]. As of November 8, 2012. *The Reign of Christ.* http://thereignofchrist.com/daniel-122/.

Gaebelein, Frank E., et. al. *The Expositor's Bible commentary With the New International Version of the Holy Bible.* Grand Rapids: Zondervan Publishing House, 1981.

Gentry, Kenneth L. *The Greatness of the Great Commission.* Tyler, TX: Institute for Christian Economics, 1990.

----------. *Before Jerusalem Fell: Dating the book of Revelation: An Exegetical and Historical Argument for a Pre-A.D. 70 Composition.* Revised ed. Powder Springs, GA: American Vision, 1998.

----------. *The Book of Revelation Made Easy.* Powder Springs, GA: The American Vision, Inc., 2008.

----------. *He Shall Have Dominion: A Postmillennial Eschatology.* Draper, VA: Apologetics Group Media, 2009.

----------. *Before Jerusalem Fell: Dating the Book of Revelation.* Fountain Inn, SC: Victorious Hope, 2010.

----------. *The Book of Revelation Made Easy: You Can Understand Bible Prophecy.* Powder Springs, GA: American Vision Press, 2010.

----------. *The Olivet Discourse Made Easy.* Draper, VA: Apologetics Group.com, 2010. Kindle Edition.

Hanegraaff, Hank. *The Apocalypse Code: Find Out What the Bible Really Says About the End Times and Why It Matters Today.* Nashville: Thomas Nelson, 2007.

Harding, Ian D. *Taken to Heaven by AD 70: A Preterist Study of the Eschatological Blessings Expected by the First Christians at the Parousia of Christ circa AD 70.* Bradford, PA: International Preterist Association, 2005.

Hartman, Lars. *Prophecy Interpreted: The Formation of Some Jewish Apocalyptic Texts and of the Eschatological Discourse Mark 13 Par.* Lund: Gleerup (1966), 187-90.

Howard, T. L. *"The Literary Unity of 1 Thessalonians 4:13-5:11,"* GTJ 9 (1988): 163-90.

Hughes, Philip Edgcumbe. *The Book of the Revelation: A Commentary.* Grand Rapids: Eerdmann, 1990.

Hyldahl, Niels. "Auferstehung Christi – Auferstehung der Toten (1 Thess. 4:4, 13-18)," In: *S. Pedersen [Hrsg.]. Die Paulinische Literatur und Theologie* (TeolSt 7) (1980), 130.

Ice, Thomas, and Kenneth L. Gentry. *The Great Tribulation, Past or Future?: Two Evangelicals Debate the Question.* Grand Rapids, MI: Kregel Publications, 1999.

Jordan, James B. *The Vindication of Jesus Christ: a Brief Reader's Guide to Revelation.* Monroe, LA: Athanasius Press, 2008. Kindle Edition.

Keathley, Hampton, IV. "Introduction to the Parables." As of August 8, 2017. *Bible.org.* https://bible.org/seriespage/introduction-parables.

Kik, J. Marcellus. *An Eschatology of Victory.* Phillipsburg, NJ: Presbyterian and Reformed Publishing Company, 1971.

King, Max R. *The Cross and the Parousia of Christ: The Two Dimensions of One Age-Changing Eschaton.* Reprint Edition. Warren, OH: Parkman Road Church of Christ, 1987.

Ladd, George Eldon. *A Commentary on the Revelation of John.* Grand Rapids: Eerdmans, 1972.

----------. *The Presence of the Future.* Grand Rapids: Eerdmans, 1974.

Leithart, Peter J. *The Promise of His Appearing: An Exposition of Second Peter.* Moscow, ID: Canon Press, 2004.

Lövenstam, O. Evald. *Jesus and 'this Generation': A New Testament Study.* Coniectanea Biblica. New Testament Series 25. Stockholm: Lund, 1995.

Marshall, I. Howard. *1 and 2 Thessalonians.* Grand Rapids: Eerdmans, 1983.

Maslow, Abraham H. *The Psychology of Science: A Reconnaissance.* New York: Harper and Roe, 1966.

Mathison, Keith A. *When Shall These Things Be?: A Reformed Response to Hyper-preterism.* Phillipsburg, NJ: P & R Publishing, 2004.

Miller, Stephen R. *Daniel.* Nashville: Broadman & Holman. 1994.

Mounce, Robert H. *The Book of Revelation. The New International Commentary of the New Testament.* Grand Rapids, MI: W. B. Eerdmans, 1998.

Newman, Carey C. "'In Grateful Dialogue." Jesus & the Restoration of Israel: a Critical Assessment of N.T. Wright's Jesus and the Victory of God. Downers Grove, IL: InterVarsity-Press, 1999.

Nisbett, Nehemiah. *An Attempt to Illustrate Various Important Passages in the Epistles, &c. of the New Testament: From Our Lord's Prophecies of the Destruction of Jerusalem, and from Some Prophecies of the Old Testament.* London, 1787.

Orchard, J. Bernard. *"Thessalonians and the Synoptic Gospel,"* Biblica 19 (1938): 19-42.

Osborne, Grant R. *Revelation.* Baker Exegetical Commentary on the New Testament. Grand Rapids: Baker Academic, 2002.

Owen, John. *The Works of John Owen.* 16 volumes. London: Banner of Truth, 1965-68.

Piper, John. "Has the Gospel Been Preached to the Whole Creation Already?" On March 14, 2017. *Desiring God.* http://www.desiringgod.org/articles/has-the-gospel-been-preached-to-the-whole-creation-already.

Preston, Don K. *We Shall Meet Him in the Air: The Wedding of the King of Kings.* Ardmore, OK: JaDon Management, Inc. 2012.

----------. *Who is This Babylon?* Ardmore, OK: JaDon Management Inc., 2011.

Rigaux, Béda. *The Letters of St. Paul, Modern Studies.* Chicago: Franciscan Herald (1968), 539.

Russell, J. Stuart. *The Parousia: the New Testament Doctrine of Christ's Second Coming.* Edited by Edward E. Stevens. Bradford, PA: International Preterist Association, 2003.

Seyoon, Kim. *"The Jesus Tradition in 1 Thess 4.13-5.11,"* New Testament Studies 48 (2002): 231-42.

Sproul, R. C. *The Last Days According to Jesus: When Did Jesus Say He Would Return?* Grand Rapids: Baker, 2015.

Stevens, Edward E. *Expectations Demand a First Century Rapture.* Bradford, PA: International Preterist Association, 2003.

Sullivan, Michael J. "A Full Preterist Response to Kenneth Gentry's Articles: Daniel 12

Tribulation, and Resurrection and Acts 24:15 and the Alleged
Nearness of the Resurrection." As of October 24, 2012.
FullPreterism.com. http://postmillennialism.com/2012/03/
daniel-12-tribulation-and-resurrection/ on 10-24-12.

Twain, Mark. Quote from September 1897 as published in *The
National Jewish Post & Observer* for June 6, 1984.

Wanamaker, Charles A. *The Epistles to the Thessalonians: A
Commentary on the Greek Text.* Grand Rapids: W. B.
Eerdmans, 1990.

Waterman, G. Henry. *"The Sources of Paul's Teaching on the
2nd Coming of Jesus in 1 and 2 Thessalonians,"* JETS 18
(1975): 105-13

Wright, N. T. *Jesus and the Victory of God.* Minneapolis: Fortress
Press, 1996.

Ancient Sources:

The Babylonian Talmud. *Talmud Bavli: Tractate Sanhedrin 98a4.*
The Schottenstein ed. Vol. III. Brooklyn, NY: Mesorah,
2014.

Eusebius, *Ecclesiastical History* 3.5.3.

Philo of Alexandria. *Flaccus.* Vol. 25. 3.8; 4.21.

----------. *On the Embassy to Gaius.* 31.213.

Josephus. *Jewish Antiquities* 10.11.7; 18.6.10; 20.8.5; 20.97-98.

----------. *The Wars of the Jews* 2.14.5; 4.9.2; 6.2.1; 6.5.3. 6.94.

Tacitus. *The Annals of Imperial Rome.* Trans. Michael Grant.
London: Penguin Books, 1989

About the Author

Dr. Brock D. Hollett is a physician and psychiatrist in Bradenton, Florida. He received a Bachelor of Science in Middle School Education from the University of Central Missouri, a Master of Divinity from Midwestern Baptist Theological Seminary (SBC), and a Doctor of Osteopathic Medicine from Kansas City University of Medicine. He also worked toward an interdisciplinary Ph.D. in Religious Studies and History at the University  of Missouri—Kansas City. He is currently an adjunct professor of biblical studies and science at Southeastern University in Bradenton, Florida. His areas of special interest include eschatology and Jewish studies. He and his wife Staci have four daughters and they attend Bayside Community Church in Bradenton, Florida.